T0301412

The Political Economy of Wages and Unemployment

For Simon.

The Political Economy of Wages and Unemployment

A Neoclassical Exploration

William Oliver Coleman

The Australian National University

Edward Elgar

Cheltenham, UK • Northampton, MA, USA

Published by
Edward Elgar Publishing Limited
The Lypiatts
15 Lansdown Road
Cheltenham
Glos GL50 2JA
UK

Edward Elgar Publishing, Inc.
William Pratt House
9 Dewey Court
Northampton
Massachusetts 01060
USA

A catalogue record for this book
is available from the British Library

Library of Congress Control Number: 2010925964

ISBN 978 1 84844 657 1

Typeset by Servis Filmsetting Ltd, Stockport, Cheshire
Printed and bound by MPG Books Group, UK

Contents

Principal notation

B   real bonds
C   consumption
E   the efficiency of labour
I   investment
K   capital
L   labour
M   the money supply
P   the money price level
R   resources
U   utility
V   the money wage
W   wages bill
Y   national product
b   labour input requirement
c   the proportion of labour force covered by regulation
d   the rate of depreciation
e   the elasticity of labour demand to the real wage
h   hours worked
i   the nominal interest rate
k   the capital–labour ratio
l   the labour–capital ratio
p   probability
q   the average product of capital
r   the resources–capital ratio
t   the tax rate
w   the real wage
x   total market expenditure
c^* consumption/workforce
k^* capital/workforce
l^* work/workforce
Θ the elasticity of efficiency to the wage rate
Λ intermediate input
Π profit bill
Σ the supply of labour
δ the rate of time preference

η   index of neutral technical progress
θ   overmanning factor
κ   index of capital augmentation
λ   index of labour augmentation
μ   the real price of resources
π   the profit share of national product
ρ   the rate of profit
σ   the elasticity of technical substitution
ς   the semi-elasticity of intertemporal substitution
τ   the unemployment benefit contribution
υ   the rate of unemployment

Acknowledgements

I would like to thank Susie Nguyen and Tom Phelan for their careful reading of large parts of the manuscript.

I would like to acknowledge the benefit of presenting parts of the draft to seminars of the Faculty of Economics and Politics, the University of Cambridge; the School of Economics, the Australian National University; the Economics Program, the Australian National University; the School of Commerce, the University of South Australia; the School of Economics, the University of Wollongong; the School of Accounting, Economics and Finance, Deakin University; the School of Economics, the University of Adelaide; the School of Economics, the University of Western Australia; the Department of Economics, the University of Queensland; the Department of Economics, Monash University; the 20th and 22nd Conference of the History of Economic Thought Society of Australia; the 40th Conference of the UK History of Economic Thought Society; the 38th and 26th Australian Conference of Economists; and the 2nd Australian Macroeconomics Workshop

The writing of this book was materially assisted by the Research Incentive Grants Scheme of the College of Business and Economics, Australian National University. It was also aided by the tranquillity and cordiality of the Kioloa Campus of the Australian National University, where a large part was written. The same thanks are owed to New College of the University of New South Wales, and the Women's College of the University of Sydney.

I should also express my debt to conversations with Declan Trott, Henry Ergas, Paul Oslington and Andrew Leigh.

1. The problem labour monopoly might solve

A PROBLEM AND A POTENTIAL SOLUTION

The abiding theoretical problem of macroeconomics asks, 'Why is there unemployment?'

The Classical economists sought to answer this question by invoking a resistance in real wages to the reduction necessary to eliminate unemployment; 'real wage rigidity'. But why real wages should be rigid was not answered. And why unemployment was intermittently pliant to something entirely non-real – monetary policy – could not be answered within their tenets.

Keynesian economics, by contrast, answered the question of unemployment by invoking nominal wage rigidity. As explicated by means of the IS-LM model, Keynesian doctrine held that rigidity in the money wage would explain both the existence of unemployment, and its apparent sensitivity to monetary policy.[1] This last sensitivity was important because it suggested a remedy for unemployment – monetary and fiscal policy – that was more politic than socially unpopular wage cuts. And perhaps this was enough for the Keynesian account of unemployment to displace the Classical one.

The Keynesian account, however, met an increasing dissatisfaction with the passing of the post-war decades. It was difficult to reconcile wage rigidity (especially nominal rigidity) with labour market participants that are both rivalrous and rational. And without wage rigidity, how could socially costly, 'involuntary' unemployment exist? It increasingly appeared to theorists that there was an inconsistency in the conjunction of involuntary unemployment, optimization and labour market competition. Thus in the post-war debates over Keynesian economics there loomed ever larger an apparent imperative to make a choice between the elements of a seemingly inconsistent triad: unemployment, optimization and labour market competition; to select some, and drop at least one.

One possible choice was to retain optimization and competition, and as a consequence to discard involuntary unemployment. This choice was exemplified best in Real Business Cycle models, but is also implicit in 'search models' of unemployment. This choice was a wholly satisfactory response to all economists, save those who believed in the reality of involuntary unemployment.[2]

A second possible response would be to retain competition and involuntary unemployment, but to abandon the tenet of optimization as it is usually understood in economics. The considerable current appeal of 'behavioural economics' has opened up an avenue for this response (Bewley 1999). But despite the undeniable resonance of behavioural ideas, a circumspection about relinquishing standard notions of optimization, both as a tool and as an intellectual discipline, has prevented these approaches from being truly accepted.

There was a third possible choice: to retain involuntary unemployment by abandoning not optimization, but competition. This is the choice the present inquiry will make. This book will evaluate the merits of discarding the tenet of labour market competition, but retaining optimization, for the purpose of explaining unemployment and the conditions of employment.

The book, then, explores the macroeconomic implications of an 'optimizing' restraint on competitive forces within the labour market. To put it another way, the present work is concerned with the behaviour of the macroeconomy when the labour force acts collectively, so to choose the best terms for its labour.

This 'anti-competitive' collective behaviour of the labour force that we are concerned with might, for the sake of concision, be denoted 'labour monopoly', a term which is unfortunate on account of its exaggeration, yet has no better alternative. But 'labour monopoly' will not be taken here as a literal analogy to business monopoly or collusion. Rather, it is interpreted as something that operates by means of the democratic electoral mechanism, where the regulations of working conditions (wage rates, hours, work intensity) are selected by an electoral process. The book, then, is concerned with, in a single phrase, the macroeconomic implications of 'electorally optimal' labour regulation.

The present work contends that such optimal restrictions on labour market competition can provide insight into involuntary unemployment. More specifically, it is argued that such optimal labour restriction implies a degree of real wage rigidity, and therefore unemployment. The power of the simple hypothesis of wage income maximization to account for real wage rigidity is a leading theme of this work.

It will also be shown that 'electorally optimal' labour regulation promises to explain several features of the labour market beyond wage rigidity. It will be argued that it also accounts for the volatility of the real wage, and not just rigidity. 'Electorally optimal' labour regulation also provides rationalization for the existence of an excess demand for labour, and not just an excess supply of labour. It suggests an explanation of an inefficient state sector existing alongside an efficient private sector. It advances grounds for the existence of a minimum wage in place of a universal regulation of wages. It puts forward a motivation for restrictions on hours worked, as well as unemployment. It suggests how unemployment benefits might be a key feature of the enforcement of wage rigidity.

Finally, the last chapter will additionally argue how labour monopoly might explain nominal wage rigidity, and not just real wage rigidity. The argument there turns on the hypothesis that nominal wage rigidity secures an increase in the flexibility of real wages, which secures in turn an expansion in the demand for labour. Thus a degree of nominal wage rigidity is in the interest of labour. This last linkage of labour monopoly to nominal wage rigidity has wider implications. For, as Keynes argued, money non-neutrality is intimately bound up with the phenomenon of 'effective demand', wherein an increase in saving will not automatically produce a matching increase in investment. Thus 'labour monopoly' may be very central to the phenomenon of effective demand.

I conclude that the labour monopoly both promises to complete the Classical explanation of unemployment – by predicting when, why and how real wages will be so rigid; but at the same time also better secures Keynesian insights, by explaining how money rigidity might be in the interest of the labour monopoly.

AN OVERVIEW OF THE UNDERTAKING

The book is an exercise in macroeconomic analysis, and in keeping with that it invokes the assumptions commonly found in macroeconomic analysis: aggregate production functions; a closed economy; homogeneous labour; homothetic and identical utility functions; and homogeneous output. The adoption of these stark and strong assumptions is justified by their simplicity, neutrality and, in some measure, by their prevalence. Nevertheless, it is worth registering that key aspects of the approach deviate from what are now virtually doctrinal norms, and this will doubtless cause frustration in some readers. I make no assumption of market equilibrium; but allow equilibrium to occur, or not occur, depending on whether it serves the labour interest or not. I make no assumption of competition in labour markets; but allow competition to occur, or not occur, depending whether its non-occurrence advances the labour interest or not. Finally, I do make an assumption of the existence of a labour interest distinguished from other economic interests; I do not assume that away by supposing homogeneity in endowments.

The political economy deployed here is as stark as the chosen macroeconomic apparatus. I generally use a median voter model; and sometimes a model of unanimity, or perfect consensus. In either case I am supposing that interests bear directly on decision-making, rather than being intermediated by way of a political class. I therefore neglect the strong recent tendency of political economy to model the democratic process as a principal–agent problem (for example Grossman and Helpman 2001), with voters as the principal, and politicians as the (wayward) agents. Thus the democracy I analyse here is a successfully direct democracy; a democracy without politicians. Assuming a political economy of this kind undoubtedly involves a loss; the principal–agent paradigm both resonates in the face of the burgeoning 'professional' political class, and has borne fruit in analytic terms. But all modelling is selection.

This book, then, splices to the median voter model the common assumptions of the macroeconomist, and investigates what results for labour market outcomes. It analyses these not in passing, but head on. So it could be entitled, 'Taking labour collusion seriously'. 'Seriously', but not comprehensively, or even 'generally'. Any attempt at some 'total theory' of labour monopoly would be hopelessly inflated. Instead the text provides 'a box of models', each focusing on a particular analytic issue. Thus the text does not proceed by way of the elaboration of an ever more general model, but moves through a sequence of vistas, as the analytic standpoint is shifted from one direction to another.

This sequence is not arbitrary.

The book's analysis opens in Chapter 3 with a 'maximally simple' model, involving a perfectly homogeneous workforce, a division of the population into workers and capital owners, and the collective choice of the wage rate by the workforce to maximize their interest. This is shown to provide an immediate rationalization of wage rigidity, overmanning and restricted hours. The easy success of such a simple model raises the prospect of an equally simple explanation of unemployment, by means of labour monopoly, even in more elaborate models.

The strong simple conclusion of rigidity that flows from a maximally simple wage bill maximizing model loses its hold once that model is extended. Chapter 4 shows that shocks to technology, taxes and input prices may yield not rigidity but volatility in wages; a volatility that *preserves* the level of employment in the face of labour demand shocks. But it is also argued that this wage volatility is a potential merit of the labour monopoly approach, for part of the phenomenon of 'wage stickiness' is not only the wage not responding to unemployment ('rigidity'), but also the wage responding to 'not unemployment' ('volatility').

Chapters 5–9 may be seen as investigations as to what predictions of rigidity and volatility survive sophistications of the simpler models that yielded them.

In Chapter 5 it is shown that rigidity and volatility may extend into situations where wage rate decisions must proceed from a compromise between the labour interest and capital interest; the situation of bargaining. The key difference from simple labour monopoly is found to be that the bargained wage, rather than being kept from falling to its competitive model, may be kept from rising to its competitive level, and yield an excess demand for labour as a result.

It is then argued in Chapter 6 that rigidity can in some degree survive the allowance of intertemporal considerations, and the recognition by the labour interest that a high wage rate will impact on investment, and so on future wage incomes. The recognition of this impact clearly threatens the coherence of the labour monopoly story by suggesting a potential coincidence of interest between capital and labour – as labour seeks to fatten the capitalist goose that will lay the golden egg it wants. But the chapter concludes that the allowance of intertemporal considerations at most only partly aligns the interest of capital and labour, and may not do so at all.

Chapter 7 argues that a larger threat to wage rigidity lies not so much in the workforce saving income, but in it owning capital. It is found that the workforce's ownership of capital not only dilutes the reward to raising the wage rate, but also creates an incentive to abandon all regulation of wage rates, and instead pursue the labour interest by managing capital along non-profit-maximizing lines.

Chapter 8 reinforces Chapter 7 by demonstrating that the existence of a value of leisure also promises to subvert wage regulation, by showing that the labour interest is better served by placing a maximum on hours worked rather than a minimum on wage rates. But it is also shown that the difficulties of enforcing restrictions on hours worked may make optimal a regime of wage regulation conjoined with unemployment benefits. The analysis of this chapter therefore concludes with the suggestion that unemployment benefits are integrally tied up with the regulation of real wages for the benefit of labour monopoly.

Chapter 9 is perhaps the key chapter in terms of relating the present approach to the contemporary world in which wage regulation is infrequently universal, but instead confined to minimum rates for low-paid labour. This chapter uses a simple, tractable model of heterogeneous workers to show how a majority of purely self-interested voters may find it optimizing to establish a minimum wage, at the cost of unemployment to those covered by it. Further, it shows that this action will rigidify the average rate of wages throughout the economy. Thus even where a majority of wage rates are set by competition, labour monopoly can operate so as to create unemployment and destroy overall wage flexibility.

The last two analytic chapters, 10 and 11, discard the standard neoclassical demand for labour function that has been maintained since Chapter 3, and adopt non-standard labour demand functions to assist the assessment of fiscal and monetary shocks in the context of labour monopoly. Chapter 10's analysis of fiscal shocks is subversive of Keynesian policy precepts. But the analysis of monetary shocks in Chapter 11 is moderately congenial of Keynesian policy, as it yields a theory as to why a labour monopoly might have an incentive to stop nominal wage rates from adjusting to money shocks

THE CRUX

If there is an overarching message of the present work it is that the phenomenon of unemployment is what economists 'should expect'. For they do expect self-interest to operate, and the interest of labour is oftentimes to overprice and underutilize labour. Thus the analysis contends that unemployment is a contrived surplus; an oversupply contrived for the benefit of a particular interest; a surplus that can be compared to 'wine lakes' and 'butter mountains'. Unemployment, then, is one manifestation of the commonplace and endemic distortion of government for the purpose of sectional gain; no different at bottom from rent control, or price supports, or empty 'bridges to nowhere'.

In assimilating unemployment to the 'commonplace and endemic distortion of government policy' the analysis evidently undertakes the 'banalization' of the unemployment problem. The present analysis (almost) wholly lacks the implicit assumption of the 'pathos of unemployment' that has characterized almost all analyses since 1936. At the same time it remains some distance from the severity of the Classical economists, as the present analysis lacks that school's sting of implicit admonishment. For the present analysis does not see wage rigidity as a matter of stubbornness or stupidity, but rationalizes it as a strategy that maximizes an interest: the labour interest, the predominant interest of the greater part of the population for the greater part of their lives.

The analysis is also banalizing of unemployment in another sense. Since about 1930 influential theories of unemployment have often had a degree of intellectual daring. Thus Keynes – the most conspicuous illustration of this proposition – devised a world where increases in (productive) capital impoverished, and increases in (unproductive) pieces of legal tender enriched. His Hayekian opponents blamed the slump on excessive money supply creation, even as the Great Depression exhibited severe monetary contraction. New Classical economists, with a near equal cognitive valour, declared involuntary unemployment to be non-existent, or meaningless. Their New Keynesian adversaries, with less daring but with every show of confidence in the utility of their technical elan, devised defences of involuntary unemployment in terms of tales of coconut trees.

In the present study, by contrast, an elementary intellectual resource – the theory of monopoly – is brought into play, and deployed, in a manner that is familiar to economists, to rationalize the existence of positive-priced resources that are in excess supply.

The present work's use of the theory of monopoly makes for another difference to the response of economists in the face of unemployment. The theory of monopoly implies that the social problem of unemployment is in large measure a problem of interests, not ideas. Unemployment is not comparable to, say, the outbreak of a previously unknown infectious disease. Such a problem calls for ingenuity to advance the scientific understanding of the disease. The solutions, if you like, are knowledge solutions. But in the labour monopoly theory there is little room for a 'knowledge solution' to the social problem of unemployment. The solution is constitutional: to prevent a special interest, even if a very large special interest, from creating unemployment for its own benefit.

This relative redundancy of knowledge solutions is perhaps one reason why the labour monopoly approach has not absorbed more attention of economists. For what can economists offer to the world but what they know? Yet there, unarguably, is another reason for the hesitations of economists; the labour monopoly approach has experienced logical difficulties over the many decades it has been pursued. The next chapter reviews the mixed success of attempts to advance a labour monopoly explanation of unemployment.

NOTES

1. Following Leijonhufvud (1968), 'Keynesian economics' is understood to be distinguished from 'the economics of Keynes'.
2. Someone may be said to be involuntarily unemployed when they have not chosen to be unemployed. To put the concept with greater precision, someone is involuntarily unemployed if: (a) they are not employed; (b) there exists an employer who would employ them on terms on which they would be willing to be employed; and (c) they and the employer are aware of each other's wishes. Like all concepts, the notion of involuntary unemployment has a theoretical habitat that best suits it, and that is one of perfectly informed price- and wage-taking agents. It might be better called 'excess supply of labour unemployment'.

2. The fall and rise of labour monopoly theory

This book contends that that the phenomenon of the collective choice by the workforce of its terms of labour helps explain unemployment, and kindred labour market dysfunctions. The present chapter traces the fluctuating fortunes of this thesis over the twentieth century. It recounts and explains the disappearance of 'labour monopoly' theory in the wake of the Keynesian revolution, and its sudden re-emergence in 1980s, after the passing of the doctrinal conflicts of the Keynesian era.

The chapter goes on to suggest that, despite the revival of labour monopoly theory since 1980, it holds no more than an indefinite and subsidiary position in macroeconomics today. It is at most merely a rationalization of neo-Keynesian 'fixed wage' macroeconomics; and in the minimum it comprises no more than several splinters in the kaleidoscopic state of contemporary macroeconomics.

The chapter further suggests that the labour monopoly doctrine remains encumbered by unresolved questions raised by the twentieth-century debates over the approach. Put in general terms, the questions amount to: can the well-developed theory of monopoly in product markets be simply and successfully transposed to labour markets? Or will any such attempt founder on the characteristics that distinguish labour markets from product markets?

In addition to these uncertainties about the theoretical coherence of the labour monopoly approach, the approach has been enervated by doubts about its applicability given the steep decline in trade unionism, and the retreat of labour market regulation.

The chapter's review of the travails of labour monopoly doctrine since the Keynesian Revolution airs the arguments, both favourable and hostile, that have surrounded the doctrine. It thereby sets the scene for this work's undertaking: to illustrate how a labour monopoly theory of unemployment can be devised that is squarely integrated into macroeconomic theory, that eludes several theoretical objections to the labour monopoly approach, and that is not reduced to irrelevance by recent trends.

THE KEYNESIAN CIRCUMVENTION

Macroeconomics germinated in the Keynesian revolution of the 1930s; a decade in which mass unionism arrived (noisily) in the United States, and was quietly insinuating itself into the governance of Great Britain. Yet the Keynesian revolution neglected anticompetitive behaviour in labour markets. In the *General Theory*'s marvellously detailed 2300 entry index there are precisely three references to trade unions. Evidently, in Keynes's mind trade unions were of very faint significance

One might hazard at least three reasons for Keynes's neglect of trade unions.

Firstly, Keynes was a 'post-Marshallian' in his intellectual capital, and there was little in the Marshallian bequest on unions. Marshall makes only 'fleeting' and 'brief' references to trade unions in his *Principles* (Petridis 1990).[1] Marshall believed his *Principles* was 'not a fitting place for a study' of trade unions, or business combinations. Why not? They were, he claimed, 'little more than eddies' of 'the deep silent stream of competition'; in other words, conspicuous but unimportant.[2] The analytical difficulty that trade unions gave him was certainly a second contributing reason: 'In Marshall's papers at Cambridge there is ample evidence that he continued to grapple with the economic analysis of trade unions with the intention of making it a substantial part of his volume II to follow the *Principles*' (Petridis 1990, 26). That second volume, of course, never appeared.[3] Overall, Marshallianism had little to contribute about unions. A telling indication of the infertility of Marshallianism is Pigou's *Theory of Unemployment* of 1933: it might be expected to say something about the issue of unions and unemployment, but says exactly nothing.[4]

On the other hand Keynes's intellectual ally Joan Robinson had just three years before the *General Theory* opened up the investigation of imperfect competition in product markets, with entirely Marshallian concepts and tools; concepts and tools that were very suggestive of the analysis of imperfect competition in labour markets. In addition, John Hicks in the previous year, and bearing a heavy debt to Marshall, published his *Theory of Wages* (1932), in which he devotes 100 pages to trade union power, industrial disputes and germane topics. Critically, he proposed a cogent solution to the problem of determining the wage rate bargain between union and firm (Hicks 1932, 141–5), a problem that had defeated Marshall, Edgeworth and Pigou, but yielded to his own fresher intuition.

Thus, it seemed that Keynes's younger peers had crafted tools that Keynes could put to use in macroconomic theorizing. But neither Keynes, nor those peers, did so. Robinson maintained that explanations of trade union behaviour in terms of economic forces were 'very long, very complicated and very unconvincing' (Robinson 1947 [1936], 174). And at a theoretical level Hicks had almost nothing to say about 'labour monopoly' in the face of competitive firms. His consciousness of product monopoly ('monopolistic combination is very common in all parts of the economic system'), his doubts about trade union power and his slighting of trade union rationality would have made 'labour monopoly' an unpromising topic to him.

There is a second and stronger ground for Keynes's neglect of trade unions: Keynes, always the topical author, would have let his thoughts be coloured by the circumstances of the decade. In 1930s' Britain trade unionism was quiescent in the aftermath of the defeat of the 1926 General Strike. It was the era of Sir Walter Citrine, an electrician by trade, who by 1936 was the pre-eminent figure in the British Trades Union Congress (TUC). Phlegmatic in personality, and moderate in his positions, Citrine's ultimate goal was to make trade union structures an integral part of the governance of Britain, almost a branch of government. It was partly as a consequence of this outlook that Citrine was knighted (by Ramsay MacDonald) in 1935, and ennobled in 1946. It was also partly as a consequence of this outlook that he was also on good terms with Keynes: good enough to be allowed by Keynes's wife Lydia to visit him during his long illness in 1937; good enough for Keynes to keep him briefed him on the proceedings of the Macmillan Committee of 1930; good enough for both to be members of the small Consultative Council to the Treasury 1940–43, where their mutual confidence smoothed the introduction of Pay As You Earn (PAYE) in the face of resistance from the factory floor (Citrine 1964). In the era of Sir Walter Citrine, British trade unionism may not have been good copy, but it was cooperative rather than wilful.

The third (and undoubtedly the most important) reason for Keynes's neglect of trade unions was that an emphasis on unions would be completely at odds with Keynes's message. It will be recalled that the notion of high wages as the source of unemployment was squarely rejected by Keynes at the opening of the *General Theory*. Consequently, he could not entertain any thesis that the deliberate high pricing of labour by 'wage-making' unions might be the source of unemployment

Keynes's rejection of deliberate high pricing of labour by 'wage-making' unions required some dialectical ingenuity, since his rejection could not be a matter of simple denial. This was because Keynes freely allowed – insisted upon[5] – a negative relation between employment and the real wage.[6] And having allowed this negative relation, there logically opens the possibility of self-seeking unions raising real wage rates, at the cost of unemployment, in return for an increase in total wage incomes.

Keynes had two ways of parrying this suggestion.

The most ambitious deflection was to contend that it was not possible for self-seeking unions to raise real wage rates for the sake of an increase in total wage incomes. To emphasize the point: it was not just that unions did not raise real wage rates; they could not. Why not? Because while wage bargains are struck in money, real wages were decided by the price level, which is not a choice variable of unions. Thus unions could not choose the real wage.

But Keynes was overreaching his model in advancing such an impossibility thesis. In bald contradiction of his thesis, a basic property of his model is that higher money wages will – subject to 'slips betwixt the cup and the lip' – increase real wages. This is because an increase in money wages will reduce the real money supply, and thereby necessitate a higher interest rate: a proposition rightly known as the 'Keynes effect'. In IS-LM terms, the LM curve is shifted upwards by a higher money wage. As long as the IS curve is not vertical, output will fall, and so real wages will rise.[7]

Thus Keynes's attempt to argue unions out of the *General Theory* is vulnerable to criticism by his own logic. And this was unreservedly granted by Joan Robinson just months after the *General Theory*. After explaining the 'Keynes effect' to her readers in the *Essays in the Theory of Employment*, Robinson goes on:

> Thus a combination of Trade Unions sufficiently strong to control the level of money wages would be faced with the problem of balancing a gain in employment against a loss in real wages, and they might be supposed to aim at establishing what appears to them to be the optimal level of employment. (Robinson 1947 [1936], 27)

Joan Robinson is here squarely raising the relevance of labour monopoly within Keynes's framework. But she curtly shies from pursuing the thought. 'In practise, as we have argued, Trade Union policy is not conceived in these terms' (ibid., 28).

In what terms, then, is trade union policy to be conceived? Here we arrive at Keynes's second, less ambitious parry of the significance of unions: unions are passive with respect to changes in real wages. More precisely, they are passive with respect to changes in real wages brought about by changes in the money prices of goods: 'They [trade unions] do not resist reductions in real wages which are associated with increases in aggregate employment . . . no trade union would dream of striking on every occasion of a rise in the cost of living' (Keynes 1936, 15).

To us this is not a very impressive generalization. With our experience of the two generations subsequent to 1936, we would allow that unions might, indeed, 'dream' of striking on occasion of a rise in the cost of living that was unaccompanied by a compensating wage rise. They might even have done so.

Be that as it may, the tenet Keynes successfully imparted to his contemporary readers was that unions were one of the inert gases of economic life, and played no role in its active chemistry. Thus self-identified Keynesians, that is, those who took the *General Theory* as their principal stimulus, accepted the Master's dictum on the irrelevance of imperfect competition in labour markets.

The upshot was that an interest in labour markets in the context of the new macroeconomics came from an oblique angle; not from a 'macroeconomic awareness' stimulated by the Depression but from an attention to microeconomic problems, animated by the 'imperfect competition revolution'.

THE NEXUS BETWEEN RIGIDITY AND IMPERFECT COMPETITION

In the early 1930s there rolled in a great wave of interest in imperfect competition, on the crest of which were the theoretical works of Robinson and Chamberlin, and the empirical work of Gardiner Means. This wave was a reflection of a sharpening of the general perception of the economic system as a monopolized one; a 'world of monopolies' in Joan Robinson's phrase.

One expression of this sense of the ubiquity of monopoly was a certain train of thought in the United States – most closely associated with Gardiner Means (1935a and 1935b) – as to why the Great Depression was so severe; a train of thought that was very ambiguously related to the almost simultaneous Keynesian revolution. This tendency of thought judged the rigidity in industrial prices as culpable in making the Depression so distressful;[8] a rigidity that was held to be tied up (somehow) with the great size of the firms that any realistic analysis would allow for. An example of analysis that airs this last supposition is 'Monopoly power and price rigidities' by J.K. Galbraith (1936). The one enduring analytical contribution of this tendency of thought was the kinked demand curve by Galbraith's colleague Paul Sweezy (1939).

This tendency of thought did not recoil from applying the 'rigidity as market power' logic to trade unions:

> 'on the matter of labor costs . . . these too are a manifestation of monopoly power. The removal of free competition in the labor markets (for which on other grounds we may find ample justification) has enabled labor leaders to choose high rates or 'prices' in preference to a larger volume of employment or 'sales'. (Galbraith 1936, 472)[9]

Evidently, there were both salient similarities and salient differences, between this 'monopoly power as price rigidity' school and Keynesianism.

On one hand they both renounced classical economics, and both shared a belief that laissez-faire was defunct. And they both rejected price flexibility as a policy *solution* to depression.[10] Nevertheless, 'monopoly power as price rigidity' constituted an explanation of the severity of depression that turned on insufficient flexibility in prices, and in some measure wages also; and that was a doctrine that would be congenial to the Classical economists, but to which Keynes was explicitly hostile. To Keynes inflexibility in prices was irrelevant to the Depression, and he underlined that by assuming away all market power or 'rigidity' in his own theoretical account of it. In fact, Keynes suspected that flexibility would be counterproductive, a proposition that was keenly supported by his foremost American epigone, Alvin Hansen (1940).

This conjunction of similarity and difference made for the possibility of a hybrid growth. At the intersection of realistic study of labour markets – that freely allowed for the significance of market power and trade unions – and the new Keynesian analysis, there lay the possibility of a quickening of a macroeconomics that took both unemployment and trade unions seriously.

One person in whose mind this possibility germinated was Martin Bronfenbrenner. In 1938–39 he believed that: 'the Keynesian and the price-flexibility insights in macroeconomics . . . appeared to me not fundamentally opposed. I felt that they could and should be unified (with substantial aid from imperfect competition) in a way which would eliminate their inconsistencies' (Bronfenbrenner, quoted in Samuels and Medema 1990, 88).

This quickening was surest in Galbraith's good friend John Dunlop (1914–2003). Upon completing his PhD at Berkley in labour issues, Dunlop spent 1937 at Trinity College, Cambridge, with D.H. Robertson as a tutor. What resulted was a set of empirical papers about the macroeconomics of wages, employment and unemployment. One of these went straight to the heart Keynes's claim of a negative co-movement between real wages and money wages; a claim Keynes justified on the grounds that an increase in employment would raise nominal wages (as labour is bid up), but reduce real wages (as the marginal product of labour is driven down). In 'The movement of real and money wage rates' (1938) Dunlop concluded that, contrary to Keynes, a rise in employment would increase real wages, as well as money wages. He explained such a rise in real wages in the face of falling marginal productivity by reference to a fall in the degree of monopoly during the upswing; and to 'trade union wage-rate policy'. Dunlop gave his greatest attention to the second; in his account, unions are active. The 'passivity thesis' of Keynes is refused:

> a detailed study of negotiations indicates that, with but one qualification, trade unions have been as willing to strike for advances in wage rates when the cost of living has risen by more than a 'small' amount as to strike for the maintenance of a wage rate when threatened with a reduction. (Dunlop 1938, 426)

Nevertheless, in Dunlop (1938) there is no model of trade union behaviour. However, a stark vision of trade unions was soon to be advanced by Henry Simons, and 'Old' Chicago.

SIMONS, DUNLOP AND LEONTIEF: THE GENESIS, AND NEMESIS, OF LABOUR MONOPOLY THEORY

It was Henry Simons (1889–1946) who led Chicago's charge against Keynesian macroeconomics in the ten years after the *General Theory*. He is remembered today for formulating the need for 'rules' in the conduct of monetary policy. What is forgotten is that in a series of papers (1942, 1944) Simons launched an anti-union polemic, in which he blamed the malaise of the US economy in the late 1930s on unions, and painted a deeply pessimistic vision of the post-Second World War world in which unions were to be the enforcers of a collectivist regime. He preferred to refer to trade unionism as 'syndicalism': the doctrine 'aims at the possession of the means of production . . . through general strikes, terrorism, sabotage, etc . . .'. He believed that the menace of syndicalist expropriation was the cause of the weakness of investment that America experienced in the late 1930s, not the 'maturity' of its economy as Hansen alleged.

Keynesians would have rejected Simons's picture of the ravages of labour monopoly, but would not have felt much need to rebut it. To Keynes, unions were neither beneficent nor harmful. Simons's views instead found traction in the mind of Dunlop, who in a 1940 visit to the University of Chicago discussed with Simons his vision of labour unions. The upshot was the analytic content of *Wage Determination under Trade Unions* (1944) which on its first page presents itself as a reasoned response to the 'provocative' positions of Simons.

Dunlop complains that unions are dismissed as a complication by mainstream economists, and 'relegated' to labour economists. He wants to bring them into the mainstream, and explore maximizing models of them. He does so by applying to them the Robinsonian apparatus for the analysis of imperfect competition. The union is a labour monopolist seeking to maximize the wage bill,[11] and consequently the elasticity of demand is critical: 'Trade union leadership, in effect, must make estimates of the elasticity of the demand for labour over very short periods, the cycle and the longer run' (Dunlop 1942, 292).[12]

But Dunlop's models had little issue in terms of macroeconomics.

The claims of both 'realism' and 'theory' partly accounted for this infertility.

Dunlop himself was a 'realistic' economist; without leaving academia he was soon engrossed in public administration, ultimately becoming a US Secretary for Labor under Gerald Ford. With this 'realism' he could not be satisfied with his schematic models of union behaviour. 'One of the more dangerous habits of mind that economic theory may create is an imperialism that insists that all aspects of behaviour, particularly any activity related to markets, can be explained by models with the usual economic variables' (Dunlop 1944, 5). More than 50 years later he said of his analysis: 'it is simply not true that unions push up wages as these models suggest' (Kaufman and Dunlop 2002).

There was also some damage from theoretical considerations.

In Dunlop the union's maximand was the wages bill:

$$\max_{L} w(L)L \qquad w'(L) < 0 \qquad (2.1)$$

This obviously ignored the cost of leisure forgone by wage earners, but this could be easily rectified by adding an expression for the disutility of labour:

$$\max_{L} w(L)L - d(L) \qquad d'(L) > 0, d''(L) \geq 0 \qquad (2.2)$$

Such an amended maximand would exactly parallel the Robinsonian analysis of product demand:

$$\max_{Q} p(Q)Q - c(Q) \qquad c'(Q) > 0, c''(Q) \geq 0 \qquad (2.3)$$

Thus, if one adopted (2.2), one could exactly transpose Robinsonian product monopoly theory to the situation of labour monopoly. Yet (2.2) remains a long distance from a tolerable utility function. For it supposes a constant marginal utility of consumption, and increasing marginal disutility of work; thus the worker is risk-neutral in consumption, has an infinite elasticity of intertemporal substitution; and does not treat leisure as a normal good.

There is a second difficulty in the Dunlopian maximand: it uses aggregate employment, L. Thus all workers are identical. Dunlop himself disliked this assumption of homogeneity of union members and their interests which allows a union to be treated as a maximizing agent: he considered it 'mischievous' to ignore the coalitional aspect of unions.

A third difficulty with the maximand is that it ignores the probabilistic character of each worker's maximand when faced with a risk of unemployment. The labour monopoly story of unemployment is that the wage is above the competitive level, with the consequence that each worker might be either employed or unemployed. Dunlop's use of the wages bill seems to assume that all members are equally rationed in work. It is a model of 'short time' rather than employment and unemployment.

Even if we allow the Dunlopian maximand as valid, the theory that drew upon it had other difficulties. In 1946 Leontief set off a mine under the basic assumption behind the supposed culpability of trade unions for unemployment: the basic presumption that what a labour monopoly does is to take advantage of an inelastic demand for labour by setting a price for labour above the competitive level, thereby increasing total wage incomes but also reducing the demand for labour, and creating unemployment. In Leontief's analysis such behaviour amount to a false maximization. In Leontief's analysis the truly maximizing union would not create anything that could be easily recognizable as unemployment.

Consider a trade union which can set the wage as a 'diktat' to wage- (and price-) taking firms. It will face a labour demand curve that will generate an inverted u-shaped relation between wages bill and employment; a 'wage bill hill' (Figure 2.1).

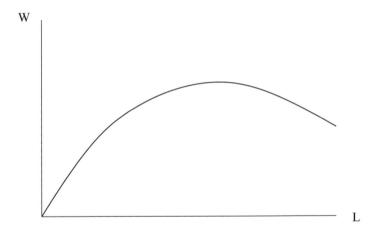

Figure 2.1   A wage bill–employment trade-off

Suppose the union has preferences over consumption and leisure, producing upward-sloping indifferences curve between the wage bill (= consumption) and labour (= not-leisure). The rational union, it would appear, selects the point on the wages bill hill that yields it the highest utility (Figure 2.2).

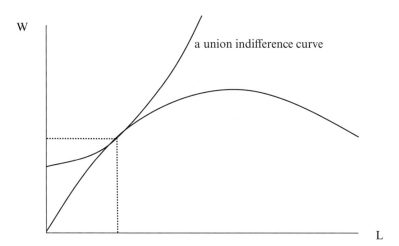

Figure 2.2   The optimal choice of the labour monopoly?

This outcome corresponds to a certain wage rate, that is measured in Figure 2.3 by the slope of ray from the origin that intersects the combination of employment and wages bill chosen by the union.

This 'optimal' wage exceeds the marginal rate of substitution. This can be seen from Figure 2.3, where the slope of the indifference curve measures the marginal rate of substitution between consumption and leisure. Evidently, the opportunity cost of leisure (the wage) exceeds the value of

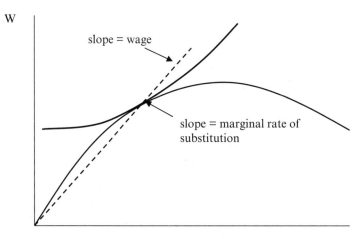

Figure 2.3   The wage rate under labour monopoly?

leisure (the marginal rate of substitution). A wage-taking worker would wish to choose less leisure; there is involuntary unemployment.

However Leontief (1946) argued that this wage diktat 'optimum' is, in fact, suboptimal; both firms and labour monopoly could do better for themselves. To see this, we begin by noting that the optimal employment decision of a group of competitive firms is describable as the point of tangency between the ray from the origin measuring the wage (in the manner of Figures 2.3 and 2.4), and the 'iso-profit' curve that is tangent to the ray.[13]

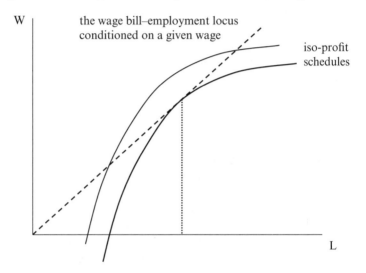

Figure 2.4   Profit-maximizing employment for a given wage

We can now infer that the iso-profit curve associated with the 'optimum' is not tangental to indifference curve associated with the 'optimum': it intersects (Figure 2.5).

Evidently, it would pareto-improving to move 'north-east' into the area bounded by the intersection of the two curves. It is pareto-improving to have more wages and more employment than the apparent labour monopoly optimum. Both union and firms can do better than the wage diktat 'optimum'.

Efficient consumption–leisure combinations could be secured by the union imposing a wage rate and employment level. Thus, by appropriate choices of both w and L, both firms and union can be made better off. This is not to say that both will be made better off. The union now chooses a wage bill–employment pair to maximize utility. Not surprisingly, the union will always choose the wage bill–employment pair such that wages

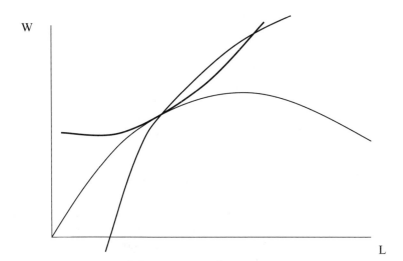

Figure 2.5   The union indifference curve and the iso-profit curve intersect

consume all of product. Thus the union takes the zero profit locus of firms as their constraint.

What is the upshot? The Leontief union solves:

$$\max_{L} Q(L) - d(L) \qquad (2.4)$$

and the optimal choice of employment is characterized by:

$$Q'(L) - d'(L) = 0 \qquad (2.5)$$

The union chooses employment such that marginal product of labour equals the disutility of labour. This is of course the perfectly competitive, and welfare-efficient, solution. Evidently, by driving the logic of the rational self-interested 'labour monopoly' so hard, Leontief had arrived in a world that seemed unlike the one the critics of labour monopoly were concerned to explain. 'Labour monopoly' had been invoked (almost always by its critics) to explain (involuntary) unemployment, that was assumed to be socially inefficient, and certainly detrimental to the welfare of the unemployed. But Leontief's analysis concludes that if the union chooses both the wage and employment then there is no contraction of employment relative to the perfectly competitive outcome. Furthermore, there is no social inefficiency. And the union's action is in the interests of its members. Further, in Leontief it is not even clear whether there is 'unemployment' in the obvious sense of more job seekers than job offers, for the whole spectacle of the 'job offer' has gone. It is no longer the firm that offers employment to labour, but the union that instructs the employer how many to employ.

Ultimately, 'labour monopoly' theory was extinguished not by Dunlop's concern for realistic assumptions, or by Leontief's skill in the theoretical fast track, but from an unexpected source; a source that contended that most important thing to bear in mind about unions was their unimportance.

THE IMPACT OF THE UNION AND NEW CHICAGO

In 1951, near (if not quite at) the high tide of American labour unionism, a symposium on unions was held in Washington, DC that included the leading lights of the time – Milton Friedman, Edward H. Chamberlin, Gottfried Haberler and Paul Samuelson – the proceedings of which were published under the title *The Impact of the Union* (Wright 1951).

Chamberlin's (1951) contribution to the symposium, 'The Monopoly Power of Labour', is an onslaught on unions. 'Strikes are a form of warfare' that involve 'mass coercion or, possibly mass violence', and are an inevitable corollary of collective bargaining. Overall, the posture is sympathetic with Henry Simons a few years earlier.

What might have been deemed unexpected (at the time) is the contribution of Milton Friedman, 'Some comments on the significance of labor unions for economic policy' (1951).

Friedman adheres to the Chamberlin union-as-cartel interpretation of unions: 'labour unions and enterprise monopolies are conceptually similar effects' (1951, 206). Nevertheless, Friedman contends that: 'laymen and economists alike tend, in my view, to exaggerate greatly the extent to which labor unions affect the structure and level of wage rates . . . [most unions] have had only a negligible effect on wage rates' (1951, 204, 215).

Friedman argued for this contention on empirical and theoretical grounds.

His empirical grounds consist of simple comparisons of growth rates in wages in more-unionized and less-unionized situations: the US Civil War, the First World War and the Second World War. That is, he compares war with no unions, war with a few unions, and war with many unions. But despite this difference in unionization there is no difference in real wage growth. He then compares growth rate in wages in 'domestic service' and autoworkers 1939–47; in other words, a comparison of an un-unionized with a highly unionized workforce. But servants' wages rose 172 per cent, while autoworkers rose only 98 per cent.

Friedman's theoretical ground for the 'negligibility' of unions is that any monopoly has power only insofar as the demand for its product has some inelasticity, and that there exist, claims Friedman, 'devious and subterranean channels' that render the demand for labour 'highly elastic'.

The end point of Friedman's reasonings was that competiveness was not merely a desirable thing; it was real thing. Friedman was rejecting the presumption of the imperfect competition revolution: that monopoly was 'normal' (or even 'natural'). To Chamberlin, 'monopoly profits exist very generally throughout the economy'. But to Friedman: 'After a visit recently to Europe [1947?], I came back saying I was going to tell my students after this that America has perfect competition everywhere' (quoted in Dow and Abernathy 1963).

It was the naturalness of competition and unnaturalness of monopoly that led Friedman to conclude that unions are in large part political creations, and that any 'unemployment in the union area would be largely offset elsewhere' where competition ruled as normal (Friedman 1951, 227).

Friedman's response was methodologically representative of his method of combat. He was not seeking to defeat his adversary on theoretical terrain; he found the union-as-monopoly formulation wholly satisfactory, and did not enter the theoretical difficulties exposed by Leontief, or any of Dunlop's more particular critics. Rather, Friedman used empirical significance as his weapon of choice.

Friedman's position was not idiosyncratic. He was speaking characteristically of the Chicago School, in its post-war reformulation, following the death of Simons in 1946, under his own leadership and facing the totally new problems of the post-war world.

A striking illustration of that reformulation – that shift – may be found in the thought of H. Gregg Lewis (1914–92), a member of the Chicago Economics Department from 1939 – the first of the 'post-Second World War' generation – and 'perhaps the founder of modern labour economics' (Ashenfelter 1994, 138).

Lewis was also a student and admirer of Henry Simons (he wrote Simons's obituary in 1946 in the *American Economic Review*), and his first entry into labour market issues – 'The labor-monopoly problem: a positive program' (1951)' – evoked the title of Simons's 1936 book *A Positive Program for Laissez Faire*; a book in which Simons had identified labor unionism as one of the many manifestations of monopoly that 'should not be tolerated in a free society' (Biddle 1996, 179). Lewis opens by declaring that in Simons's work, 'the ill [of unionism] was diagnosed, but the measures for relief not prescribed' (1951, 277). He proposed his relief measure: outlawing any union-negotiated agreement that covered more than one firm. By law unions had to be single-firm in membership and scope of action. The action in concert by workers across an occupation, or an industry, was to be illegal.

This aggressive posture towards trade unionism did not endure. One of Lewis's memorialists records that within a few years:

> Rather than inveighing against the union monopoly problem he was taking its measure with what he considered to be the tools of the impartial scientist . . . Lewis' theoretical analyses of unionism led him to conclude contra Simons, unions themselves were not necessarily inconsistent with competition. (Biddle 1996)

The relentless use of 'labour-monopoly' as a synonym with 'trade union' was now spurned. In fact, by 1965 Lewis had developed a conception of competitive unionism, where a union is a business – a negotiation business – and union members are its customers (Lewis 1965).[14]

DEMISE

Keynes's neglect of trade unions constituted a vulnerability that the adversaries of Keynes might have usefully exploited. Nevertheless, in the formulation of the modern 'Chicago School' that took place around 1950, anti-competitive behaviour in labour markets was consciously minimized by the leading adversary of Keynesian policies. The upshot of the transformation of 'Old' Chicago into 'New' Chicago was that the (surely vulnerable) Keynesian position on the irrelevance of unions was neglected by their most salient opponents. The end result was that the foundational debates of the late 1930s and 1940s, that structured macroeconomic discourse in the twentieth century, eliminated unions from mainstream macroeconomics.

In my interpretation, unionism was written out of macroeconomic thinking for 50 years on account of two contrary, but ultimately congruent, reactions to the imperfect competition revolution. To Keynesians, the empirical significance of imperfect competition was unimportant: to Chicago it was all-important. Consequently, to Keynesians the significance of unionism would only be a distraction from their overarching message, while to 'Chicago', as formulated in the post-war era, any significance of unionism would be positively at odds with their message. This left space for a common cause: throughout the sparring in the post-war generation, one tenet that Keynes and Chicago could agree upon was the macroeconomic inconsequence of imperfect competition in labour markets.

In the post-war generation interest in the nexus between unions and unemployment retreated to the ideological margins; for example, Hutt

(1930) and Hayek (1980). With good reason, one advocate of the 'labour monopoly' approach could in 1981 ask: 'Whatever happened to the monopoly theory of labour unions?' (Reynolds 1981). In fact, it was about to happen all over again.

REVIVAL

In retrospect, it was a brilliant stroke by Friedman to discard 'labour monopoly' and to stake all on 'money'. Keynesian policy had under-estimated the significance of money. At the same time the conservative critics of unions in the mid-twentieth century had overestimated their import. Whether through a lucky strike, or sound analysis, or sensitive intuition, Friedman's 1951 paper seems to have anticipated the long, deep and (fairly) steady decline in trade unionism in the United States, and elsewhere.

But Chicago's forsaking of labour monopoly ultimately had some un-expected intellectual reverberations. Chicago's very destruction of Keynes's claims – its reduction of his 'general theory' to a miscellany of freak cases – had made it more accepted that, within the bounds of standard theory, labour market competition and involuntary unemployment were mutually exclusive. Wage flexibility would surely ensure full employment.

How could those who took involuntary unemployment as significant dysfunction respond? One response was to reject 'existing, standard theory' – and strive to obtain a theory of involuntary unemployment even within in the context of labour market competition (see De Vroey 2004 for a survey of these efforts).

A different response was to accept the alleged mutual exclusivity of labour market competition and involuntary unemployment, but – faced with the choice between labour market competition and involuntary unemployment – to take involuntary unemployment as real, and labour market competition as illusory; and to explain involuntary unemployment in terms of imperfect competition in the labour market; and to do so not out of an aspiration to rid the world of that imperfect competition, but out of a wish to reinforce the reality of involuntary unemployment and the wage rigidity, by giving it an adequate microfoundation.

It was through this logic that in the 1980s the macroeconomic signifi-cance of monopolized labour markets became the subject of substantial research. It was in that decade that Solow wrote of a 'true renaissance' in the search for 'adequate' labour microfoundations for 'mainstream macroeconomics' (that is, neo-Keynesian economics) 'with alternative models appearing monthly' (Solow 1985, 411).[15] Early highlights of this literature include McDonald and Solow (1981), where those two authors ask 'why fluctuations in the demand for labour should so often lead to large changes in employment, and small . . . changes in the real wage' (McDonald and Solow 1981, 896).

Taking up a Dunlopian 'simple monopoly union', where the union sets the wage by diktat, they infer that the optimal wage is related to the elasticity of demand, and they note that if elasticity of demand is a given: 'the wage will be rigid during business cycles and fluctuations will fall entirely on employment' (p. 899).

Thus in the 1980s, the very phenomenon that Keynes belittled – unions – was brought in to shield from assault what was left of the Keynesian intellectual bequest. This is not the gentlest irony in the history of economic analysis.

This surge of interest was sustained beyond the demise of the Keynesian–Monetarist dispute, and into the 1990s. There were two principal developments.

Firstly, the long overdue application of the theory of the Nash bargain (first advanced in 1950) to the interaction of the labour monopolist and a labour monopsonist (for example Layard and Nickell 1990).[16]

Secondly, the development of the aggregate wage-setting/aggregate price-setting (AWS/APS) model (see, for example, Booth 1995). This model combined price-making (but wage-taking) firms that set prices, and wage-making (but price-taking) unions that set wages. The interaction of these two behaviours produces unemployment. However, in the most common formulation, AWS/APS assumed the price-setting behaviour of firms to be such that the real wage is invariant to employment.[17] Thus in the most common formulations of AWS/APS the price-making power of firms is invoked to eliminate the choice of the real wage by unions. It might be said that the 'second imperfect competition revolution' of the 1980s (Brakman and Heijdra 2004), that is plainly one inspiration for the AWS/APS model, has negated the impact of labour monopoly as much as the 'first' of the 1930s did.

THE FOUNDATIONS OF MONOPOLY POWER

By the close of the 1990s a disparate set of models had found their way into textbooks (see for example, Heijdra and van der Ploeg 2002; Carlin and Soskice 2006), coinciding with a loss of momentum in the revival.

The loss of momentum in labour monopoly must have been encouraged by a burgeoning interest in a radically novel interpretation of the processes of employment and unemployment. Whereas Chicago and (we have seen) Keynes were happy to assume the existence of competition by firms for labour, and competition by labour for jobs, this new interpretation favoured totally disregarding the competition by firms for labour, *and* the competition by labour for jobs. This literature, that has been christened 'equilibrium unemployment theory' (Pissarides 2000), is perhaps more effectively invoked by the tag of 'matching function'. In this vision the labour market is seen as vast tableau of numerous but wholly disconnected bilateral encounters between isolated firms and workers. On a homogeneous plane there randomly wander isolated workers who collide unpredictably with isolated chunks of capital – 'a match'. And upon bumping the two parties arrange a trade of labour for wages according to the Nash bargain.

This 'matching function' vision of employment and unemployment is remote from Keynes, Chicago and any issue of the Walrasian–Marshallian market vision. It is also remote from the labour monopoly explanation of unemployment. For it is not an 'excess supply of labour' account of unemployment; it is not an account of the unemployment of 'too many applicants for available jobs'. Rather, the 'matching function' economy consists of a plenitude of tiny bilateral monopolies; a single firm on one side, and a single worker on the other, each able to say 'take it or leave it'. By contrast the notion of labour monopoly relies on a 'unilateral monopoly'; competition on one side, and a lack of competition on the other: the absence of competition in the supply of labour, and the presence of competition in the demand for labour. And in this difference the merit, we believe, lies with the labour monopoly. If labour monopoly exaggerates the competition of firms for labour, the matching function surely underestimates that by completely disregarding it. If labour monopoly exaggerates the collusive behaviour of workers, the matching function approach surely underestimates that by completely abolishing it. It is a paradox that the same generation that has seen the world so intensely interconnected by informational and geographical mobility has seen a powerful trend propose the bilateral encounter as a paradigm of economic life. It is proposed that we are to understand this present world in terms of the passing encounter between buyer and seller; a situation that the classical economists placed as belonging to the most rudimentary economic existence; the case where you are on 'Lake Superior in a steam-boat, making your way to an unsettled region 800 miles ahead of civilization, and consciously with no chance at all of purchasing any luxury whatsoever for the space of ten years to come', and you find 'one fellow-passenger, whom you will part with before sunset, has a powerful musical snuff-box' that 'you are vehemently desirous to purchase' (De Quincy, quoted in Mill 1848 [1878]).

But apart from the development of theoretical alternatives to the market conception of the economy, the loss of momentum in labour monopoly was plausibly hastened even more by the atrophy of collusive behaviour in the labour market in the 1990s, manifested in the crash in union membership, and the withering of labour market regulation. A body of theory that had been launched on rhetoric of realism now seemed outmoded by the newest realities. In a world of $200 000-a-day 'executive compensation'[18] what grip can 'labour monopoly' have on our attention?

On several grounds, however, it does.

Even if we are to take the decline of 'labour monopoly' as a permanent reality, we evidently require a theory of imperfectly competitive labour markets to explain the decline of imperfectly competitive labour markets. The present inquiry is suggestive of such a theory. Further, the trends of past decades may yet be reversed, and in modest measure have been.[19]

Nevertheless, the trends of recent decades raise the question: how securely is anti-competitive behaviour bottomed in generalities of human conduct?

As is well known, collusive conduct is dogged by the problem of the defector. If it is better for all to collude than to compete, then it is still better to compete oneself while others collude. The cartel, it seems, will be undermined by the defector, the cheat and the entrant. And the Nash equilibrium concept provides an impressive theoretical warrant for this contention. If we assume price is the instrument, and abstract from product heterogeneity, then the Nash equilibrium (that is, Bertrand solution) is none other than the competitive equilibrium. Thus any labour cartel that is conceived in analogy with the product cartel is a flimsy device.

It has been suggested that collusion as an equilibrium might be established by supposing the adherence to an anti-competitive 'code' by the members of the labour cartel (for example Booth 1985). This suggestion operates by positing a modification of the stance of labour to restrictions on competition. Up to this point it has been implicitly assumed that the labour interest takes a starkly instrumental attitude to restrictions on competition; these restrictions are valued insofar as they are a means to the end of higher incomes. And, as we have just noted, these restrictions may not be a robust means to that end. To invoke the existence of a code is to suppose that as far as the labour interest is concerned, restrictions on competition in the labour market are an end in themselves; they are rewarding in themselves. To put the thought another way: labour competition is deemed offending, galling, costly in itself. This hypothesis is a straight road to the establishment of collusion as an equilibrium.

It is not the path taken in this work. It is not taken because we can posit another 'code' that is less demanding on our credence, that with equal success will dissolve the threat of defection and make collusion effective.

This is the code of law-abidingness. This code, which makes legal sanctions effective, will permit, and in a democracy make possible, the use of the ordinary law of the land against defection. Thus rather than invoking the informal code of anti-competitiveness, collusion is founded upon a more general code of law-abidingness, which will allow the effectuality of laws passed to limit competition in the interests of the majority.

So we arrive at our vision of labour interest securing collusive conduct by the law. In this vision unions differ from the 'labour monopoly' literature. Unions are not seen as coming from below, by economic logic of an industry-level situation. Their foundation is not seen as lying in some labour supply analog of the foundation of typical monopolists or oligopolists. In our vision unions are 'legal' rather than natural monopolies; more political constructs rather than 'market structures'; far closer to lobbies or political parties than oligopolistic firms.

We therefore purport to see through 'the veil of unions', to the politically empowered mass franchise below, using the law by what means it can to further its economic interest. That mass might use that power to establish trade unions as 'legal monopolies' with special rights: rights to visit workplaces, collect fees, hold picket-lines, obtain preference for union members, be exempt from certain common-law actions, and have privileged access to tribunals. However, in the present vision, this mass power equally might discard unions as a means to their ends, and instead rely on direct 'labour regulation' to determine the terms of sale of labour. The true locus of the 'labour monopoly' is not the union; but in democracy.

The present work does not propose to make a conceptual tool out of 'democracy', but some clarificatory remarks on how the word is being understood are in order. The essence of democracy is a stress on power-spreading. This begs the question: how much power-spreading? The minimum spread of power that is consistent with democracy is majoritarianism. Analytically, this may be captured through median voter mode. The maximum of power-sharing is perfect consensus, or unanimity: a decision can only be made with complete agreement. The analytic tool here is the theory of the bargain; where a decision requires the consent (obviously) of all parties.

These answers, too, inevitably beg questions. What determines the extent of the franchise? What determines the extent of plural voting (one voter having more votes than the other) – either in black-letter law, or in practical effect? Once these have been answered, there remains the fact that majoritarian decision-making is troubled by the 'paradoxes of democracy'. But this is not a treatise on democracy, and there is no attempt here to answer these questions. We restrict ourselves to modelling democracy by the median voter model or one of the many models of bargaining.

NOTES

1. Stigler: 'Marshall's *Principles of Economics* . . . devoted one chapter out of 55 to monopoly' (1985, 91). Marshall also allocated the final chapter of *Elements of Economics of Industry* to 'trade-unions': 'The power of Unions to raise general wages by direct means is never great' (Marshall 1892, 392). References to trade unions are scattered throughout Marshall's descriptive *Industry and Trade* of 1919, but there is no focused analysis. In Stigler's view, Marshall's lack of interest in labour monopoly was typical of nineteenth-century economics: 'if one were to canvass all the books and articles in economics up to 1900 . . . one would conclude monopoly was not a serious problem'.
2. A suggestion Friedman was to concur with in his crucial 'Comments' of 1951.
3. Marshall's unpublished use of his international trade theory to analyse labour mon-opoly was pursued by Pigou, but only to underline the 'indeterminacy' of the wage rate in a bilaterally monopolized labour market (Pigou 1905). On this point Pigou did little more than establish that there existed a lower bound to the wage rate, below which both profit and labour's surplus would fall; and an upper bound to the wage rate, above which both profit and labour's surplus would fall.
4. To find an expression of the 'Classical' economists' diagnosis of unemployment and wages one would need to leave the intellectual confines of Cambridge, and consult Clay (1929a, 1929b).
5. Shortly after the *General Theory*'s publication, Keynes wrote that diminishing marginal products were 'one of the very few incontrovertible propositions of our miserable subject!' (quoted in Brown 1991, 441).
6. Joan Robinson had brought out sharply that the neoclassical theory of factor demand is overturned by the existence of monopsony. But Keynes believed he could make all the points he wished without reference to monopsony.
7. Keynes himself allows this chain of causation from the money wage to the real wage in his discussion of the attempts of the Australian Arbitration Commission to peg real wages (Keynes 1936, 269–71). See Coleman et al. (2006, 100) and Aspromourgos (1997).
8. Means: 'If all prices had been flexible it is doubtful if we would have had a serious depression after the stock crash of 1929. When prices are rigid, however, a general drop in demand has quite different and most disastrous results' (1935a, 405). In a sympa-thetic vein, Means (1935b [1992]) traces the major causes of the Depression to a conflict between those factors (many and various) that necessitated 'great and rapid economic readjustments', and factors that 'decreased flexibility'.
9. Means (1935a, 402) included the 'inflexibility . . . of salaries and often of labour rates' in his vision of an economy dominated by 'administered prices'.
10. Means did not see price flexibility as a solution to depression, since flexibility was unattainable; inflexibility was 'inherent in modern technology'.
11. The analysis of this maximand was not original to Dunlop. Some years before Martin Bronfenbrenner, a University of Chicago PhD taught by Simons and befriended by Douglas, published a paper in which a union maximizes aggregate wages given a Cobb–Douglas function and an unemployment benefit (Bronfenbrenner 1939).
12. But Dunlop is also Robinsonian in that he wants to place the union within 'a world of monopoly': a world in which the labour buyer might be a monopsonist, and a world in which the product seller might be a monopolist (Dunlop and Higgins 1942).
13. The iso-profit curve plots the combination of wage bill and employment that yields equal profits.
14. This congenial vision of trade unionism had long earlier been articulated by John Stuart Mill (1869).
15. Layard, Nickell and Jackman (1991), Creedy and MacDonald (1991) and Sanfey (1995) provide surveys of the range of research. See also Oswald (1982), Carruth and Oswald (1987), Kaufmann (2002) and Swanson and Andrews (2007).

16. An early application of the Nash bargaining model to trade unions (de Menil 1971) seems to have been isolated.
17. This is represented by a 'horizontal' APS curve in employment real wage space (for example Carlin and Soskice 2006, 112). One reviewer of Carlin and Soskice has judged that the horizontal nature of this curve 'comes close to an act of faith' (Naylor 1992).
18. 'Wall Street kings get by on $200 000 a day', *The Age*, 8 March 2008.
19. In ballots held at the time of 2006 US Congressional elections six states approved increases in the minimum wage.

3. How a wage bill hill creates a wage rate floor

This chapter lays the analytical foundation for the present inquiry into labour monopoly by establishing how far one may travel in explaining wage rigidity and unemployment by means of a 'maximally simple' modelling of labour monopoly. This chapter, therefore, outlines a model of the macroeconomy in which the workforce neither uses money, owns capital, saves income or values leisure, but in which it collectively choose the terms of sale of labour in order to maximize its total wage incomes.

The chapter's leading conclusion is that models of wage bill maximization reach a considerable distance in explaining unemployment. For in such models the maximization of wage incomes can be achieved by imposing a rigid 'floor' to the real wage rate, and thereby making full employment, in defined circumstances, unattainable. Further, the optimality of a rigid wage floor survives elaborations of the very simplest model to allow, for example, for pockets of labour market competition, the existence of monopolistic and monopsonistic firms, the presence of risk aversion and the payment of efficiency wages.

The chapter also brings out that there exist other strategies for the maximization of wages incomes, apart from a downwardly rigid wage floor. It is shown that, in a wide variety of circumstances, both a maximum to hours worked and a regime of overmanning are just as effective as a wage floor in maximizing wage incomes.

THE MAXIMALLY SIMPLE MODEL: WAGE BILL MAXIMIZATION

We begin by outlining a simple model that will be a point of reference throughout the present work.

Assume a single output that is produced by two factors, by means of the familiar constant returns to scale production function.

$$\frac{Y}{K} = q\left(\frac{L}{K}\right) \qquad q' > 0 \qquad q'' < 0 \tag{3.1}$$

$$Y = \text{output}, \ L = \text{labour}, \ K = \text{capital}$$

Capital is homogeneous, and 'putty' like.

Firms are perfectly competitive with respect to both the price at which they sell output, and the wage at which they buy labour. Consequently, the real wage rate equals the marginal productivity of labour, that is a function of the labour–capital ratio.

$$w = q'(l) \qquad l \equiv \frac{L}{K} \tag{3.2}$$

and so:

$$\frac{L}{K} = l(w) \qquad l(w) = q'^{-1}(w) \tag{3.3}$$

The population is composed of a number of 'pure capital owners'; persons endowed with capital, but no labour; and Σ identical workers who are endowed with one unit of time, but (in this chapter) no capital. We suppose the economy is a one-period economy, with no point in saving, so the consumption function of the ith worker is:

$$C_i = wL_i \tag{3.4}$$

Utility is obtained from consumption only:

$$U = u(C) \tag{3.5}$$

Finally, the supply of labour is 'monopolized'. The terms of the sale of all labour are the prerogative of a single unitary agency, the labour monopolist, directed by a majoritarian process, in which the (decisive) median voter is an employee.

The simple model can be made even simpler, if we were to assume constant marginal utility:

$$U_i = C_i \tag{3.6}$$

and, in consequence, the labour monopolist wishes to maximize $wL_i = C_i$.

The maximization of wL_i may be secured by the labour monopoly by various means. Here we consider just three instruments the labour monopolist might use: 'work rationing', 'job lotteries' and 'overmanning'.

Work Rationing

The labour monopoly may pursue its goals through a 'work ration'. Under a 'work ration' system, the labour monopoly restricts the number of hours each worker works. Literally perceived, each worker is given some 'work ration', of h hours. More concretely this 'work ration' can interpreted as a union imposing a short-time rule, or a legislature placing a maximum on hours. But, critically, there is no restriction on the wage rate as such, and so the wage rate adjusts until the demand for labour equals the aggregate of work rations, Σh.

The work ration (that is, hours per person) selected by the labour monopoly is constrained to be the same for all workers, and so would equal L/Σ. Thus the labour monopolist's problem is:

$$\max: w\frac{L}{\Sigma} \tag{3.7}$$

This maximization amounts to the maximization of the wage bill, $W \equiv wL$. As the wage equals the marginal product of labour, $q'(l)$, it follows:

$$\max_{l}: q'(l)\frac{L}{\Sigma} = q'(l)l\frac{K}{\Sigma} \tag{3.8}$$

The choice problem therefore confirms with the classic Robinsonian treatment of monopoly maximization that takes quantity as the choice variable. Thus l, the labour–capital ratio, is chosen so that $\partial W/\partial l = [q'(l) + lq''(l)]K = 0$, and the 'marginal wages bill' is set to zero. The problem's diagrammatic solution is given in Figure 3.1, which depicts a Robinsonian 'marginal wages bill' schedule.

But as the elasticity of labour demand, $e \equiv -w\partial L/L\partial w$, equals $-q'(l)/lq''(l)$, the first-order condition of maximization may be helpfully written as:

$$e(l) = 1 \qquad \text{First-order condition (FOC)} \tag{3.9}$$

and the second order as:

$$\frac{\partial e(l)}{\partial l} < 0 \qquad \text{Second-order condition (SOC)} \tag{3.10}[1]$$

Thus in this representation the FOC requires employment to be chosen to equate the elasticity of demand for labour to one. The SOC requires

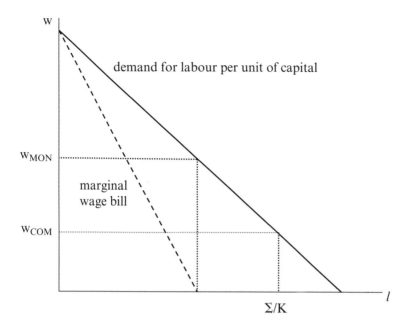

Figure 3.1   A Robinsonian representation of labour monopoly equilibrium

a negative dependency of e on employment, a negativity that becomes significant at various points in later argument. The problem's solution in terms of elasticity is represented diagrammatically in Figure 3.2.

It is worth underlining that under certain conditions the optimal 'work ration' per worker, $l_{MON}K/\Sigma$, may be secured by the labour monopoly directly choosing the wage rate, rather than by choosing the work ration. For any chosen wage implies a certain total demand for labour. And if we also suppose that: (1) small chunks of the total L, 'jobs', are randomly allocated across workers; (2) this random allocation occurs not just once in the period, but many times in the period (say every 'day' of the 'year'); and (3) each random allocation is independent, then with a sufficiently large number of random allocations each worker will receive (approximately) the same amount of total work, $l_{MON}K/\Sigma$. Thus a work ration is implicitly chosen by the choice of w. The only difference is the regularity of the ration: instead of each worker working less every 'day', as under a short-time regime, each worker will now experience some 'days' when they do not work at all, and are 'unemployed', having missed out on a job that day. Nevertheless, all expect to experience the same number of 'days' of unemployment in a given 'year' thanks to the randomness of job offers.

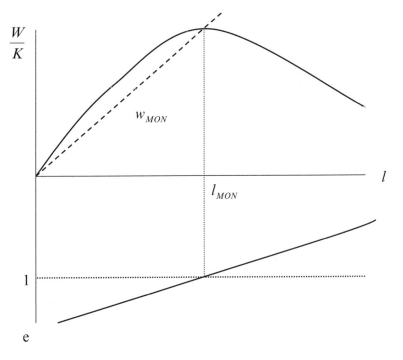

Figure 3.2   An elasticity representation of labour monopoly equilibrium

Thus under certain circumstances we may represent the labour monopolist's problem as:

$$\max_{w}: \; wl(w)\frac{K}{\Sigma} \qquad\qquad (3.11)$$

Using w as the choice variable manner instead of labour – a Cournotian rather than Robinsonian approach – proves to have advantages at some points, and we will explore it here.

Given that $e = -l'(w)w/l(w)$ the conditions of maximization may be represented as:

$$e(l(w)) = 1 \qquad \text{First-order condition} \qquad (3.12)^2$$

$$\frac{\partial e}{\partial w} > 0 \qquad \text{Second-order condition} \qquad (3.13)^3$$

Figure 3.3 plots a relation between the wages bill per unit of capital, W/K, w and e such that the two conditions are satisfied. Figure 3.3 depicts

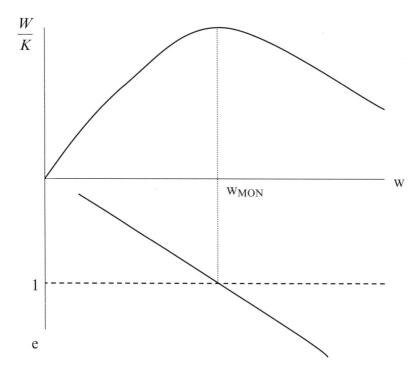

Figure 3.3   A Cournotian representation of labour monopoly equilibrium

the monopoly wage, at w_{MON}, sitting at the summit of a 'wage bill hill'. The same figure brings out an implication of the second-order condition; that the demand for labour is inelastic at any wage less than w_{MON}, and elastic at any wage in excess of w_{MON}.

Some algebraic expressions for the wage bill maximizing wage rate implied by various aggregate production function are presented in Table 3.1.

By how much will the labour monopoly wage differ from the competitive wage? Our conclusion that the demand for labour is inelastic at wage below the labour monopoly wage, combined with a knowledge of the unemployment rate, puts a lower limit in the gap. If there is 5 per cent unemployment the inelasticity of labour demand implies that a wage reduction of more than 5 per cent is required to eliminate it; thus the labour monopoly wage is more than 5 per cent above the competitive wage.

Table 3.1   *The elasticity of labour demand, the wage rate and employment under wage bill maximization for three technologies*

	Quasi Cobb–Douglas	Quadratic	CES ($\sigma = 0.5$)
$q = \dfrac{Y}{K}$	$l^\beta - \phi l$	$l\beta - l^2\phi$	$\phi\dfrac{l}{\beta + l}$
$e(l)$	$\dfrac{\beta - l^{1-\beta}\phi}{\beta[1 - \beta]}$	$\dfrac{\beta}{2l\phi} - 1$	$\dfrac{1 + \dfrac{\beta}{l}}{2}$
$e(w)$	$\dfrac{w}{w + \phi}\cdot\dfrac{1}{[1 - \beta]}$	$\dfrac{w}{\beta - w}$	$\dfrac{1}{2 - 2\sqrt{\dfrac{\beta w}{\phi}}}$
w_{MON}	$\dfrac{1 - \beta}{\beta}\phi$	$\dfrac{\beta}{2}$	$\dfrac{\phi}{4\beta}$
l_{MON}	$\left[\dfrac{\phi}{\beta^2}\right]^{\frac{1}{\beta-1}}$	$\dfrac{\beta}{4\phi}$	β

Note:
For the CES function with an unconstrained σ, the elasticity of labour demand is:

$$\sigma[l^{\frac{\sigma-1}{\sigma}}\beta + 1], \text{ where } q = \phi[l^{\frac{\sigma-1}{\sigma}}\beta + 1]^{\frac{\sigma}{\sigma-1}}. \text{ Thus } \frac{l\partial e}{e\partial l} = \frac{[\sigma - 1][1 - \pi]}{\sigma},$$

and $\dfrac{\partial ew}{\partial we} = [1 - \sigma]\left[\dfrac{1 - \pi(w)}{\pi(w)}\right].$

Non-'standard' monopoly equilibria

The monopoly equilibrium that is depicted in Figures 3.2 and 3.3, and described by the first- and second-order conditions – and which yields both positive profits and an excess supply of labour – we will call the 'standard monopoly equilibrium'.

This standard monopoly equilibrium need not exist.

It may not exist because the first-order condition, $e = 1$, may not be satisfiable. e might be parametrically < 1; as in the production function, $q = 1 - \phi/l^\beta$ where $e = 1/[1 + \beta] < 1$. Alternatively, e might be parametrically > 1; as in the Cobb–Douglas function, $q = l^\beta$, where $e = 1/\beta > 1$. In both the cases there is no wage bill 'hill' with a summit, but merely a one-sided slope, either perpetually rising with employment ($e > 1$), or perpetually falling ($e < 1$).[4]

If $q = 1 - \phi/l^\beta$, and e is less than one for all wage rates, then the wage bill would increase with every increase in the wage rate. This seems to yield the absurdity that employment is optimally reduced to zero. But this absurdity is prevented by allowing for another constraint: that the profit rate must exceed zero if any wages are to be paid at all: $\partial Y/\partial K = 1 - \phi[1 + \beta]l^{-\beta} > 0$. This implies a minimum magnitude for employment $l > [\phi[1 + \beta]]^{1/\beta}$. Thus the wage bill-maximizing labour monopolist drives down employment to a level such that profit is zero, and the marginal product of labour equals the average product of labour. As this amounts to a total expropriation of capital income, this solution to wage maximization appears extreme. But it is nevertheless a labour monopoly equilibrium; the equilibrium is simply not the 'standard equilibrium' that the (unconstrained) optimization condition describes.

If $q = l^\beta$ and the elasticity of labour demand is greater than one for all wage rates, then every decrease in the wage rate would result in an increase in the wage bill, until full employment is reached. In this case the monopolist maximizes the wage bill by setting the wage equal to the competitive level, and obtaining full employment. This is a labour monopoly equilibrium, but it is not the 'standard' one, and it is identical to the competitive equilibrium.

Can we establish the conditions under which a 'standard' monopoly equilibrium exists, and under what conditions it does not exist? Parameterizing the elasticity of technical substitution permits some conclusions. Recall that the standard 'Hicksian propositions' (Hicks 1932, 242–4), include:

$$e = \frac{\sigma}{\pi} \tag{3.14}$$

$$\sigma = \text{elasticity of technical substitution} \equiv \frac{\partial k}{\partial w/\rho} \frac{w/\rho}{k},$$

$$\pi = \text{profit share}, k \equiv \frac{K}{L}.$$

The elasticity of demand rises as the profit share falls; which is just a way of saying that as labour costs occupy a greater share of total expenses, the elasticity of demand for labour rises. But the profit share changes with the labour–capital ratio, according to the relative magnitude of the elasticity of technical substitution:[5]

$$if \ \sigma > 1 \ then \ \frac{\partial\pi}{\partial l} < 0 \tag{3.15}$$

and:

$$if \ \sigma < 1 \ then \ \frac{\partial \pi}{\partial l} > 0$$

The upshot is we may restate the first- and second-order conditions as:

$$\frac{\sigma}{\pi} = 1 \qquad \text{First-order condition}$$

$$\sigma < 1 \qquad \text{Second-order condition}$$

If σ is parametrically greater than 1 then clearly there can be no monopoly equilibrium: both the first- and second- order conditions are violated. Thus if labour and capital are 'too substitutable', there is no standard labour monopoly equilibrium.

If σ is parametrically less than 1 it would seem that both the first- and second-order conditions are certainly satisfied; the second automatically, and the first, too, as it would appear that w could always adjust make the profit share equal the elasticity of substitution, and so $\sigma/\pi = 1$. As the stylized facts suggest that $\sigma < 1$, this would seem to recommend the realism of the standard monopoly equilibrium, and its 'wage bill hill'.

But, in fact, there may be no standard monopoly equilibrium even if $\sigma < 1$. For even supposing $\sigma < 1$, σ/π (the elasticity of labour demand) may exceed 1 at full employment. In that circumstance increasing the wage rate above the full employment rate will only reduce the wage bill; and reducing the wage rate below the full employment rate will also only reduce the wage bill, as in this circumstance employment cannot increase in response to the reduction in the wage. Thus if $\sigma/\pi > 1$ at full employment then the monopolist will maximize the wage bill by setting the wage equal to the competitive level, w_{COM}, and obtaining full employment (see Figure 3.4). The monopoly equilibrium is a zero unemployment equilibrium; a competitive wage equilibrium.

The upshot is that even if the elasticity of technical substitution is less than 1 – as is plausible – a monopolized labour market may yield results identical to the competitive market, that is, full employment. This is no embarrassment to this model. On the contrary, it is a merit. Episodes of full employment are well known, and have sometimes been lengthy. It would be more of a discomfort to the model if it predicted the necessity of an excess supply of labour.

Circumstances that give rise to the standard monopoly equilibrium
Under what circumstances will the standard monopoly solution (that is, positive profits and an excess supply of labour) occur? And under what

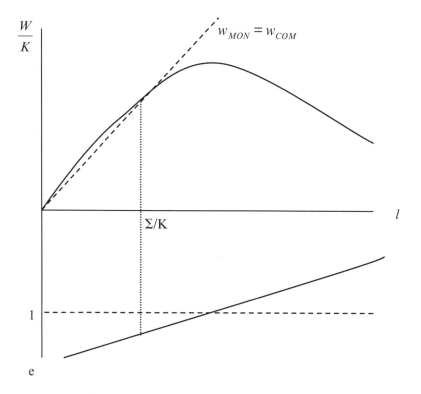

Figure 3.4   Full employment under labour monopoly equilibrium even
though σ < 1

circumstances will the monopoly equilibrium merely replicate the competitive equilibrium? The answer turns on the size of the labour force
relative to the capital stock. Given the (negative) relation between the
elasticity of labour demand and the labour–capital ratio implied by the
second-order condition, there is some critical ratio of the labour force to
capital, Σ/K, that makes the elasticity of the demand for labour at full
employment equal to unity.[6] This critical ratio satisfies:

$$\frac{\Sigma}{K} = \left[\frac{\beta\sigma}{1-\sigma}\right]^{\frac{\sigma}{1-\sigma}} \tag{3.16}$$

If Σ/K exceeds this critical magnitude then full employment spells such
a large labour–capital ratio the elasticity of demand for labour will be
less than one, and the labour monopoly will consequently choose a wage

higher than the competitive equilibrium wage. It is easy to see that, for any arbitrary size of the capital stock, there is always some increase in the labour force sufficiently large to make the magnitude of Σ/K exceed the critical ratio. In other words, there is always some increase in the labour force sufficiently large to create unemployment and a 'standard' monopoly equilibrium, where there had previously been full employment. Thus it may be said that the standard labour monopoly solution is associated with a 'sufficiently large' supply of labour.

With respect to the elasticity of technical substitution, there is always some magnitude in the elasticity of technical substitution sufficiently close to one so that $e > 1$ at full employment, and thereby makes for full employment, where there had previously been unemployment. Thus the standard solution can also be said to be associated with a 'sufficiently small' elasticity of technical substitution.[7] This conclusion hangs very easily with our intuition that the strength of any power of labour monopoly will lie in the difficulty in substituting capital for labour.

Thus any tendencies to augment capital relative to labour supply, or to increase the substitutability of labour and capital, tend to full employment; while any tendencies to augment labour relative to capital, or to the substitutability of labour and capital, tend to unemployment.

Regardless of what factors encourage a distinct labour monopoly solution, we wish to know if the actual state of affairs is

$$\frac{\Sigma}{K} > \left[\frac{\beta\sigma}{1 - \sigma}\right]^{\frac{\sigma}{1 - \sigma}}.$$

Would any labour monopoly have, in point of fact, an incentive to impose a wage different from the competitive wage? Briefly, is the demand for labour elastic at full employment?

One method of gauging the elasticity of labour demand is inductive and empirical. The tendency of these studies is to suggest that demand is inelastic (Hamermesh 1993).[8] A contrary conclusion is implied by a second method of measuring the elasticity of labour demand. This method takes advantage of Hicksian propositions (Hicks 1932, 242–4), and compares the size of σ with the size of π as, under our assumptions, the ratio of the two equals elasticity of labour demand. The empirical indications are that σ might be in the region of 0.5 and the profit share about 0.35. This is suggestive of an elastic demand. Unfortunately for this 'test', the magnitude of the elasticity of technical substitution is uncertain, and the profit share is only roughly measured.

Henceforth we will assume that the demand for labour is inelastic at full employment, and restrict ourselves to the 'standard monopoly equilibrium', the equilibrium with both an excess supply of labour and positive profits.

Job Lotteries

We have assumed that all workers receive the same 'work ration'; all workers do the same amount of work. But we can think of an alternative instrument by which a labour monopoly may seek to maximize wage incomes: 'job lotteries'. Suppose now that employment comes in packets, called jobs.[9] Jobs will be offered just once per period (a 'year'), and randomly allocated across would-be takers. If there are fewer jobs than workers, then the unlucky will not receive one. Each member of the labour force is, therefore, either employed for the entire period, or unemployed for the entire period.

The consumption outcome by any worker is now probabilistic, for a worker will consume w if employed, and 0 if unemployed. Thus, the expected utility of all workers is:

$$EU = pw \qquad (3.17)$$

where:

$$p = \text{the probability of employment.}$$

Thus:

$$\max_{w} : EU = \frac{l(w)K}{\Sigma}w \qquad (3.18)$$

This objective is evidently equivalent to wage bill maximization, just as under 'work sharing'. Thus the FOC and SOC are the same as under 'work rationing' and 'job lotteries', and so is the chosen wage – and consequently employment. Thus job lotteries produce identical results in terms of wage and employment, output and the elasticity of demand. It is true that under a system of job lotteries there now exists a distinct divide between 'the employed' and 'the unemployed', but this divide is in large measure nominal. This is because the expected utility of every worker is the same as every other worker regardless of their *ex post* employment status. Granted, those who miss out on work have a lower utility *ex post* than the employed (and a lower utility than under labour market competition). But these workers are comparable to persons who have made a gamble at favourable odds, but have (despite the favourable odds) lost. Such persons will repeat the gamble if the opportunity is re-presented. And the workers who have lost (that is, become unemployed) are content to repeat the gamble (that is, have the wage set at the monopoly level) in the next period. There is, then, none of the 'pathos of unemployment' that is typically in the representation of that phenomenon: the unemployed as victims, as sufferers. In the present modelling, the unemployed are willing victims, and willing sufferers. This conclusion is underlined by noting that the magnitude of expected utility of each worker under job lotteries is equal to the utility under work rationing, and certainly higher than under the competitive wage, despite the unemployment the monopoly wage creates. This last conclusion underlines that the labour monopoly approach casts a different light on the 'problem' of unemployment. For the workforce this 'problem' is not a problem: it is their strategy for maximizing their expected utility. For 'society as a whole' the unemployment is a problem, as national product is reduced. But for workers the abolition of unemployment by means of a wage reduction would reduce their expected utility.

Overmanning

Beyond 'work rationing' and 'job lotteries' there is a third instrument that the labour monopoly can use to secure wage income maximization: 'overmanning'.

Let us distinguish between the length of time an employee is hired ('time hired') versus the length of time actually worked ('time worked'). Under competition, the time hired will presumably equal the time worked. We might imagine, however, a labour monopoly controlling that fraction of time hired that the worker is actually working, θ: the ratio of time worked to time hired. For the labour monopoly to set θ to be less than one can be interpreted as the labour monopoly imposing a reduction in 'work intensity'. Alternatively, it can be interpreted as the labour monopoly's control 'work practises'.

The labour monopolist can shape workforce utility through its choice of θ. How so? Under the overmanning strategy the labour monopoly forgoes direct control over the wages paid for any period of time hired: w is set by competitive forces to secure full employment, and so w must equal the marginal product of per period of hire at full employment. Nevertheless, choice of θ will impact on the wage per period of hire. Specifically, a reduction in θ provides both a positive and a negative stimulus to the wage per period of hire, by giving both a positive and a negative stimulus to the output added by a given period of hire. On one hand, time worked within the period of hire falls: this is the negative stimulus. On the other hand, the reduction in time worked within an hour of hire will increase the productivity of any period that was in fact actually worked, on diminishing marginal productivity grounds; this is the positive stimulus. In summary, each worker works less during their period of hire, but produces more whenever they are actually working within that period; and the net impact on the product they add during their period of hire may be either positive, negative or zero.

It is easy to appreciate that if the productivity of labour (at the margin) has an elasticity to time actually worked of −1, then the net impact of these two stimuli nets out at zero, as the reduction in time hired will be just matched by the higher productivity of the time actually worked. But to say that productivity at the margin has an elasticity to time actually worked of −1, is to say that the elasticity of demand for labour to the real wage is one ($\partial q'l/\partial q' = 1$ implies $\partial l/\partial w \, w/l = 1$). Thus, if the (positivized) demand for labour is unit elastic to the wage, then the net impact on labour demand of overmanning is zero.

It is not difficult to appreciate that if the demand for labour is inelastic – which simply means productivity at the margin rising disproportionately with the decline in work – then the positive stimulus arising from overmanning will outweigh the negative stimulus, and overmanning will increase the wage. So to conclude: if the demand for labour is inelastic the labour monopoly will overman, and reduce θ. But by how much? Is there is no limit to the incentive to overman? Could θ be reduced to zero? The limit to the incentive is that every increase in overmanning reduces effective employment, and so we may infer from the second-order condition of maximization that every increase in overmanning will increase the elasticity of labour demand. Thus, if the demand for labour is inelastic, the labour monopolist imposes overmanning until the elasticity is driven up to one, and the incentive to overman further disappears.

More formally, let the production function be:

$$q = q(l\theta) \tag{3.19}$$

l = labour time hired, per unit of capital

$l\theta$ = labour time actually worked, per unit of capital

Then:

$$w = \theta q'(\theta l) \tag{3.20}$$

The labour monopoly wishes to choose θ so as to maximize utility, as before. But now all labour is employed, by competitive processes. So the maximization problem amounts to maximizing w.

$$\max_{\theta}: \theta q'\left(\theta\frac{\Sigma}{K}\right) \qquad (3.21)$$

The relevant first-order condition can be written as $e = 1$. Thus θ will be adjusted until the elasticity of demand for labour is one.[10] This is identical to the elasticity chosen by the 'work-rationing' labour monopolist and the 'job lottery' labour monopolist. And the wage bill is the same as in the case of work rationing and a job lottery.[11] The wage rate is lower – reflecting overmanning – but employment is higher, reflecting the absence of unemployment. In an important sense both the wage rate and employment are exactly the same as under work rationing and job lotteries. The wage paid per period actually worked is the same. And unemployment is exactly the same; for unemployment is now simply taken 'on the job'; and the amount of work actually done is the same.

There is a further parallel: as with the work ration case and the job lottery case, it may be that the monopoly equilibrium is identical with the competitive solution. For if the demand for labour is elastic at full employment, it would only reduce labour incomes to overman. Therefore, the labour monopolist does not overman. Indeed, the labour monopolist would want to underman if it could. But it cannot. Thus if at full-efficiency the demand for labour is elastic at full employment, then the labour monopolist leaves labour at full efficiency.

THE WAGE FLOOR

The previous section concluded, unsurprisingly, that the wage rate of the 'standard' labour monopoly equilibrium exceeds the competitive wage rate. This section underlines a further – and key – contention: the magnitude of the labour monopoly wage rate is completely inelastic to the supply of labour, and the supply of capital. That is, the monopoly equilibrium wage is perfectly rigid in the face of fluctuations in the supply of labour, and fluctuations of the supply of capital. Thus the labour monopoly equilibrium wage is a floor, beneath which the wage will not fall despite pressures to labour supply, or labour demand.

Rigidity in the Face of Fluctuating Labour Supply

Consider the wage bill maximization model's first-order condition.

$$e(w) = 1$$

Under our assumptions, the elasticity of demand for labour is a wholly determined by the wage rate, and the 'state of technology'. Thus we may say (if we disregard for the moment technological parameters) that the real wage varies with nothing. Specifically, w does not vary with the supply of labour. An increase in the supply of labour does not reduce the wage rate. And this is not a matter of a 'slow adjustment' of the wage rate to the new state of supply: there is no adjustment at all.

The rigidity in the chosen wage rate also extends to changes in the capital stock. An increase in capital will have zero impact on the wage rate. It is worth pausing to clarify why the wage rate is completely invariant to the capital stock: it is because is the elasticity of labour demand is completely independent of the magnitude of the capital stock. If the elasticity of labour demand was equal to one at some wage under a smaller capital stock, it will remain equal to one at that same wage under a larger capital stock.

Concomitant with the zero elasticity of w to K is the unit elasticity of L to K. It is also worth pausing to clarify why the employment is unit elastic to the capital. An increase in capital must increase employment because at an unincreased level of employment the labour share of national income would have risen in the face of the higher capital–labour ratio,[12] and the elasticity of labour demand thereby increased to greater than one. Wage bill maximization requires employment to increase until the elasticity of labour demand is driven back down to one, that is, until the labour–capital ratio is what it was before.

Evidently, a sufficiently large increase in K will increase the labour share of national income so much that labour demand becomes elastic even at full employment. In that situation, the labour monopolist can do no better than accept the competitive wage.

To summarize, for a given technology, wage bill maximization puts a floor on the wage, and an L-shaped relation between the wage rate and employment emerges (Figure 3.5).

Because, in the context of less than full employment, shocks to Σ and K obviously impact upon unemployment, we may say that the wage is completely invariant to unemployment. So in a well-known representation of wage flexibility:

$$w = \alpha \upsilon + \varepsilon \qquad (3.22)$$

$$\upsilon = \text{unemployment rate}$$

where $\eta = \alpha$ indicates perfect wage flexibility, and $\eta = 0$ indicates perfect wage rigidity, wage bill maximization implies perfect wage rigidity. The wage, note, is not 'sticky'; it is perfectly rigid.

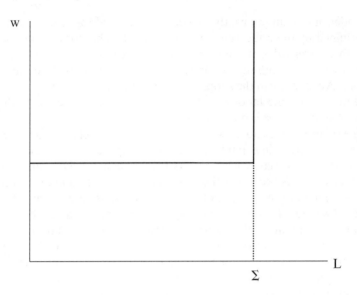

Figure 3.5   The wage floor

Monopoly, we may say in summary, provides an explanation of real wage rigidity: a rigid real wage serves the maximization of the wage bill.

RELAXING THE ASSUMPTIONS

The previous section concluded that the labour monopoly seeking to maximize total wage incomes chooses either a work ration or a wage rate, or an overmanning factor such that the elasticity of labour demand $e = 1$. This conclusion was made under a host of simplifying assumptions. How sensitive is this conclusion to these simplifying assumptions?

This section demonstrates that several of the more intrusive assumptions can be relaxed with no change in the conclusion that $e = 1$. And others may be relaxed with the only change being that e equals a parameter other than one.

Monopoly in the Product Market

Thus far perfect competition in the product market has been assumed. The existence of imperfect competition drives a potentially unstable wedge – 'the markup' – between the wage rate and the marginal product of labour. Imperfect product market competition thereby strikes at the link between the wage rate and employment, upon which all the analysis rests. An exhaustive treatment of the implications of imperfect competition is not consistent with the plan of this work. But if the labour monopoly thesis is to have any sway, it must be possible to sketch some model in which imperfect competition is introduced but the incentive of the labour monopoly to restrict employment remains. This is simply done.

Suppose there is not one product, but a large number of products of imperfect substitutability. All products are produced by the same production function. Each product is produced by a sole firm. Each firm faces a downward-sloping demand schedule, and chooses price so as to maximize profits, but does so under the assumption that other firms' prices are given. This could be interpreted as 'monopolistic competition', or it could be taken as a Bertrand oligopoly. Under these assumptions profit maximization implies:

$$P_i = \frac{e_i}{e_i - 1} MC_i \tag{3.22}$$

where

$$e_i \equiv -\frac{\partial d_i P_i}{\partial P_i d_i}, \quad d_i = \text{market demand for product } i,$$

$$P_i = \text{price of product } i$$

Thus the 'real wage', measured in any product i, is now less than the marginal product of labour in i:

$$w_i = \frac{e_i - 1}{e_i} MPL_i \tag{3.23}$$

To exploit this equality, we need a theory of the price elasticity, e_i, which in turn requires a modelling of consumer demand. Perhaps the simplest modelling that both allows a product monopoly equilibrium and satisfies the Cournot aggregation conditions is to assume all individuals having the same Linear Expenditure System (LES) demand system:

$$P_i d_i = P_i \gamma_i + \psi_i [x - \sum P_k \gamma_k] \tag{3.24}$$

$x = \text{total market expenditure on all products}$

Thus:

$$e_i = \frac{P_i \psi_i \gamma_i + \psi_i [x - \sum P_k \gamma_k]}{P_i \gamma_i + \psi_i [x - \sum P_k \gamma_k]} \tag{3.25}$$

This price elasticity must exceed one if there is to be a product monopoly equilibrium. But as long as the marginal propensity to consume ψ is positive but smaller than one then each γ must be negative if each price elasticity is to exceed one. If we suppose further:

$$\psi_i = \psi_j \text{ all } j \tag{3.26}$$

$$\gamma_i = \gamma_j \text{ all } j$$

then all commodities have the same elasticity, and so the same price. So the 'real wage' is the same regardless of what product measures it, call it w, and the labour–capital ratio is the same for all products. Thus the real wage (in whatever good it is measured) may be related to the aggregate l:

$$w = \frac{e_d - 1}{e_d} q'(l) \tag{3.27}$$

e_d = common elasticity of product demand

What does (3.27) imply for the plotting between w and l? The negative relation between l and marginal productivity is now not sufficient to secure a negative plotting between w and l; we must allow for that impact of w and l on the elasticity of product demand, and so the markup. But under the assumptions above an increase in l reduces the product demand elasticity, $e_d'(l) < 0$; thus product demand becomes more inelastic as employment rises, and the 'markup' increases with employment.[13] This increased markup simply reinforces the downward pressure that diminishing marginal productivity exerts on the real wage as employment grows. Thus the negatively sloped demand for labour remains. There remains 'a labour demand schedule' for the labour monopoly to exploit.

Yet the 'reinforcing' pressure of expanding markups on wages as employment grows means that any increase in employment is bought at a greater reduction in the real wage; that is, labour demand is more inelastic for any level of employment than under product monopoly.[14] Thus labour monopoly will choose a lower level of employment under product monopoly than under perfect competition. The upshot is that product monopoly in no way inhibits the impact of labour monopoly on employment: on the contrary, it exaggerates the negative impact of labour monopoly on employment.

Whether imperfect competition in the product market will dull the incentive to introduce labour monopoly in the first place is another question. For it is unclear whether the benefit to the workforce of labour monopoly is larger or smaller under imperfect product market competition. In one circumstance, however, the benefit is unambiguously larger: when under product competition the standard labour monopoly equilibrium is coincident with the labour competition equilibrium. In that case the benefit of labour monopoly under product competition is zero, but as labour demand under product monopoly will be inelastic at full employment under these conditions, labour monopoly will still have a benefit to the workforce. The parting suggestion is that the workforce is always hostile to imperfect product market competition, but may have a greater incentive to monopolize labour under imperfect product market competition.

Monopsony

As is well known, monopsony strikes radically at the neoclassical theory of factor demand, and produces 'paradoxes'. The acknowledgement of the empirical significance of monopsony is hard to resist, and it has become object of research (see for example Manning 2003).

The point of this section is to illustrate that monopsony can be introduced without at all reducing the incentive of labour monopoly to create unemployment.

Consider a simple model of firms facing a less than infinitely elastic supply of labour. Suppose capital is located uniformly on a straight line, cannot move, and at each location is owned by a different owner. Labour is located uniformly on a straight line, and can 'commute to work'. Critically, however, labour experiences a cost in commuting depending on the distance it travels to work, f(distance), $f' > 0$, $f'' > 0$. A worker supplies labour to the capital that offers the highest wage net of commuting costs.

With all locations symmetrical and choosing their wage, the Nash equilibrium implies that the wage rate is the same at all locations. In equilibrium people work at their local workplace, because although the wage is no higher than the neighbouring workplace, the transport costs are less. The distinctive aspect of the equilibrium is that the wage at each site is less than the marginal product. For it is easy to see that, holding the wage rates of other locations constant, the supply response of labour offered at location i to wage rate at i is:

$$\frac{\partial L_i^S}{\partial w_i} = \frac{1}{f'(L_i^S/2)} \tag{3.28}$$

The elementary theory of monopsony teaches that this positive elasticity of labour supply means that the wage in location i is less than the marginal product in location i.[15]

The critical and simple truth is that monopsony power is eliminated with the advent of the labour monopoly dictating a wage universally at all locations. Capital at any location no longer chooses its wage; it takes the wage, and demands labour according to the marginal productivity of labour. Thus the former model, where firms had no wage-making power, is restored, and the former analysis with it. Thus the presence of monopsony does not change labour monopoly equilibrium. The wage chosen will be the same; the level of employment it indirectly chooses will be the same. Thus whether labour monopoly causes unemployment is wholly independent of the strength of monopsony power. If a labour monopoly causes unemployment, it will do so regardless of whether monopsony power is strong or weak. The strength of monopsony power is irrelevant.

This is not to say that monopsony makes no difference to the impact of labour monopoly. In the absence of monopsony, labour monopolization either increases unemployment or does not increase wages. In other words, in the absence of monopsony, labour monopoly only increases wages at the cost of unemployment. This need not be the case in the presence of monopsony. In the presence of monopony the advent of the labour monopoly may increase wages without unemployment. For we know that the labour monopoly, monopsony or not, may choose full employment. But with labour monopoly the full employment wage will be the marginal product of labour, whereas under monopsony it would be less than the marginal product.

Thus the presence of monopsony makes the advent of labour monopoly more advantageous to the labour interest; the wage bill may be higher and cannot be lower. But the presence of monopsony does not make the advent of labour monopoly less socially costly.

Incomplete Coverage of Labour and Capital

Incomplete coverage of labour
So far we have assumed that the entire labour force is covered by the terms laid down by the labour monopolist. Such truly blanket coverage might seem unlikely. We are led to ask: what if the mandated terms do not apply to the entirety of the labour force? What if the members of some age group (or ethnic group, or the inhabitants of some political jurisdiction) were not covered, but were free to contract over their wage as they please, while the median worker remains covered? Will not that exemption of a certain group subvert the benefit of the coverage to the median worker? Will not the exempt reduce their wages in the face of any unemployment, and so 'exempt' themselves from unemployment? Will not this self-exemption of

some from unemployment destroy the advisability of the wage floor for the remainder of the labour force? The answer is, 'not necessarily'.

An argument that denies that less than full coverage must undermine the wage floor may be obtained by supposing that capital is mobile between all members of the labour force. The key implication of capital mobility is the equality of the profit rate for all capital, and the consequent equality of the wage rate for all workers, regardless of whether a worker is covered or not. Yet it also seems necessarily true that any unemployment will not be borne by those who are free to contract, as they can always cut their wage. The reconciliation is that all have the same wage rate, but all the unemployment is borne by those covered by the labour monopolist. And that portion of the labour force that is not covered will be fully employed.[16] Employment of the covered section, L_+, consequently amounts to the jobs 'left over' after all the uncovered part of the workforce, Σ_-, has been fully employed:

$$L_+ = l(w)K - \Sigma_- \tag{3.29}$$

If the exempt group are in a minority in the electoral franchise then the median worker is a member of the covered section, and the maximization problem becomes:

$$\max_{w}: pw = \left[\frac{l(w)K - \Sigma_-}{\Sigma_+}\right]w \tag{3.29}$$

This implies an optimal elasticity of labour demand that satisfies:

$$e = \frac{c - \upsilon}{1 - \upsilon} \approx c \tag{3.30}$$

$$\upsilon \equiv \frac{\Sigma - lK}{\Sigma}, c \equiv \frac{\Sigma_+}{\Sigma}$$

The elasticity of total labour demand approximately equals the coverage ratio, which is necessarily less than one.[17] Thus the elasticity of demand for labour is reduced relative to the case of complete coverage, and this entails a reduction in the wage rate floor. It is possible that the floor is reduced so much that full employment is obtained, and that becomes more likely the lower is c. But putting that possibility to one side, a less than complete coverage will lower the wage floor that the labour monopoly deems optimal without removing it; the wage floor and wage rigidity in the presence of unemployment still remains.

Incomplete coverage of capital

In the preceding section we supposed that some part of the labour force could charge what it liked for its labour. Now suppose that some part of the capital stock can offer to pay what it likes for labour. Which is to say that for some part of capital the wage is set not by labour monopoly, but by competitive forces, presumably because some portion of capital, K_I, is beyond the reach of the labour monopoly. To illustrate, we might imagine a 'formal sector' of the economy that is subject to the wage chosen by the labour monopoly, and an 'informal sector' that is not.

The existence of a sector of the economy where the wage is the outcome of the competition might be thought to destroy the distinct labour monopoly equilibrium that produces unemployment. For will not the informal sector absorb all those left unemployed in the formal sector? Indeed, certain modellings of this situation do destroy the whole labour monopoly approach. But there are other modellings where it remains largely in place.

First, consider a modelling that does destroy the labour monopoly's power. Suppose the labour monopolist chooses a wage in the formal sector, and jobs there are allocated randomly. And suppose anyone who does not receive a job in the regulated sector then 'goes to market' in the unregulated sector, and the wage rate there adjusts to absorb them. On our assumption that all workers are identical, the labour monopoly is concerned to maximize the expected wage of each worker; that is, the wage in the formal sector, w_F, weighted by the probability of working in the formal sector, plus the wage in the informal sector, w_I, weighted by the probability of working in the informal sector:

$$\text{Max} \quad \frac{L_F}{\Sigma} w_F + \frac{L_I}{\Sigma} w_I \tag{3.31}$$

$$\text{st} \quad L_F + L_I = \Sigma$$

L_F = employment in the formal sector, L_I = employment in the informal sector.

Thus the labour monopoly chooses the wage in the formal sector so as to maximize the sum of wage incomes in both sectors $L_F w_F + L_I w_I$, subject to the employment of the total labour supply. This implies that labour is allocated between the two sectors so that the marginal wages bill in the formal sector equals the marginal wage bill in the regulated sector:

$$\frac{\partial W_F}{\partial L_F} = \frac{\partial W_I}{\partial L_I} \tag{3.32}$$

But since the two sectors have identical production functions, the marginal wage bill will be same in each sector when employment (relative to capital) is the same in each sector.[18] But this equality of labour–capital ratios, combined with the full employment of labour, is identical to the competitive equilibrium. Thus the existence of an 'unregulated sector' – a portion of capital where the labour monopoly wage is not in force – totally destroys the distinct monopoly equilibrium. Even the tiniest size of informal sector – the most homeopathic dose of unregulated capital – appears to restore the competitive outcome.

The conclusion is powerful, as there must always be some portion of capital beyond the sway of labour monopoly. This surely amounts to the total elimination of the significance of labour monopoly. But there is an implicit assumption in the analysis that is easily challenged; there is an implicit assumption of a certain sequencing in markets. It is implicitly supposed that the market in the regulated sector is opened first, and jobs are allocated. Only then is the market in the unregulated sector opened. But why not have both sectors open for employment contracting simultaneously? Under that arrangement one can either accept a less well-paid but 'sure thing' job in the informal sector, or throw one's hat into the formal sector, and hope to get a higher-paying job. In that case the equilibrium condition would be:

$$pw_F = w_I \qquad (3.33)$$

p = probability of employment in the formal sector.

The labour monopolist wishes to maximise pw_F, or, equivalently, w_I. It is analytically convenient to suppose the maximand is w_I. By assumption w_I is not directly controlled by the labour monopolist, but by choice of L_F (through choice of w_F) the labour monopolist can manipulate the probability of employment in the formal sector, and so the relative attractiveness of the informal sector, and so the number of people choosing the informal sector, L_I, and so w_I. This chain of dependency between L_F, L_I and w_I is brought by articulating $pw_F = w_I$:

$$\frac{L_F}{\Sigma - L_I} w_F(L_F) = w_I(L_I) \qquad (3.34)$$

This implies the a dependency of L_I on L_F:

$$\frac{\partial L_I}{\partial L_F} = \frac{\partial W_F / \partial L_F}{\Sigma \partial w_I / \partial L_I - \partial W_I / \partial L_I} \qquad (3.35)[19]$$

Thus choosing L_F to minimize L_I (and so maximize w_I) implies:

$$\partial W_F / \partial L_F = 0 \qquad (3.36)$$

The upshot is that the labour monopolist wishing to maximize the wage in the informal sector chooses employment in the formal sector to maximize the wage bill in the formal sector. But the wage rate that secures that wage bill maximizing level in the formal sector is just the standard monopoly wage if all capital is regulated, w_{MON}:

$$w_F = w_{MON} \qquad (3.37)$$

So the wage rate in the formal sector is unchanged relative to complete coverage. The impact of less than universal coverage is felt in the fact that workers must allocate themselves between the formal and informal sectors so as to be indifferent between the two sectors, and satisfy:

$$w_I = p w_F \qquad (3.38)$$

The wage in the informal sector must be lower than in the formal sector to cancel the advantage that the probability of employment is higher in the informal sector than in the formal sector.[20] But w_I is not sufficiently low enough to employ all those not employed in the formal sector. w_I adjusts only enough to leave a size of L_I that yields unemployment in the formal sector large enough so that expected wage in the formal sector, pw_F, is equal to the ('sure thing') wage in the informal sector. Thus contrary to the intuitions of many, the incomplete coverage of capital – and the existence of a 'free market sanctuary' in the informal sector – cannot be said to make a wage floor pointless or irrelevant, or to eliminate the unemployment that would otherwise be caused by it. The wage floor in the formal sector is left intact, and the wage in the informal sector only falls so low as to leave those who choose the formal sector feeling that the risk of unemployment in that sector is worth the chance of a job there. It is true that the wage rate in the informal sector has a degree of flexibility absent from the formal sector; it is a negative function of the labour force per unit of capital:

$$w_I = \frac{w_F l(w_F) K_F}{\Sigma - l(w_I) K_I} \qquad (3.39)$$

But the informal wage will not fall sufficiently to prevent unemployment rising in the face of larger Σ/K.[21]

Efficiency Wages

Considerable attention has been devoted to the implications for the theory of unemployment of allowing for the possibility that a higher wage rate may induce greater labour effort, 'the efficiency wage' effect. It has been mooted that this phenomenon may be strong enough to make unemployment inescapable even in competitive labour markets. But what does the efficiency wage phenomenon spell for the behaviour of labour monopoly? It will be argued here that in the most plausible modelling of efficiency wages the previous conclusions regarding labour monopoly wholly survive an allowance for the efficiency wage phenomenon – an above-competitive wage floor with consequent socially wastefully unemployment. Efficiency wages, then, are 'news' for the competitive model, but not the labour monopoly model.

Suppose some efficiency factor, E, is a positive function of w:

$$q = q(E(w)l) \qquad (3.40)$$

This implies a profit function:

$$\rho = q(E(w)l) - wl \qquad (3.41)$$

For a given wage, profit maximizing employment implies the 'efficiency adjusted wage', w/E, equals the marginal product of the 'efficiency adjusted labour' $E(w)l$:

$$q'(E(w)l) = \frac{w}{E(w)} \qquad (3.42)$$

This produces a labour demand function:

$$E(w)l = l\left(\frac{w}{E(w)}\right) \qquad (3.43)$$

$$l\left(\frac{w}{E(w)}\right) \equiv q'^{-1}(E(w)l)$$

which is more compactly represented as a 'demand for efficiency adjusted labour' function:

$$\bar{l} = l(\bar{w}) \qquad (3.44)$$

$$\bar{w} \equiv \frac{w}{E}, \qquad \bar{l} \equiv El$$

Equation (3.44) implies an expression for the elasticity of demand for labour:

$$e = \bar{e} + \Theta - \Theta\bar{e} \qquad (3.45)$$

$$\bar{e} \equiv -\frac{\partial \bar{l}}{\partial w}\frac{\bar{w}}{\bar{l}} = -\frac{q'(El)}{q''(El)El}, \qquad \Theta \equiv \frac{wE'}{E}$$

Equation (3.45) states that in the presence of efficiency wage effects the elasticity of demand for labour is a function of Θ and $\bar{e}$. Θ is a measure of the strength of the efficiency wage effect; it is the elasticity of E to w. $\bar{e}$ is the elasticity of the demand for efficiency-adjusted labour to the efficiency-adjusted wage. This elasticity evidently has a functional form identical to the conventional elasticity analysed earlier in this work: $\bar{e}$ behaves identically to conventional elasticity analysed earlier, save that efficiency-adjusted labour governs its magnitude, not labour as such. Thus, assuming the elasticity of technical substitution is less than one, $\bar{e}$ declines as efficiency-adjusted employment rises.

  $\bar{e}$ is also equal to elasticity of the demand for ordinary labour to the wage, when the impact of w on E is ignored. And this allows us to calibrate $\bar{e}$. For we are interested in labour monopoly equilibrium as distinct from labour competition equilibrium. And if there is to be a distinct equilibrium, without invoking efficiency effects, then $e < 1$ at full employment, disregarding efficiency effects. Thus if we are to take the prospect of a distinct labour monopoly equilibrium as real, and not be required to rely on efficiency wage effects to make it real, then $\bar{e} < 1$.

  It is critical and easy to establish:[22]

(a) e > 1 if *either* Θ < 1 and $\bar{e}$ > 1 *or* Θ > 1 and $\bar{e}$ < 1

(b) e = 1 if *either* Θ *or* $\bar{e}$ = 1

(c) e < 1 if *either* Θ < 1 and $\bar{e}$ < 1 *or* Θ > 1 and $\bar{e}$ > 1

However, the calculation of elasticities misses the sting of efficiency wages, for the phenomenon threatens the whole notion of a firm optimally selecting employment in the face of a wage it takes as given. For although a firm cannot pay less than the going wage, it always has the prerogative to raise the wage rate it pays, with this impact on profits:

$$\frac{\partial p}{\partial w} = q'(El)E'l - l \qquad (3.46)$$

If there was no efficiency wage phenomenon (if $E' = 0$) then (3.46) is negative, and the firm will never exercise its prerogative to raise the wage rate. But if E' is positive then $\partial p/\partial w$ may be positive. More precisely, the existence or non-existence of an incentive to raise wages depends upon the magnitude of Θ relative to one. If Θ is greater than one, and the efficiency wage effect is 'strong', then it can be concluded that $\partial p/\partial w > 0$. Every firm has an incentive to raise wages.

Thus, as long as Θ remains greater than one, no matter high the wage rate may be, it will be pressed still higher by the profit increasing wage offers of firms. Thus if Θ is parametrically > 1, w will rise indefinitely, as firms cut the efficiency-adjusted wage. In raising the wage rate, and thereby productivity still more, they will also reduce the demand for labour.[23] So to pursue the thought experiment to the limit, if Θ is parametrically > 1 then the economy will consist of a single worker being paid a fabulous wage rate, and displaying amazing productivity. A labour monopoly will not be pleased. For assuming $\bar{e} < 1$, a Θ in excess of one makes the demand for labour elastic, and every increase in the wage would only reduce the wages bill.[24] The indefinitely high wage rates that firms press for yield indefinitely low-wage incomes. The labour monopoly in these circumstances would prevent the wage rate rising. Indeed, since the demand for labour is elastic, the labour monopoly would prevent the wage rate rising above the full employment level. Here we have a picture of firms pressing to push wages to the sky, and destroy employment and wage incomes; and the labour monopoly vigilantly fastening the wage rate to its full employment level.

The fantastic picture of the previous paragraph dissolves if Θ is less than one, and the efficiency wage effect is 'weak'. For then it can be concluded that $\partial p/\partial w < 0$, and the employer will accept the going wage as the best wage they can obtain, and adjust employment to make the marginal product equal to that wage, and $\partial p/\partial l = 0$. The labour demand curve has a conventional negative slope; there will be a full employment wage, defined by $q'(E(w)\Sigma/K) = w/E(w)$. The judgement the labour monopolist will make of this full employment wage depends on whether the elasticity, $e = \bar{e} + \Theta[1 - \bar{e}]$, is greater or less than one. If $\bar{e} < 1$ then $e < 1$, and the labour monopolist obviously wishes to increase the wage. That must increase $\bar{w}$ (as Θ is now assumed to be less than one) and that reduces efficiency labour, $\bar{l}$. And that will increase $\bar{e}$, in accordance the negative relationship between $\bar{e}$ and $\bar{l}$ posited above. Thus the labour monopolist will increase the wage until $\bar{e}$, the elasticity of demand for efficiency labour, equals one, and so $e = 1$, and there is no more incentive to raise the wage. Thus if Θ is parametrically less than one, we restore the picture met many times earlier of a labour monopolist obtaining wage rises at the cost of unemployment.

Thus depending on whether Θ is parametrically less than one or greater than one, we behold two very contrasting visions of the meaning of labour market competition, or monopoly. But to suppose Θ is parametrically less than one is restrictive, and to suppose Θ is parametrically greater than one leads to fantastic results. A more plausible specification is to suppose at low w Θ is high and greater than one, but declines to less than one (as in Figure 3.6).

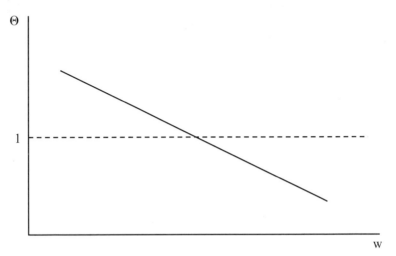

Figure 3.6   The elasticity of efficiency to the wage declines with the wage

Under this hypothesis, every increase in the wage increases efficiency, but the proportionate increase in efficiency becomes smaller relative to the proportionate increase in the wage as w rises.

What will be the plotting of W against w under this hypothesis? For a wage rate so low that Θ is in excess of one we know that the wages bill falls as w rises, since $e > 1$. Once w is so high that $\Theta = 1$, then $e = 1$, and the wage bill is stationary. For a higher wage rate still, labour demand becomes inelastic as a higher Θ takes its toll.[25] Thus the wage bill starts rising with w. But the reduction in the quantity of efficiency labour caused by the now higher efficiency wage increases $\bar{e}$, and that exerts a positive impact on the elasticity of labour demand, in accordance with $e = \bar{e} + \Theta[1 - \bar{e}]$. At some point the impact of higher $\bar{e}$ will outweigh the impact of falling Θ, and the elasticity will trough at some inelastic magnitude, and then begin to rise with still higher wage rates,[26] and ultimately reach one. The relationship between W and w is, then, a 'valley' and a 'hill', as represented in Figure 3.7.

The upshot is that there is now a distinct full employment wage, w_{FE},

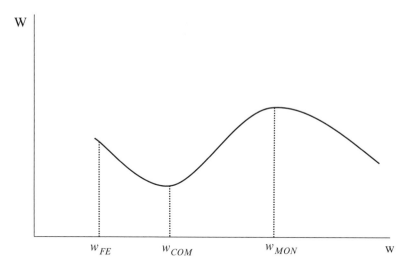

Figure 3.7   The full-employment wage, the competitive wage and the labour monopoly wage

a higher distinct competitive labour market wage, w_{COM}, and a still higher distinct labour monopoly wage, w_{MON}. In both the competitive and monopoly solutions the elasticity of labour demand equals one, but for completely different reasons. In the competitive equilibrium because $\Theta = 1$; in the monopoly equilibrium because $\bar{e} = 1$. The labour monopoly solution has a higher wage and higher unemployment. And the labour monopoly equilibrium is socially costly, as the competitive outcome is the socially efficient one by minimizing $\bar{w}$, and so maximizing $\bar{l}$.

Risk Aversion

The maximally simplest model assumed constant marginal utility. That implies risk neutrality, and a perfect substitutability between future and current consumption: both insupportable assumptions. How robust are the earlier conclusions with respect to that assumption?

The introduction of declining marginal utility of consumption – and so risk aversion – will not affect the maximizing solutions to optimal work-sharing or overmanning, since the outcomes deterministic in those situations, and consequently the consumption maximization that the preceding section dealt with, is equivalent to the maximization of the utility of consumption that we are currently entertaining. The optimal elasticity remains one.

But the presence of diminishing marginal utility – and so risk aversion – seems to affect the job lottery solution. The maximand is now:

$$EU = pu(w) = \frac{K}{\Sigma}l(w)u(w) \tag{3.47}$$

The optimizing solution now appears to be:

$$e = \frac{u'w}{u} = \text{elasticity of utility to consumption} < 1 \tag{3.48}$$

The optimal elasticity has been reduced to below unity on account of risk aversion. Thus the chosen wage is lower on account of risk aversion. The intuition of this result is simply that the prospect of unemployment is weighted more heavily than the prospect of employment, and a reduced wage is consequently preferred.

This inference however neglects the possibility of unemployment insurance. In the present framework, unemployment is a downside risk that one would be able to insure oneself against, as long as one's unemployment status is verifiable. In such a situation actuarially fair insurance would offer payout Z in the contingency of unemployment for premium z, where $z = [1 - p]Z$. Each worker chooses Z to maximize:

$$EU = pu(w - z) + [1 - p]u(Z - d) \tag{3.49}$$

$$\text{s.t.} \quad z = [1 - p]Z$$

$$Z = \text{pay out if jobless, } z = \text{premium}$$

The expected utility-maximizing choice of Z by each worker implies that $Z = w$; perfect insurance. The income of each worker, after allowing for premiums and any payouts, is pw in both the employed and unemployed state. The labour monopolist's maximization problem thereby becomes non-probabalistic. It is:

$$EU = u(pw) = u\left(\frac{K}{\Sigma}l(w)w\right) \tag{3.50}$$

This maximand is exactly the same as in the original work-sharing and overmanning cases, and again results in an elasticity of one.

Putty Clay Capital

We have assumed capital is putty. But an alternative, putty clay modelling, will sustain our previous conclusions equally effectively.

Under putty clay capital there exist an array of 'vintages' of capital, each with an exogenous output–capital ratio, and labour–capital ratio. The units of measurement of the capital of each vintage can be chosen so that the labour–capital ratio for each vintage is one. We may then index vintages by labour; so vintage i has an average product of labour Ψ_i. Or $\Psi = \Psi(L)$. Thus $w = \Psi(L)$. Thus $e = -\Psi(L)/\Psi'(L)L$. As the wage moves from its maximum magnitude to a lowest; as L moves from zero to the highest level that has any productivity at all at the margin; the elasticity moves from infinity to (almost) zero. Thus the first- and second-order conditions of wage bill maximization are satisfied; a higher wage increasing the elasticity, from zero to infinity. The elasticity may exceed one at full employment. In this situation, the monopolist chooses full employment, just as it does in situation with putty capital.

Bargaining Over Jobs as well as Wages

The 'jobs lottery' schema examined in this chapter supposes that the wage is decided by the labour monopoly, but employment is decided by firms. As this schema may result in an excess supply of labour it violates the tenet of 'efficient bargaining'. This point was made by Leontief (1946), and aired again by Solow and McDonald (1981), generating an extensive subsequent literature on the labour monopoly that efficiently bargains over jobs as well as the wage (see Oswald 1993).

As Leontief's analysis brought out, any requirement that bargaining be efficient has devastating implications for any labour monopoly explanation of unemployment. In the framework of present chapter the efficient labour monopoly strategy would require firms to employ the whole labour force fully, and pay a wage equal to the average product of labour. More exactly, labour monopoly would dictate that each firm's employment–capital ratio, l, equal Σ/K, and each firm pay a wage, $q(l)/l$. However, this strategy assumes that the labour monopoly can monitor each firm's employment–capital ratio. If this ratio is not observable, this 'efficient' strategy is not feasible. Evidently, it has been implicitly assumed here that the employment–capital ratio of each firm is not known by the labour monopoly. While this assumption doubtless exaggerates the labour monopoly ignorance of each firm's operations, to suppose instead that it has perfect knowledge of the firm's operations is surely the greater exaggeration. Henceforth, it will be assumed that the labour monopoly does not know each firm's employment–capital ratio, and is thereby restricted to bargaining over the wage.

CONCLUDING COMMENT

The present chapter has shown that in a very simple model wage bill maximization implies unemployment and wage rigidity. A very simple explanation of unemployment in terms of rational restrictions on competition suggests itself. It is true that the excess supply of labour consequent on wage bill maximization does not necessarily require the partitioning of the workforce into employed and unemployed; in the maximally simple model the labour monopolist would be just as rewarded by a tactic of work rationing or overmanning, both of which share equally the reduction in work among all. It is also true that the wage rigidity result does not survive all elaborations considered here (for example product monopoly). But these elaborations also include cases (for example monopsony) where, as far as the labour monopolist is concerned, job lotteries dominate both work rationing and overmanning. We are left with the primacy of job lotteries, and the consequent thought that labour monopoly can explain not only waste of labour (excess supply), but also its concentration on one part of the workforce; and not only a wage above competitive levels, but also its rigidity of shocks.

NOTES

1. $$\frac{\partial^2 W/K}{\partial l^2} = q'(l)\frac{e'(l)}{e^2} + q''(l)[1 - 1/e] = q'(l)\frac{e'(l)}{e^2} \text{ at } \frac{\partial W/K}{\partial l} = 0.$$

2. The conclusion that e = 1 does presuppose e is a continuous function of w, and that $l(w)$ is everywhere differentiable. Obviously, this need not be the case. And so there may not be a wage bill hill (that is, an inverted U), but a wage bill peak (an inverted V). In this circumstance 'the' elasticity of demand is not uniquely defined at the maximum. But this seems like a freak event.

3. $$\frac{\partial EU}{\partial w} = [l + w\frac{\partial l}{\partial w}]\frac{K}{\Sigma} = l[1 - e(w)]\frac{K}{\Sigma}.$$

    $$\frac{\partial^2 EU}{\partial w^2} = -le'(w)\frac{K}{\Sigma} + l'[1 - e]\frac{K}{\Sigma} = -le'(w)\frac{K}{\Sigma} \text{ at } \frac{\partial U}{\partial w} = 0.$$

4. The second-order condition may also be violated. There may be no wage bill hill, but a 'valley', or (possibly) a perfectly flat plain; if $q = \ln(l)$ then $W = 1$ for all w.

5. If $q = \phi\left[l^{\frac{\sigma-1}{\sigma}}\beta + 1\right]^{\frac{\sigma}{\sigma-1}}$ then $\pi = \dfrac{1}{\beta l^{\frac{\sigma-1}{\sigma}} + 1}$.

6. The critical magnitude of Σ is that such that $\sigma/\pi = 1$ when $L = \Sigma$. Given that at full employment

    $$\pi = \frac{1}{1 + \beta\left[\dfrac{\Sigma}{K}\right]^{\frac{\sigma-1}{\sigma}}}$$

when technology is CES and the elasticity of technical substitution is parametric, then the critical magnitude of the ratio of population to capital is defined by

$$\sigma = \frac{1}{1 + \beta\left[\dfrac{\Sigma}{K}\right]^{\frac{\sigma-1}{\sigma}}}.$$

7. As $\pi < 1$, $\sigma/\pi > 1$ as $\sigma \to 1$. A sufficiently small σ may also secure an elastic demand for labour at full employment, reflecting the larger share of costs accounted for by labour if σ is small.
8. Hamermesh (1993, 82–5) reports 34 studies of the elasticity of the demand for labour 'using data on aggregates or large industries'; 31 yield a point estimate less than one. Regrettably for the present purpose, the definition of 'the elasticity of labour demand' found in these studies often deviates from that used here. The capital stock is always taken as a given in the present conception of labour demand.
9. We will suppose 'a job' consists of employment for a period equal to the worker's endowment of time, 1. The easiest way to rationalize employment coming in such job 'packets' is to suppose each employment contract has a fixed cost. This fixed cost will presumably be borne by capital under labour monopoly, but capital owners will minimize it by seeking maximum work from each employee.
10. FOC

$$q''\left(\frac{\theta\Sigma}{K}\right)\left[\frac{\theta\Sigma}{K}\right] + q'\left(\frac{\theta\Sigma}{K}\right)$$

$$= q''\left(\frac{\theta\Sigma}{K}\right)\left[\frac{\theta\Sigma}{K}\right]\left[1 + \frac{q'\left(\dfrac{\theta\Sigma}{K}\right)}{q''\left(\dfrac{\theta\Sigma}{K}\right)\dfrac{\theta\Sigma}{K}}\right] = q''\left(\frac{\theta\Sigma}{K}\right)\frac{\theta\Sigma}{K}[1 - e] = 0$$

SOC

$$-q''\left(\frac{\theta\Sigma}{K}\right)\frac{\theta\Sigma}{K}\frac{\partial e}{\partial\theta} + \partial\frac{q''\dfrac{\theta\Sigma}{K}\dfrac{\partial e}{\partial\theta}}{\partial\theta}[1 - e] > 0, \text{ and so } \frac{\partial e}{\partial\theta} > 0$$

11. Under overmanning

$$W/K = \frac{\Sigma}{K}w = \frac{\Sigma}{K}\theta q'\left(\frac{\theta\Sigma}{K}\right).$$

Under work rationing $W/K = lq'(l)$. The elasticity of labour demand under overmanning and work rationing are both equal to one;

$$\frac{q'\left(\dfrac{\theta\Sigma}{K}\right)}{-q''\left(\dfrac{\theta\Sigma}{K}\right)\left[\dfrac{\theta\Sigma}{K}\right]} = 1 = \frac{q'(l)}{-q''(l)l}.$$

Thus $l = \theta\Sigma/K$. Thus the wage bill under overmanning equals the wage bill under work rationing.

12. This draws on (3.14) and (3.15). It is assumed that the elasticity of technical substitution is less than one.

13.   Greater l means greater x. And

$$\frac{\partial e_i}{\partial x} = \frac{\psi\gamma[1 - \beta]P_i}{[P_i\gamma + \psi[x - \sum P_k\gamma]]^2} < 0,$$

given our assumption that $1 > \beta > 0$, and $\gamma < 0$. But how might we understand this decline in price elasticity as total expenditure rises? Let the negative γs be understood as endowments, and the ds as market expenditures, so that consumption of any good i is the sum of the market purchase of i plus the endowment of i. Under this interpretation, the LES system is one of constant shares of the value of consumption, that obviously implies the consumption of any good is unit elastic to price. Market demand, by contrast, is elastic to own price, as market demand must take all the burden of any increase in price. But as x, total market expenditure, rises the value of endowments become less important, and so market demand becomes less price elastic.

14.   Elasticity of labour demand under product monopoly

$$\equiv -\frac{w\partial l}{l\partial w} = -\frac{\dfrac{e_d - 1}{e_d}q'(l)}{l\left[\dfrac{[e_d - 1]}{e_d}q''(l) + \dfrac{e_d'(l)}{e_d^2}q'(l)\right]} = \frac{e}{1 + \dfrac{e_d'(l)}{[1 - e_d]}e} < e$$

The relative inelasticity of labour demand implies that employment must be lower in the presence of product monopoly. The wage bill maximizing wage rate, notice, could be either higher or lower.

15. $q'(L_i^S/K_i) - f'(L_i^S/2)L_i^S = w_i$ indicates the supply of labour that is profit-maximizing capital at location i. But the amount of labour that is chosen to be supplied at i is a function of the wage rates at all locations; $w_i = g(w_1, \ldots w_N, L_i^S)$. These two yield a best response function of w_i for the given $w_1, \ldots w_N$. But as all N firms are symmetrical, the w_i and L_i^S outcomes will be the same. Thus: $w = q'(\Sigma/N/[K/N]) - f'(\Sigma/N/2)\Sigma/N$.

16.   Like ideas were explored in the context of international trade in Brecher (1974).

17.   The elasticity of demand for covered labour will still be one.

18. $$\frac{\partial W}{\partial L_F} = q'(l_F) + l_Fq''(l_F) = q'(l_I) + l_Iq''(l_I) = \frac{\partial W}{\partial L_I} \text{ implies: } l_F = l_K$$

19.   Second-order conditions are satisfied. If L_F is chosen minimize L_I then $\partial L_I/\partial L_F$ must move from negative to positive as L_F increases. But $\partial W_F/\partial L_F$ is moving from positive to negative as L_F moves past the stationary point. Therefore second order conditions require $\Sigma \partial w_I/\partial L_I - \partial W_I/\partial L_I$ be negative around the stationary point. This requirement is satisfied as $\Sigma \partial w_I/\partial L_I - \partial W_I/\partial L_I = [\Sigma - L_I][\partial w_I/\partial L_I] - w_I < 0$.

20.   The labour monopoly would mrefer a simultaneous opening of the two labour markets. In the simultaneous opening the wages bill in the formal sector is not reduced at all compared to sequenced opening; and in the informal sector it is reduced by less, because employment rises by less.

21. $$\frac{\partial w_I}{\partial \Sigma} = -\frac{w_I}{\Sigma - l(w_I)K_I - w_Il'(w_I)K_I} < 0; \frac{\Sigma \partial w_I}{w_I\partial \Sigma} = \frac{-\Sigma}{\Sigma - L_I + e_IL_I} \approx -1$$

$$\frac{\partial L_I}{\partial \Sigma} = \frac{\partial L_I}{\partial w_I}\frac{\partial w_I}{\partial \Sigma} = \frac{-l'(w_I)K_Iw_I}{\Sigma - l(w_I)K_I - l'(w_I)K_Iw_I} < 1$$

22. (a): $e = \bar{e} + \Theta - \Theta\bar{e} = \bar{e} + \Theta[1 - \bar{e}] = \Theta + \bar{e}[1 - \Theta]$. Thus if one of Θ and $\bar{e}$ is less than one, and the other is greater, then the elasticity amounts to a weighted average of one and another number greater than one, and such an average must exceed one. (b): Obvious. (c): If contrary to hypothesis $\Theta < 1$, $\bar{e} < 1$ and $\bar{e} + \Theta - \Theta\bar{e} > 1$ then $\Theta[1 - \bar{e}] > 1 - \bar{e}$, and so $\Theta > 1$. Contradiction.

23. The last raises the possibility could Θ and $\bar{e}$ be so much greater than one that e becomes 'negative'; that is, a higher wage makes a larger level of employment profit-maximizing. This is possible; as long as Θ and $\bar{e}$ are both greater than one. But if $\bar{e} < 1$, it is impossible.

24. The elasticity of the demand for labour will become only more elastic with w. Proof: the rise in w will reduce $\bar{w}$ and so increase $\bar{l}$, and so reduce $\bar{e}$. But $\partial e/\partial\bar{e} = 1 - \Theta < 0$ if $\Theta > 1$. Thus the fall in $\bar{e}$ as w rises pushes e still higher.

25. $\dfrac{\partial e}{\partial w} = \dfrac{\partial\bar{e}}{\partial w}[1 - \Theta] + \dfrac{\partial\Theta}{\partial w}[1 - \bar{e}] = \dfrac{\partial\Theta}{\partial w}[1 - \bar{e}] < 0$ at $\Theta = 1$, as $\dfrac{\partial\Theta}{\partial w} < 0$ and $\bar{e} < 1$.

26. If $\Theta < 1$ then $\partial\bar{l}/\partial w < 0$ and so $\partial\bar{e}/\partial w > 0$. Consequently

$$\frac{\partial e}{\partial w} = \frac{\partial\bar{e}}{\partial w}[1 - \Theta] + \frac{\partial\Theta}{\partial w}[1 - \bar{e}]$$

may now be non-negative. As w grows and $\bar{e}$ grows it will eventually become zero (the elasticity has troughed), and then become positive.

4. Why the floor will fluctuate

Chapter 3 developed a conclusion of considerable apparent significance: average wage income is made the largest by keeping labour costs completely rigid in the face of shifts to the demand for labour caused by changes in the capital stock. Thus the stylized fact of wage rate rigidity in could be explained very simply by reference to wage income maximization.

Chapter 3's analysis, however, might be deemed 'too successful' in explaining rigidity. For it predicts an adamantine rigidity in the wage even in the face of the most drastic excess supply of labour. Wage rates are absolutely motionless short of full employment.

A closer examination of the implications of wage bill maximization for rigidity is therefore warranted. This chapter consequently digs deeper into the reactions of the wage bill maximizing labour monopolist to shifts in the demand for labour, and extends the analysis of that response to shocks to technology, the terms of trade, taxes and the supply of other factors.

This chapter concludes that the rigidity found in Chapter 3 need not extend to all shocks to labour demand; under a labour monopoly wage rates need not be rigid in the face of all shocks to labour demand. Indeed, there are shocks in which the labour monopolist finds it optimal to leave employment completely unchanged, and have the wage rate take all the burden of adjustment. It is concluded that the labour monopolist commonly has two distinct strategies to maximize the wage bill: one that fixes the wage, and one that fixes employment. The first strategy amounts to minimizing the movement in wage, and 'maximizing' the movement in employment, and is rational in the face of some shocks, including those examined in Chapter 3. This strategy can be called a 'wage rigidity strategy'. The second strategy amounts to minimizing the movement in employment, and to 'maximizing' the movement in the wage rate, and we will see that it is rational with respect to certain other shocks. This may be called a strategy of 'wage volatility'.

Thus this chapter fills out the rationalization of the stylized facts of wage behaviour in terms of optimizing constraints on competition. For those stylized facts extend beyond simple 'rigidity' – the zero response of the wage rate to unemployment – to comprehend also 'volatility' – the positive response of the wage rate to 'not-unemployment'; the responsiveness of wages to factors other than the pressure of excess supply. It is this allowance for the rationality of a strategy of volatility that explains motion in the wage rate short of full employment. To explicate these thoughts in terms of a wage adjustment equation:

$$w = \alpha \upsilon + \psi \varepsilon \qquad (4.1)$$

Whereas Chapter 3's analysis rationalized $\alpha = 0$ (rigidity), the present chapter additionally rationalizes $\psi > 0$ (volatility).

A CONTRAST IN LABOUR DEMAND SHOCKS

The potential for wage bill maximization to yield both wage volatility and wage rigidity is well introduced by returning to the labour monopolist's optimization condition. Recall that a labour monopoly using 'job lotteries' to maximize members' welfare chose the wage so that:

$$-\frac{wl'(w)}{l(w)} = 1 \qquad (4.2)$$

On the face of it, this expression gives no warrant for a general rigidity in the wage rate in respect of a shift in labour demand. For inspection reveals that the preservation of that equality in the face of a shift in labour demand is consistent with w rising, w falling or w staying the same. It also reveals that the preservation of that equality in the face of a shift is consistent with L rising, L falling or L staying the same. Finally, an increase in both w and L is also possible.[1] The only observation that (4.2) disallows as a consequence of an (outwards) shift in labour demand is a fall in both w and L; but that is no more than a direct implication of the definition of an 'outward shift in the demand for labour', and owes nothing to the wage bill maximization as such.

Is wage bill maximization, then, a contentless theory? No, it is not. Wage bill maximization is saved from being contentlessness by the fact that shifts in the demand for labour possess a certain structure conferred by the source of that shift, and the existence of that structure allows contentful inferences. What this chapter underlines is how different types of underlying shock will impart different structures to the shift in labour demand, with different implications for the response of the wage bill maximizing wage rate.

To bring out the range of possible responses, two particular structures to the shift to labour demand are highlighted and contrasted. The first, which we might call a 'demand' shock, amounts to a uniform proportionate increase in employment, at all wage rates. The second, a 'demand price' shock, consists of a uniform proportionate increase in the wage rate for levels of employment.

Diagrammatically, a 'demand' shock can be represented by uniform proportionate horizontal shift in the labour demand function. Algebraically, demand shock is represented by a change in φ in:

$$L = \varphi l(w) K \tag{4.3}$$

Evidently, then, elasticity of the demand for labour in the context of demand shocks is:

$$e = -w\frac{l'(w)}{l(w)} \tag{4.4}$$

We see that the magnitude φ is completely irrelevant to the elasticity; and so the choice of w that makes e = 1, is completely independent of the magnitude φ, the 'demand shock' factor. There is wage rigidity in the face of this type of labour demand shock. This is the result seen in Chapter 3.

Diagrammatically, a 'demand price' shock can be represented by uniform proportionate vertical shift in the labour demand function. Algebraically, a 'demand price' shock is represented by a change in ψ in:

$$L = l(w\psi) K \tag{4.5}$$

Evidently, the elasticity of the demand for labour in the context of demand shocks is:

$$e = -w\psi\frac{l'(w\psi)}{l(w\psi)} \tag{4.6}$$

Clearly, there is a unique magnitude of $w\psi$ that secures e = 1. And that magnitude is completely independent of the magnitude of ψ. So if ψ rises, $w\psi$ is unchanged at its unique optimal value; w moves inversely with ψ. And as $w\psi$ is unchanged in the face of changing ψ, L must be unchanged in the face of changing ψ. We conclude that in the face of a negative labour 'demand price' shock wage bill maximization dictates 'employment rigidity', and a concomitant change in the wage rate to secure that rigidity. We are now encountering a strategy of minimizing the movement in L, and maximizing the movement in w; a strategy of 'wage volatility' rather than wage rigidity.

The term 'wage volatility' is used here rather than 'flexibility', with intent. For flexibility is suggestive of equilibration, but the strategy of wage volatility is no more hospitable to equilibrium that wage rigidity. Yes, under wage volatility wage rates are 'flexible' downwards in the face of a negative shock; a negative labour shock will be met with a reduction in wages so large that employment is completely unchanged.

But it is equally true that wage rates are 'flexible upwards': a positive labour shock will be met with an increase in wages so large so that employment is completely unchanged, no matter how large unemployment may be. Thus the strategy of volatility lends itself to equilibration no more than a strategy of rigidity. Both serve equilibration in certain circumstances (a favourable shock under rigidity, an unfavourable shock under volatility); and both are inimical to equilibration in other circumstances (an unfavourable shock under rigidity, a favourable shock under volatility).

It is worth underlining that these two shocks – the 'demand' shock (producing a strategy of a stable wage and unstable employment) and the 'demand price' shock (producing a strategy of an unstable wage and stable employment) – emphatically do not exhaust all possible structures to shifts in labour demand. The two do not even exhaust all structures that yield 'rigidity' and 'volatility'; other structures can produce wage volatility. But the contrast between 'demand' and 'demand price' shocks makes the point we are seeking: even by allowing for just these two structures, wage bill maximization allows for the wage rate to take none of the shock, or all of it.[2]

The task is to examine the response of the wage bill maximizing wage rate and employment for a variety of real shocks characteristic of macro-economic turbulence. I will collect these shocks under four headings:

- technology;
- supplies of other factors;
- the terms of trade;
- taxation.

TECHNOLOGICAL SHOCKS

Consider technological change that consists of the augmentation of the 'effective' quantity of labour or capital:

$$\frac{Y}{\kappa K} = q\left(\frac{\lambda L}{\kappa K}\right) \tag{4.7}$$

λ = index of labour augmentation

κ = index of capital augmentation

and consequently:

$$w = \lambda q'\left(\frac{\lambda}{\kappa}l\right) \tag{4.8}$$

$$e = e\left(\frac{\lambda}{\kappa}l\right) \tag{4.9}$$

Table 4.1 summarizes the responses of interest to technological shocks under wage bill maximization.

Table 4.1   Elasticities of incomes to types of technical change under wage bill maximization

Type of technical change	w	L	W	Y	w/λ	ρ
Purely capital-augmenting	0	1	1	1	0	1
Equally capital- and labour-augmenting	1	0	1	1	0	1
Purely labour-augmenting	1	−1	0	0	0	0

Capital-Augmenting Technical Change

Table 4.1 indicates, unsurprisingly, that any technological change that is purely capital-augmenting is equivalent to increase in the capital stock. The wage 'floor' is completely invariant to capital-augmenting technical progress, while employment is proportional to the index of capital augmentation. Thus with respect to purely capital-augmenting change the labour monopolist adopts a wage rigidity strategy. This can be rationalized as a wage bill maximizing response to what amounts to a 'demand' shock, and a uniform horizontal shift to labour demand:

$$L = \kappa l(w)K \qquad w = q'\left(\frac{l}{\kappa}\right) \tag{4.10}$$

Neutral Technical Change

If technological change augments labour and capital equally, so that technological change is 'neutral' between labour and capital, and $\lambda = \kappa = \eta$, then:

$$L = l\left(\frac{w}{\eta}\right)K \qquad w = \eta q'(l) \qquad (4.11)$$

Evidently, such 'Hicks-neutral' technical change amounts to a 'demand price' shock, and accordingly the labour monopolist adopts a strategy of wage volatility. More specifically, the wage rate is increased by the rate of neutral progress, leaving employment unchanged.[3]

Labour-Augmenting Technical Change

If technological change is purely labour-augmenting then the wage rate increases by the amount of labour augmentation, and employment falls by the rate of labour augmentation.

How may one understand the negative response in employment to labour augmentation? Observe first that labour augmentation is of ambiguous advantage to the labour interest, according to the theory of labour demand. For while it will increase the demand price of labour at the elastic portion of the labour demand schedule, it will reduce the demand price of labour at the inelastic portion of the labour demand schedule. And it will leave the wage rate unchanged at the level of employment where labour demand is unit elastic.[4] This last borderline case is the relevant one, for in labour monopoly (unlike in the competitive market) the wage is set so that the demand for labour is unit elastic. Thus – unlike in the competitive market – the wage bill maximizer will necessarily experience zero change in labour demand in the face of labour-augmenting technical progress at the former wage.

But the maximizing reaction of the labour monopolist makes that dull picture still darker. For the theory of labour demand also implies that labour augmentation will reduce the elasticity of the demand for labour at any given level of employment. The upshot is that demand is now inelastic at those levels of employment at which it was formerly unit elastic.[5] Thus the wage bill maximizer will rationally respond to changed labour demand conditions by raising the wage rate in the face of now inelastic demand, and thereby by reducing employment as a consequence of labour-saving technical progress. Thus it might be said that the problem of labour monopoly in face of labour-saving technical progress is not the wage being rigid, but it being *flexible in the wrong direction* as far as the elimination of unemployment is concerned. Wage rates go up in the face of an unchanged demand for labour.[6]

The situation is illustrated in Figure 4.1.

Two further consequences of the response to labour augmentation are worth underlining.

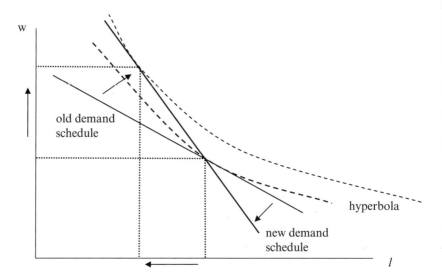

*Figure 4.1   The shift in the demand for labour by labour-augmenting
technical progress*

First, the fact that the quantity of labour falls by as much as its effectiveness has risen implies that the effective quantity of labour is unchanged,
and so national product does not change. An anti-social aspect of the
labour monopoly is very apparent here: an improvement in technology
that would certainly increase national product in the competitive model,
now reduces employment insufficiently so as to leave national product
unchanged.

Second, the optimal response to labour augmentation implies that the
chosen wage bill is exactly unchanged. Thus in the face of pure labour
augmentation, the labour monopolist adopts neither a 'wage rigidity,
employment volatility' strategy, nor a 'wage volatility, employment rigidity' strategy, but a third strategy that keeps the wage bill rigid in the face
of shocks by means of appropriate volatility in both 'employment' and
'wages'. Consonant with this, Figure 4.1 suggests (and inspection of the
expression for labour demand confirms) that labour augmentation is
neither a horizontal nor a vertical shift, but amounts to an equal-sized
negative horizontal shift (demand shock), and a positive vertical shift
(demand price shock). This is the diagrammatic manifestation of a third
strategy of rigidity: wage bill rigidity.

To summarize this section: wage rates are rigid only in the face of those
technological shocks that are purely capital-augmenting. Nevertheless,

the simple wage rigidity result survives in another form, in reference to the wage per effective unit of labour, w/λ. No matter whether technological change is purely capital-augmenting, purely labour-augmentating, or some arbitrary mix of the two, the wage rate per unit of effective labour is completely unaffected. Thus the 'productivity-adjusted wage rate' (that is, the cost of one unit of effective labour, w/λ) is rigid to all forms of technological progress considered above.

SHOCKS TO FACTOR SUPPLIES

The previous section has stressed that in the face of technology shocks wage volatility may be observed instead of wage rigidity. Is wage rigidity also menaced by shocks to factor supplies? Chapter 3 underlined that in the context of a two-factor production function the wage bill maximizer will keep the wage perfectly rigid in the face of shocks to supplies of capital or labour. But is this result just an idiosyncrasy of a model with two factors of production? Will this result survive in the face of changes in the supply of some third factor? Under moderately broad conditions, the answer is 'yes'.

The argument can be conducted without any assumption about what the third factor actually is, but the most resonant interpretation is to suppose that third factor – call it R – is some kind of labour not part of the 'labour monopoly'. Specifically, it is perhaps most meaningful to suppose that R is unskilled labour, who on account of lack of citizenship, or some other disqualification are not part of the electorate. Given this interpretation, the analysis suggests, perhaps contrary to expectation, that under conditions that are specific but not special an increase in the supply of unskilled (politically marginalized) labour will not change the wage rate of ordinary labour that maximizes the incomes of ordinary labour.

To launch the argument we will take advantage of the fact that any constant returns to scale three-factor production function can be represented as dependency of the average product of capital on l, and $r \equiv R/K$:

$$q = q(l, r) \qquad (4.12)$$

$$r \equiv \frac{R}{K}$$

Wage bill maximization implies:

$$e = -\frac{q_l(l, r)}{l q_{ll}(l, r)} = 1 \qquad (4.13)$$

We can infer that in the face of an x per cent increase in both K and R the optimization condition (4.13) will be preserved by a matching x per cent equal increase in L. Thus an equiproportionate increase in K and R leaves l and r unchanged, and so the wage rate is unchanged. So the wage bill maximizing wage rate is invariant to equiproportionate increases in K and R: wage rigidity survives for a 'balanced' increase in both factor supplies. This is true for any balanced increase of n factors.[7]

But can the wage rate be rigid in the face of an 'unbalanced' increase in the supply of one of the factors? Not surprisingly, sufficiently strong assumptions can secure an affirmative answer. Thus the results of the maximally simple model are reproduced if we suppose that r and l enter separably into production:

$$q = \omega(l) + \vartheta(r) \qquad (4.14)$$

and so resource intensity has no impact on the marginal product of labour, and no impact on the wage bill maximizing wage rate.[8]

But the rigidity of the wage rate to increases in a third factor does not require the extreme assumption of separability. Table 4.2 presents adaptations of the three production functions used previously in Chapter 3. In none of the three is there separability; but in all three the wage bill maximizing wage rate is still completely invariant to the supply of R. Table 4.2 shows that the expression of the wage bill maximising wage rate for each production function is solely a function of parameters.[9]

Table 4.2   The wage bill maximizing wage with a third factor

	Quasi-Cobb–Douglas	Quadratic	CES ($\sigma = 0.5$)
q	$l^{\beta}r^{\gamma} - \phi l$	$l\beta - l^2\phi - \gamma\dfrac{l^2}{r}$	$\dfrac{l}{\beta + l + \dfrac{l}{r}}$
w_{MON}	$\dfrac{1-\beta}{\beta}\phi$	$\dfrac{\beta}{2}$	$\dfrac{1}{4\beta}$

For these three production functions the wage bill maximizing wage rate is completely invariant to R (and K), and the only impact of an increase in resources is an increase in employment. How can this be understood? One way of understanding it is first to register that all three production functions of Table 4.2 can be represented as:

$$q = y\left(\frac{g(r)}{l}\right)l \qquad (4.15)$$

Such a production function can be rationalized as one where R and K produce an intermediate good, call it F, that then cooperates with labour to produce final output, Y:

$$Y = Ly\left(\frac{F}{L}\right) \qquad F = g\left(\frac{R}{K}\right)K$$

To illustrate concretely, imagine R (unskilled labour) and K (equipment) produce a tangible good, F, that is used by L to produce a final good or service.[10] The key point is that the final good is produced by just two factors – L and F – and we know from Chapter 3 that in such a two-factor production function the wage is rigid to the fluctuation to both labour and factor with which it works.[11] In Chapter 3 the factor which worked with labour was K, and here it is called F. So the wage is rigid with respect to the supply of F. And consequently the wage is rigid to fluctuations in supply of any factors which produce F, namely R and K.[12]

The 'realism' of such a modelling of technology is hard to judge.[13] It might be more useful to note that wage rigidity only requires that technology can be interpreted in this way. The significance of this is that a given technology can be interpreted in several different ways. Thus the CES function:

$$Y = [L^\gamma + K^\gamma + R^\gamma]^{1/\gamma} \qquad (4.16)$$

can be interpreted as K and R producing some intermediate input for L to transform into the final good.[14] But (4.16) equally permits the interpretation of production so that K and L produces an intermediate input for R to transform into the final good. (And it equally permits the interpretation of production as R and L producing an intermediate input for K to transform into the final good.) The key result here, then, is that a modelling of technology as standard as the CES modelling implies wage rigidity in the face of fluctuations of the third factor, R.[15]

In spite of the wage rigidity in some common technologies, it merits underlining that the wage rigidity result is in no way 'general'; the wage bill maximizing rate might instead fall with the third factor. To illustrate this possibility: if the third factor is a perfect substitute for labour then an increase in its supply will reduce the wage bill maximizing wage rate.[16]

Of course, to conclude that a labour monopolist will change the wage (in any direction) in response to an increase in the supply of some substitute implicitly presupposes that the labour monopolist cannot control the price of that substitute. For if the labour monopolist could do so then the labour monopoly would do best by eliminating the substitute by pricing it completely out of the market. But if there is a physical complementarity between L and R – as there is in all the production functions in Table 4.2 – the labour monopoly would not price out the third factor, even if it could control its price. On the contrary, it would welcome the expansion of that third factor's supply. But it would not let the wage rise in the face of such an expansion, as would happen under a competitive labour market. Rather the labour monopoly will peg the wage so that the third factor's enlarged supply impacts on only employment.

SHOCKS TO THE TERMS OF TRADE

The price at which home output is sold to the world, and the price at which inputs are bought from the world, are commonly seen as a source of economic turbulence. How will the labour monopolist choose to adjust, or not adjust, the wage rate in the face of shocks to these?

To begin with a polar case, suppose all output is exported, and all consumption is imported. In this situation the demand for labour remains a function of the product wage. But the wage rate that the labour monopolist cares about is the wage evaluated in terms of the import good, $w\,tot$, tot = value of home output in terms of (imported) consumption good. Thus labour monopolist's problem is max $l(w)w\,tot$. Clearly changes in 'the terms of trade', tot, have no impact on the maximizing magnitude of the product wage, w; and consequently no impact on employment. 'The terms of trade' in this modelling is irrelevant to the demand for labour, and so must be irrelevant to the labour monopolist's maximizing choice of employment. The terms of trade remain of concern to the workforce, because as a consequence of the rigidity in w, the wage in terms of the consumer good, $w\,tot$, will be 'volatile', and will rise and fall with the value of output in terms of the import good.

Now consider the case where the import good is solely an input into home production. In other words the third factor, R, is sourced wholly from overseas at a price in terms of home output, μ, given by world markets. To illustrate, R might be a form of energy ('oil') that is imported from world markets. The goods and factor price-taking firm maximizes:

$$q(l, r) - wl - \mu r \tag{4.17}$$

yielding two optimization conditions:

$$q_l(l, r) = w \qquad (4.18)$$

$$q_r(l, r) = \mu$$

This is two equations in two unknowns and implicitly determines the two relative factor demands, l and r, as functions of w and μ. We are interested in the demand for labour per unit of capital:

$$l = l(w, \mu) \qquad (4.19)$$

as it implies:

$$\frac{W}{K} = wl(w, \mu) \qquad (4.20)$$

Clearly, the wage rate that maximizes the wage bill is completely independent of the capital stock; so rigidity of the real wage with respect to the capital stock is completely restored.

What of the impact of a change in the price of resources? Is the wage rigid or volatile or something else? Some of the specific production functions we have trialled have this property, as Table 4.3 reveals.

Table 4.3 The wage bill maximizing wage and employment with an imported input

	Quasi-Cobb–Douglas	Quadratic	CES ($\sigma = 0.5$)
q	$l^\beta r^\gamma - \phi l$	$l\beta - l^2\phi - \gamma\dfrac{l^2}{r}$	$\dfrac{l}{\beta + l + \dfrac{l}{r}}$
w_{MON}	$\dfrac{1 - \gamma - \beta}{\beta}\phi$	$\dfrac{\beta}{2} - \sqrt{\gamma\mu}$	$\dfrac{[1 - \sqrt{\mu}]^2}{4\beta}$
l_{MON}	$\left[\left[\dfrac{\mu}{\gamma}\right]^\gamma\left[\dfrac{\phi}{\beta^2}[1 - \gamma]\right]^{1-\gamma}\right]^{\frac{1}{\gamma-1+\beta}}$	$\dfrac{\beta}{4\phi} - \dfrac{\sqrt{\gamma\mu}}{2\phi}$	β

With quasi-Cobb–Douglas technology the wage is entirely rigid with respect to the change in resource prices. And for this reason employment falls in the face of higher resource prices. But in the quadratic technology we see the wage rate falling in reaction to higher resource price, yet not enough to prevent some negative impact on employment in the face of resource price shocks. In the CES technology, with $\sigma = 0.5$, the wage drops sufficiently in the face of a resource price shock that employment is completely insulated; there is complete 'wage volatility'. (This result extends to all magnitudes of σ.) The CES style production function brings out the potential for either wage stability or wage volatility on the part of the labour monopolist. Recall that if the supply of the third factor was perfectly inelastic then under a CES technology the wage was completely rigid, and employment would vary with the quantity of resources. But if the supply of resources was perfectly elastic then under a CES the wage is sufficiently flexible that there is zero response to the change in the price of resources.

TAX SHOCKS

The capacity for labour monopoly to generate wage volatility is further underlined by considering the response of labour monopoly to tax shocks. This reveals a behaviour quite different from what we would expect if real wage rigidity was simply a defensive psychological posture, a stubborn insistence in holding whatever one has. Such a stubbornness about the magnitude of 'take-home pay' would surely make the labour interest as aggressive in seeking wage rises in response to income tax increases as, say, in seeking money wage rises in response to price increases. A similar stubbornness would see wage rates insensitive to the imposition of payroll tax. This section demonstrates, however, that the wage bill maximizing labour monopolist will choose not wage rigidity in the face of tax shocks, but wage volatility, letting wages adjust so as to leave employment completely unaffected.

Income Taxes

The simplest case is an income tax. Supposing the labour monopolist is interested in maximizing take-home pay, they will maximize:

$$\frac{W[1 - t]}{K} = [1 - t]wl(w) \qquad (4.21)$$

Evidently, the w that maximizes the right hand side is invariant to the magnitude of t. Thus the wage bill maximizer does not respond by trying to claw back.

Payroll Taxes

The profit maximization condition if payrolls are taxed is:

$$w[1 + t] = q'(l) \qquad (4.22)$$

Thus:

$$\frac{W}{K} = w[1 + t]l(w[1 + t])$$

As W/K depends solely on $w[1 + t]$, there is some magnitude of $w[1 + t]$ that maximizes W/K. Changes in t will not change that magnitude; it will only change the associated magnitude of w. Thus an increase in t will depress w by the same amount, leaving $w[1 + t]$, and so employment, unchanged. This is wage volatility. Or to be more exact, it is volatility in the effective wage to the worker, but rigidity in the effective wage paid by the employer.

We conclude that the imposition of an income tax will not induce the labour monopolist to try to claw back the tax from the employer, by raising wages, and thereby cutting employment. And the imposition of a payroll tax will not reduce employment, as the labour monopolist lets the tax pass on to employees. In both, taxes will have zero impact on employment, as the effective wage received by the worker falls by the full amount of the tax, leaving the effective wage paid by the employer unchanged.

Several questions are begged in the above analysis. We are supposing that an income tax is being imposed despite the labour interest being in control of the legislature. If it controls the legislature, why not extract all revenue from capital?

CONCLUDING COMMENT

Whereas Chapter 3 pictured labour monopoly theory as very definite in its conclusions, this chapter represents labour monopoly as far more plastic and extensive in its possibilities. Whereas in Chapter 3 wage rigidity was an apparently all-pervasive characteristic of labour monopoly, now it is seen that wage volatility is also characteristic of labour monopoly.

A strategy of volatility might seem incongruent with the regulatory power by means of which we have supposed labour monopoly as operating, for regulations do not seem to be 'volatile'. But it is the effect of regulations on real wages that counts, and a stable schema of regulation may yield volatility in real wages. To illustrate; a regulation that the money wage, V, be rigid may yield the requisite real wage volatility in the face of shocks. To illustrate, notice that in the face of technology shocks the labour monopolist wage rule is simply:

$$\dot{w} = \lambda \qquad (4.23)$$

or:

$$\dot{V} = \dot{\lambda} + \dot{P} \qquad (4.24)$$

Invoking a simple Quantity Theory relation:

$$\dot{M} = \dot{Y} + \dot{P} \qquad (4.25)$$

and inferring from Table 4.2:

$$\dot{Y} = \dot{\kappa} \qquad (4.26)$$

we have:

$$\dot{M} = \dot{\kappa} - \dot{\lambda} + \dot{V} \qquad (4.27)$$

Thus a rigid money wage, $\dot{V} = 0$, will produce the requisite volatility (or rigidity) in real wages if the money supply grows in accordance with the excess of capital augmentation over labour augmentation. This provides a clue as to where 'volatility' in policy might occur: in monetary policy.

NOTES

1. Let there be a shift out in labour demand, so that $l_1(w) > l(w)$ for all w. It is possible that under wage bill maximization this shift will leave the wage rate unchanged, as $w = w_1$ is consistent with the optimization conditions $-w_1 l'_1(w_1)/l_1(w_1) = 1 = -wl'(w)/l(w)$, as long as $-l'_1(w) > -l'(w)$. And it is also possible that employment is left unchanged under wage bill maximization, as $l(w) = l_1(w_1)$ is consistent with $-w_1 l'_1(w_1)/l_1(w_1) = 1 = -wl'(w)/l(w)$ as long as $-l'_1(w) < -l'(w)$.

2. In speaking of the 'contrast' between a demand shock and a demand price shock, it is acknowledged that a given shock could simultaneously be both a 'demand' shock, and a 'demand price' shock. That would be the case if the demand for labour was of the form $L = \gamma w^{-\xi}$, and the shock was to γ. But this demand for labour function exhibits a parametrical elasticity of demand, which is inconsistent with the 'standard monopoly equilibrium', and so not of interest here

3. Inspection of $W/K = \eta q'(l)l$ indicates that the wage bill maximizing level of employment is invariant to the magnitude of η.

4. Proof: just as $w = q'(l)$ implies

$$\frac{dw}{w} = -\frac{1}{e}\frac{dl}{l}, \text{ so } \frac{w}{\lambda} = q'(\lambda l) \text{ implies } \frac{dw}{w} - \frac{d\lambda}{\lambda} = -\frac{1}{e}\frac{d\lambda}{\lambda}$$

at an unchanged level of employment. And so, at an unchanged level of employment, if $e = 1$ then $dw/w = 0$.

5. Proof: since

$$e = \frac{\sigma}{\pi(\lambda l)} \text{ and since } \frac{\partial\pi}{\partial\lambda} > 0 \text{ (as long as } \sigma < 1), \text{ then } \frac{\partial e}{\partial\lambda} < 0 \text{ for a given } l.$$

Therefore at the former wage bill maximising level of l, e falls from 1 to less than 1.

6. Inspection of the expressions for the total wage bill:

$$\frac{W}{K} = \frac{w}{\lambda}l\left(\frac{w}{\lambda}\right) \quad \text{or} \quad \frac{W}{K} = \lambda lq'(\lambda l)$$

reveals that wage bill maximization is a matter of the optimal choice of w/λ. Thus the wage bill maximizing wage rate rises proportionately with the index of labour augmentation. Further, $W/K = \lambda lq'(\lambda l)$ implies that wage bill maximization is a matter of the optimal choice of λl; 'effective' labour per unit of capital. Thus l declines proportionately with the index of labour augmentation.

7. Let $q = q(l, r, A/K...)$, then wage bill maximization implies:

$$-\frac{q_l\left(l, r, \dfrac{A}{K}...\right)}{lq_{ll}\left(l, r, \dfrac{A}{K}...\right)} = 1.$$

8. Optimization then implies:

$$e = -\frac{q'(l)}{lq''(l)} = 1$$

Evidently R has no impact on L/K, and so the wage. And K has no impact on L/K, and so the wage.

9. It is easy to see from (4.13) that a sufficient condition for wage rigidity in the face of factor supplies is:

$$lq_{ll} = \psi q_l + \xi$$

This amounts to the marginal wages bill being a linear function of the wage rate. This condition is true of all of the production functions in Table 4.2.

10. In this rationalization of the technology the marginal productivity of K and R are increased by L on account of the 'good' produced by K and R adding more final output when operated more intensively by L. Thus the complementarity L has with R and K is not a manifestation of what happens at the F production stage, but at the Y production stage.

11. As a further upshot, the elasticity of employment to R will equal to R's share of non-wage income, and the elasticity of employment to K equals K's share of non-wage income.

12. $$w = y\left(\frac{g(r)}{l}\right) - \frac{g(r)}{l}y'\left(\frac{g(r)}{l}\right). \text{ Thus: } \frac{W}{K} = ly\left(\frac{g(r)}{l}\right) - g(r)y'\left(\frac{g(r)}{l}\right).$$

Wage bill maximization implies:

$$\frac{\partial W/K}{\partial l} = y\left(\frac{g(r)}{l}\right)\frac{g(r)^2}{l^2} - \frac{g(r)}{l}y'\left(\frac{g(r)}{l}\right) + y''\left(\frac{g(r)}{l}\right) = 0$$

This solves for an optimal $g(r)/l$ which in turn implies an optimal w. That optimal w is solely a function of technology: the wage bill maximizing wage rate w is parametric.

13. An objective indicator of this modelling's coherence with reality is the extent to which the sharing out of non-wage incomes between K and R is independent of the size of L:

$$\frac{\partial Y}{\partial R} = g'(r)y'\left(\frac{g(r)}{l}\right) \text{ and } \frac{\partial Y}{\partial K} = [g(r) - rg'(r)]y'\left(\frac{g(r)}{l}\right)$$

$$\frac{\frac{\partial Y}{\partial R}R}{\frac{\partial Y}{\partial K}K} = \frac{rg'(r)}{g(r) - rg'(r)}$$

The relative size of rent and capital incomes is purely a function of R/K. The irrelevance of the size of L to the division between K and R of the total of income received by K and R is the economic sign that R and K are producing separately from L.

14. $Y = [L^\gamma + K^\gamma + R^\gamma]^{1/\gamma}$ implies

$$\frac{Y}{L} = \left[\frac{1 + \left[\frac{R}{K}\right]^\gamma}{[L/K]^\gamma} + 1\right]^{1/\gamma} = \left[\left[\frac{\left[1 + \left[\frac{R}{K}\right]^\gamma\right]^{1/\gamma}}{L/K}\right]^\gamma + 1\right]^{1/\gamma}.$$

Thus $g(r) \equiv [1 + r^\gamma]^{1/\gamma}$ and $y\left(\frac{g}{l}\right) \equiv \left[\left[\frac{g}{l}\right]^\gamma + 1\right]^{1/\gamma}$

15. Other CES style functions exclusively imply one representation or another. Thus $Y = [[K^\theta + R^\theta]^{\gamma/\theta} + L^\gamma]^{1/\gamma}$ exclusively implies a technology where R and K produce an intermediate good that cooperates with labour to produce final output.

16. If R is a perfect substitute for L then there is effectively a single price for both L and R. But R is always fully employed, so: $L = l(w)K - R$. Consequently,

$$\frac{W}{K} = wl(w) - wr \text{ and } e(w) = 1 - \frac{r}{l(w)}. \text{ Thus, } \frac{\partial w}{\partial r} = \frac{-1/l}{e' - l'} < 0.$$

5. How bargaining may build a ceiling instead of a floor

Chapters 3 and 4 were concerned with how the wage rate might be shaped by a majoritarian political process, in which the median voter is a wage earner. The two chapters concluded that the wage rate formed by such a process would exhibit both the rigidity and the volatility characteristic of labour markets.

A defect in the assumption of a majoritarian process deciding the wage is that it amounts to supposing that the wage rate is subject to a 'dictatorship of the median worker', in which the labour force's most preferred wage rate is unilaterally imposed on employers. Not only does such a 'dictatorship of the median worker' grossly exaggerate the present strength of the labour interest, but it also misses democracy's requirement for a degree of consensus amongst its composing and rival constituencies: neither the spirit nor the practise of democracy coincides with '50 per cent plus one taking all'. If we think in terms of two constituent political interests – 'capital' and 'labour' – this appetite of democracy for consensus suggests that both interests must participate in the shaping of the wage rate.

This chapter therefore moves to analyse the situation where neither rival interest can simply impose its most preferred restriction on market forces by the sole virtue of being a majority. Instead any such restriction of the labour markets must be agreed upon by both interests. So in terms of historical narrative of labour conditions we move away from 'victories', 'milestones' and 'landmark judgements' and towards 'compromises' and 'compacts'. In electoral terms we move away from France's Popular Front of 1936, to Sweden's Saltsjöbaden agreement of 1938.[1] And we ask, in particular, how much of the wage floor, so prominent in Chapter 3 and 4, survives the requirement that rival interests agree on the wage rate; how much will it survive the introduction of the employer's interest into the wage-setting process?

The analysis of two simple but relatively transparent bargaining models – the Zeuthen and the Hicks models – suggests that the wage phenomenon of rigidity (and volatility), may or may not survive in an environment of bargaining. Allowing the profit interest to bear on the wage decision may make the wage more flexible and less rigid (or volatile) than when it was the choice variable of a 'labour monopoly'. But not necessarily so.

A more definite, if unsurprising, conclusion is that to allow the profit interest to bear upon wage determination will reduce the level of the wage. Indeed, it may reduce the wage rate so much that there is an excess demand for labour. Thus allowing for both interests to bear on the wage decision raises the possibility of something not previously encountered in the analysis: an excess demand for labour, a phenomenon that no labour monopoly would ever have any incentive to create, and which is, of course, inconsistent with competitive labour markets. So whereas thus far we have considered the shaping of labour markets by political processes as productive of an excess supply of labour, it may now produce an excess demand for labour. Instead of political processes stopping the wage rate from falling to its competitive level, we see in this chapter that the political process may stop the wage rate from rising to its competitive level; the political processes yields a 'ceiling', rather than a floor.

WAGE RIGIDITY AND VOLATILITY UNDER THE ZEUTHEN BARGAIN

The problem of the explaining the bargain struck between a single seller and a single buyer was first scientifically broached by the inaugural generation of English neoclassicals, Jenkin, Edgeworth and Marshall (see Creedy 1986, 44–5; Dimand and Dimand 1996, 54–80); but without concluding with any solution to the problem.

The first cogent solution of the problem of the bargain was advanced by Zeuthen (1930). It was expressed in terms of a wage negotiation, and is immediately adaptable here.[2]

In Zeuthen the wage rate is assumed to be decided by an agreement between two groups: one representing the labour interest, and one representing the capital interest. The spirit of the present work would recommend that the groups be seen as political parties, but in keeping with the literature on Zeuthen, we will call them the Union and the Confederation. If these two parties do not reach agreement on a wage rate then no employment takes place; there is a 'stoppage', and both the profit bill, Π, and the wages bill, W, are zero. Given an agreed wage rate, the volume of employment is decided by the individual capital owner, and so the demand for labour per unit of capital is, as before, $l(w)$.[3] Through this labour demand function, each wage offer maps into a certain Π and W; and so each side offering a wage rate comes down to the Confederation offering the Union some wage bill, W_C, and the Union offering the

Confederation some profit bill, Π_U. The question is, what offers will result in mutual agreement?

In Zeuthen the germ of the answer lies in supposing that each party compares a 'sure thing' with a gamble; the 'sure thing' that is provided by accepting its adversary's offer, with the gamble instead insisting on its own offer – a gamble that may yield their adversary's belated capitulation (which is the upside of the gamble) or their renewed defiance, and a consequent stoppage (which is the downside of the gamble). Clearly a key ingredient in this comparison is the 'concession probability': the probability that the other side will concede in the face of your refusal of their offer. The decision problem for any given side can be formulated as the comparison of the actual concession probability with the 'critical concession probability' that would leave the given side indifferent between the 'sure thing' – accepting its adversary's offer – and the gamble; refusing its adversary's offer and insisting on its own. Given that the income of each side is zero if agreement is not reached (and there is a consequent stoppage) it is easy to see that under risk-neutrality these critical concession probabilities satisfy to:

$$W_C = p_U W_U \qquad \Pi_U = p_C \Pi_C \qquad (5.1)$$

p_U = the critical concession probability to the Union

p_C = the critical concession probability to the Confederation

W_C = wage bill conditional on Confederation's offer

W_U = wage bill conditional on Union's offer

Π_U = profit bill conditional on Union's offer

Π_C = profit bill conditional on Confederation's offer.

These expressions underline that the critical concession probability is not a forecast, an expectation or a cognitive entity of any kind; it is constructed solely from current and objective phenomenon, and operates as a kind of 'supply price of militancy'. It states the minimum probability of success from gambling on militancy that you require if you are to be willing to gamble on militancy. For if the actual chance of success from militancy (that is, the actual concession probability) exceeds this critical concession probability, then you benefit from militancy, and so you are militant.

So how might the critical concession probability compare to the actual concession probability? It would not be coherent to suppose that this critical concession probability of both sides is less than the actual probability, for then both sides would choose militancy, and consequently both sides would be certain of the worst outcome (zero income). It also appears incoherent to suppose that this critical concession probability of both sides exceeds the actual probability. For then both sides choose capitulation, which makes nonsense of each side's capitulation.[4]

The upshot is that one side must have a critical probability lower than the actual probability (and be militant); and the other must have a critical concession probability greater than the actual probability, and so will concede. To illustrate, if:

$$\frac{W_C}{W_U} > \frac{\Pi_U}{\Pi_C} \qquad (5.2)$$

then it is clear that the Union's critical concession probability is higher than the Confederation's, and so it is the Union that concludes militancy is not worth it, and concedes.

But the Union has some influence over the critical probability of the Confederation. For the Union can nudge the critical probability of Confederation upwards – and so nudge the Confederation into a posture of concession – by reducing its own wage demands. The Union may be able to increase Π_U by reducing W_U so that:

$$\frac{W_C}{W_U} < \frac{\Pi_U}{\Pi_C} \qquad (5.3)$$

and the Confederation is now left conceding to the Union's new offer. That, as far as the Union is concerned, has to be an improvement on conceding to the Confederation's offer. In order for the Union to achieve this – to reverse the inequality – the reduction W_U must secure a larger proportionate increase in Π_U. So as long as Π_U goes up by more than W_U goes down, the Union can turn the tables. That is, as long as the Union can increase the product $W_U \Pi_U$, it can induce the Confederation to concede.

The Confederation replies in the same way, and nudges the critical probability of Union upwards – and shifts it into a posture of concession – by increasing its wage offer so that:

$$\frac{W_C}{W_U} > \frac{\Pi_U}{\Pi_C} \qquad (5.4)$$

By a parallel argument to that used before, it can be seen that the Confederation will turn the tables as long as it can increase the product $W_C \Pi_C$.

In summary, the two sides will each compete to push the other into having the higher critical probability, and will do so until the product of the wage bill and profit bill cannot be expanded. Thus the Zeuthen outcome maximizes:

$$W\Pi \tag{5.5}$$

But as:

$$\Pi = \Pi(W) \quad \text{and} \quad \Pi'(W) = \frac{1}{e-1} \tag{5.6}^5$$

the maximization of $W\Pi$ implies:

$$e = 1 - \frac{W}{\Pi} < 1 \tag{5.7}$$

Thus equilibrium in the Zeuthen bargain is a matter of securing an optimal elasticity of labour demand, just as it was under a 'dictatorship of the median voter'. But under the Zeuthen bargain the equilibrium elasticity of demand is less than one. Smaller, in other words, than under labour monopoly (see Figure 5.1).

In the particular case of parametrical elasticity of substitution, σ, the expression for elasticity of labour demand under the Zeuthen bargain confirms to:

$$e_{ZEUTHEN} = \frac{2\sigma}{1 + \sigma} \tag{5.8}$$

Evidently $e_{ZEUTHEN} < 1 = e_{MON}$, as long as $\sigma < 1$, and the chosen wage is lower under the Zeuthen bargain than under labour monopoly 'diktat'.

But while the floor is lower under a Zeuthen bargain, the wage is nevertheless a 'floor' decided without regard for the size of the labour force, the size of the capital stock, or the wage rate that would fully employ the labour supply:

$$e(w) + \frac{1 - \pi(w)}{\pi(w)} = 1 \tag{5.9}$$

This floor has the same potential for 'volatility' of the floor found under wage bill maximization. To illustrate, the equilibrium condition (5.9) may be written:

$$e\left(\frac{\lambda}{\kappa}l\right) + \frac{1 - \pi\left(\frac{\lambda}{\kappa}l\right)}{\pi\left(\frac{\lambda}{\kappa}l\right)} = 1 \tag{5.10}$$

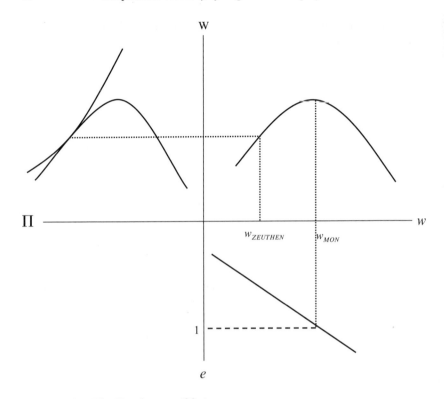

Figure 5.1   The Zeuthen equilibrium

That implies a unique magnitude of $\lambda l/\kappa$, just as the equilibrium condition for labour monopoly, $e(w) = 1$, implied a unique magnitude of $\lambda l/\kappa$. Thus the response of L to technological shocks will be precisely the same under the Zeuthen bargain as under wage bill maximization of Chapter 4. Specifically, we can infer that under the Zeuthen bargain there will be 'wage volatility and employment stability' in the face of neutral technological shocks; the wage rate shall respond to shocks so that employment is exactly unchanged. And we can infer in the face of purely labour-augmenting technological progress that there will be 'wage volatility and wage bill stability'; the wage rate rises so that the wage bill is exactly unchanged.

To summarize, the wage rate is lower under the Zeuthen bargain, and so unemployment is less 'likely', under bargaining. But if there is unemployment, then the wage rate will be just as rigid, or volatile, as under a wage 'diktat'.

All in all, allowing for the profit interest to bear upon the wage decision does not eliminate the wage floor.

WAGE RIGIDITY, VOLATILITY AND EVEN SOME FLEXIBILITY UNDER THE HICKS BARGAIN

While Zeuthen's model receives respectful nods from modern bargaining theorists (Harsanyi 1956), the Hicks model is largely ignored.[6] This is unfortunate because Hicks scrutinizes the mechanism of optimization that must lie beneath any bargain more closely and searchingly. The Hicks bargain lends itself to application beyond the (perhaps unusual) case of formal constitutional requirement of consensus, and towards the ever-present case where two interests are in a latent – and potentially violent – struggle to subjugate each other.

A Rational Reconstruction

Hicks's account of his theory (1932, 140–46) is brief, verbal and informal. It includes a single figure, but no mathematics. To the present author it 'seems reasonable', without the reasoning being very clear. It is a representation of an intuition, rather than a proof of some theorem. This section attempts to obtain a rationalization of Hicks by advancing a certain interpretation of Hicks that deploys some of the moves that a modern theorist might make, including references to 'symmetry', 'belief equilibria' and 'credible threats'. In order to get more effectively at rationalization, we begin by casting the bargaining problem in quite general terms, and then proceeding to wage bargaining

In the present interpretation, the key to the Hicks bargain is the appreciation that the decision to agree with one adversary is itself a choice; one made in the light of a comparison with the alternative: the attempted subjugation of the opponent. Thus Hicks's analysis turns on the proposition that there are two ways to settle a clash of wills: the two parties can agree, or they can fight it out. Hicks's analysis, then, is concerned with the rational choice between those two alternatives; the rational choice we must often make between accord and coercion, between peace and war.[7]

The root of the logic of choice between peace and war lies in the fact that there are benefits and costs to both alternatives. Victory in war consumes resources, but concludes in the plunder of the adversary. Peace economizes on the resources spent in war, but forgoes the spoils of ultimate victory. Thus victory may be preferred to peace, or peace may be preferred to victory.

To get a grip on these preferences, we make some particular assumptions. We suppose there is some object of dispute between two parties, D and Δ. The object of dispute might be a border that divides a certain valuable territory between two countries. In the Zeuthen approach, if the two parties cannot agree then neither side gets anything; it is as if the contested territory is left vacant. But in Hicks's approach the alternative to agreeing about it is fighting over it. We assume that any war ends with the 'complete victory' for one side, in the sense that the victor is free to impose whatever terms it likes, and to its maximum advantage. In the example we have been using, the victor wins the entire territory, and the loser loses all.[8]

We assume that the winner of struggle is the party that devotes the more resources to the struggle; the side that spends more on its armed forces. We also suppose that the amount of resources is a choice variable. It is not that a side is 'endowed' with some given amount of 'struggle resources'. Rather, each side can purchase any amount of struggle resources at a fixed price; and the price is the same for both parties. Thus the 'cost of victory' for any side, X, is how much it believes it must spend to outspend its adversary in a war.

If victory has a cost, peace also has its price. For any peace terms will involve awarding at least some territory to the other side, even if only an epsilon amount. The 'price of peace' for any side is the value of what that side forgoes by the peace terms relative to the value of what it would have obtained by victory. The general point is that the peace terms might be severe, or they might be generous, but they will always have some 'price'; something forgone relative to outright victory.

If we let the 'terms of peace' be measured by a number, then the 'price of peace' to D can be expressed as function of those terms. Suppose we index the peace terms so that zero is the best outcome for D; this would be the case if the peace terms were indexed by the proportion of territory awarded to Δ. Then the price of peace to D is a positive function of the peace terms (Figure 5.2).

It is not difficult to appreciate that the maximum cost of victory D will be prepared to incur for any given peace terms is the corresponding 'price of peace': the value of what is forgone by accepting peace terms rather than obtaining outright victory. Thus the horizontal axis can be also labelled 'the cost of victory', indicating the cost of victory that would leave D indifferent between accepting the peace terms and instead fighting for victory.

In Hicksian terminology Figure 5.3 plots the 'concession curve'. This curve indicates the maximum amount D would be willing to pay to have victory rather than those peace terms. It is clear that the concession curve constitutes a boundary between two zones of preference: D preferring victory to peace, and D preferring peace to victory, as Figure 5.3 illustrates.

The same exercise can be repeated for Δ, but since the interests of D and Δ are directly conflicting – and an improvement in peace terms for D

peace terms

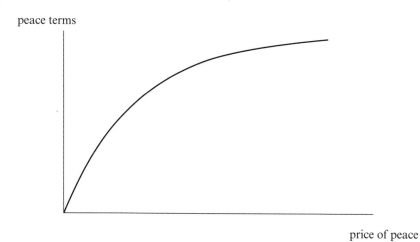

price of peace

Figure 5.2   The price of peace as a function of peace terms

peace terms

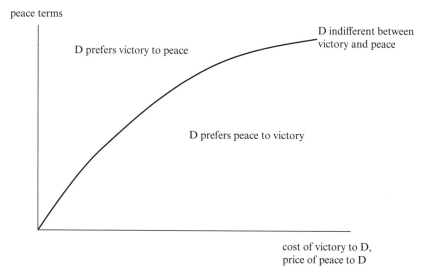

Figure 5.3   D's concession curve

is a deterioration in peace terms for Δ – the concession curve for Δ slopes downwards (Figure 5.4).

Hicks's principal contention seems to be that from the data represented in Figures 5.3 and 5.4 one can derive an equilibrium peace terms, and an equilibrium belief in the cost of victory, shared by both countries.

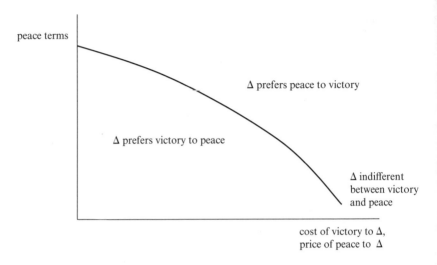

Figure 5.4   Δ's concession curve

We begin by observing that since Δ and D have exactly the same opportunities to win – they both face the same price of 'struggle resources' – it
seems sensible that in equilibrium both must have the same belief as to
the amount of resources that will secure victory. Thus we do not have to
distinguish between the cost of victory to Δ and the cost of victory to D;
there is just one, commonly shared estimate of the cost of victory, and so
the concession curves of Δ and D can be plotted on the same figure, and in
doing so we can obtain the plotting of preferences of Δ and D over peace
and war implied by various peace terms and costs of victory (Figure 5.5).
    Can we obtain combinations of peace terms and the cost of victory that
would constitute an equilibrium?
    Quadrants I, III and IV seem to provide only non-equilibria combin-
ations.
    Quadrants I, III and IV are inconsistent with peace. This is because
if both sides are to agree on peace terms then both must consider that
the terms are better than the cost of victorious war. But in all points in
Quadrants I, III and IV at least one party thinks they could do better by
paying the cost necessary to win a war.
    But Quadrants I, III and IV are also inconsistent with war.
    Quadrant IV may suggest war. But what Figure 5.5 states of any point
in Quadrant IV is solely that D would be better off by refusing the peace
terms implied by that point, and spending the amount indicated by that
point in the pursuit of victory, on the assumption that the indicated
amount would secure victory. But can that assumption be true? If D

peace terms

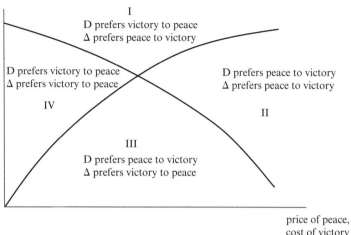

Figure 5.5   The Hicks solution

believed it to be true, then Δ would believe it to be true. But if they both believed that spending that amount would achieve victory, then spending that amount would not achieve victory for either. There is, then, no 'equilibrium in beliefs' in Quadrant IV .

Quadrant I may also suggest war. For at any point in that quadrant D judges that they would be better off by refusing the peace (and spending the amount indicated by the cost of victory corresponding to that point) but Δ, by contrast, does not consider that victory, acquired at the cost of victory corresponding to the point, superior to peace. But while to Δ's mind peace is preferred to victory, *victory is still preferred to defeat.*[9] So if it is 'war', Δ will spend to win. But if both spend the indicated amount then neither outspends the other, and neither achieves victory. There is no 'equilibrium in beliefs' here. War in Quadrant III seems to be disqualified as an equilibrium by a comparable argument.

What of the quadrant we have so far ignored, Quadrant II? Here we have both sides preferring peace to victory for a great range of peace terms. Here there are apparently an abundance of peace term possibilities. But one can argue that the lack of 'credible threats' disqualify all the points on II as disequilibria. Take any point in Quadrant II. What Figure 5.5 states is that D would be better off by accepting the peace terms indicated by that point rather than spending the amount indicated by that point in the pursuit of victory. D might embrace the peace terms corresponding to that point. But what is D's alternative? Their only alternative is a war in which victory is so costly that winning it would make them worse off. Therefore D has no credible threat to make to Δ to the effect: 'If you don't accept this division of the territory proposed by the peace terms, then we are content to go to war and dispossess you of all the territory.' D has no credible threat to the effect: 'We are offering these terms; and if you do not take them, you will regret it.' So why would Δ take them? Quadrant II offers no equilibrium either.

We conclude that the only equilibrium seems to be at the intersection of the concession curves, where the price of peace is the same for both sides. At the peace terms implied by that intersection, victory is not preferred to peace; so the peace can survive. But peace is not preferred to victory, and that lends credibility to the peace terms, as they are not undermined by the belief that the other side would rather accept some other peace terms than go to war. Each side can credibly say to the other: 'If you don't accept this division, then we are content to go to war.'

An Algebraic Representation

To represent the equilibrium algebraic terms, let ι be the index of the peace terms, that vary from 0 to Ω; where $\iota = 0$ is the most favourable to D, and $\iota = \Omega$ is the most favourable to Δ. Let $P_D(\Omega - \iota)$ be the pay-off of peace to D conditional on peace terms, ι, whereby $P'_D > 0$. And $P_\Delta(\iota)$ be the pay-off of peace to Δ conditional on peace terms, ι. whereby $P'_\Delta > 0$. Let $V_D = $ pay-off of victory to D, $V_D \equiv P_D(\Omega)$. Similarly for Δ.

'Belief equilibrium' requires:

$$X_D = X_\Delta \tag{5.11}$$

and optimization requires:

$$X_D = V_D - P_D(\Omega - \iota) \tag{5.12}$$

$$X_\Delta = V_\Delta - P_\Delta(\iota)$$

thus:

$$V_D - P_D(\Omega - \iota) = V_\Delta - P_\Delta(\iota) \tag{5.13}$$

Equilibrium occurs at the peace terms ι that make the price of peace equal. At the equilibrium what D forgoes by accepting the terms rather than achieving victory equals what Δ forgoes by accepting the terms rather than achieving victory.[10]

The Hicks Wage Bargain

Hicks expounded his theory in terms of a bargain over the wage between employees and employers. Let us cast the interpretation of the Hicks bargain we have advanced in terms of a bargain specifically over wages.

The Union and Confederation can either agree over w, or resort to a struggle. Victory for the business confederation will entail a wage rate of zero; that is the most advantageous wage rate to the business confederation, and it gets the whole of output. Victory for the Union is the wage rate that maximizes the wage bill, w_{MON}.

What constitutes the 'struggle' here? Perhaps the most meaningful analogy to war is a political struggle: a struggle for control of the coercive, legislative power of the state.[11] The dimensions of this struggle can be numerous. They could include campaigns to win public opinion, bribes for politicians, and election campaigns. If the Confederation wins that struggle and seizes control of the state, it passes a law reducing the wage rate to zero. If the Union wins that struggle and seizes control of the state, it passes a law imposing a wage rate equal to the wage bill maximizing rate. So:

$$V_C = Kq\left(\frac{\Sigma}{K}\right) \tag{5.14}$$

$$V_U = w_{MON}l(w_{MON})K \tag{5.15}$$

If the wage dispute is settled by agreement then the pay-off for workers is $wl(w)K$, and the payoff for capital owners is $[q(l(w)) - wl(w)]K$. Thus:

$$P_C = [q(l(w)) - wl(w)]K \tag{5.16}$$

$$P_U = wl(w)K \tag{5.17}$$

The Hicksian logic, we have argued, maintains that in equilibrium the 'price of peace' is the same for both:

$$V_U - P_U = V_C - P_C \tag{5.16}$$

or

$$w_{MON}l(w_{MON}) - wl(w) = q\left(\frac{\Sigma}{K}\right) - [q(l(w)) - wl(w)] \tag{5.17}$$

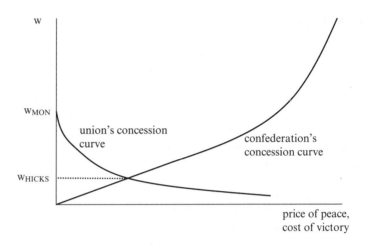

Figure 5.6   The Hicks solution for the wage rate

This solves for w, w_{HICKS}.

The solution is represented diagrammatically in Figure 5.6. The left-hand side of (5.17) is the price of peace to the Union, expressed per unit of capital; it is the concession curve for the Union. The right-hand side of (5.17) is the price of peace to the Confederation, expressed per unit of capital; it is the concession curve for the Confederation.

The wage rate is less than the wage bill maximizing wage rate, w_{MON}, and greater than zero.

The wage rate is such that that the 'concession' the Confederation has given – the difference between the maximum profit rate and the actual profit rate – equals the concession Union has given – the difference between the maximum wages paid per unit of capital and the actual wages paid per unit of capital. So it may be described as a system of equal absolute concessions.

The comparative statics of an increase in Σ

The Hicks wage is not one of perfect wage rigidity.

An increase in the supply of labour will reduce the wage rate. Employment will increase, but not by as much as the increase in labour supply.[12] Thus a higher labour supply produces a lower wage, and higher unemployment.

Diagrammatically, an increase in Σ will not shift the Union's concession curve, but will shift the Confederation's concession curve outwards. The Union's concession curve is unaltered: both its pay-off to peace, and the pay-off to victory, are unchanged; the wage income for any given wage offered as peace terms is unchanged, and the wage income from the monopoly wage imposed in victory is unchanged. So the maximum amount the Union would be willing to pay secure victory rather than accept given peace terms is unchanged. In contrast, the Confederation's circumstances have been altered. For while the pay-off to the Confederation of peace is unaltered for any given wage, the pay-off to victory has increased, as business gets the whole of output under victory, and that increases with the size of the labour force. So the maximum the Confederation would pay to secure victory rather than accept given peace terms, has increased. So the Confederation's curve shifts out. And the wage rate falls.

Notice that it is not that workers are 'weaker' or 'hungrier' when they are more numerous; rather it is capital that has become 'hungrier', as the pay-off to them for victory is now greater. And that greater incentive for the Confederation to win any 'war' is why the wage falls.

The comparative statics of an increase in K

An increase in the supply of capital will increase the wage rate. Indeed, it increases the wage so much that employment may actually fall; employment increases only if $e < 1/[1 + \upsilon/2]$.[13] Thus a higher capital stock produces a higher wage, and perhaps unemployment. Since the demand for labour is inelastic, the wage bill must have increased, and so the labour interest has definitely been advantaged by the increase in capital, but the benefit may bring a decline in employment.

Diagrammatically, an increase in K will not shift the Union's concession curve, but will shift leftwards the Confederation's concession curve. An increase in the supply of capital will not shift the Union's concession curves because, for any given wage offered as peace terms, the pay-off to peace per unit of capital and the pay-off to victory per unit of capital are unchanged.

But an increase on K will shift the Confederation concession curve leftwards. Intuitively, this is because for any given wage offered as peace terms, the pay-off to victory is increased by a lesser proportion than the pay-off to peace. And this is because of diminishing marginal returns to capital: business gets the whole of output under victory, but that is inelastic to the capital stock. The upshot is that the cost of victory that would leave it just worth peace is reduced to the Confederation.

The solution wage rate has a zero elasticity to equiproportionate increases in the supply of capital and labour. Thus the wage rate is invariant to any 'balanced' increase in capital and labour. Such balanced increases produce an equiproportionate increase in employment; thus an increase in the supply of labour takes the wage sting out of the increase in capital, permits an expansion in employment, and prevents an increase in the unemployment rate.

Vacancies not Unemployment

We have earlier concluded that the bargained wage floor will be lower than the labour monopoly wage floor. How much lower? Table 5.1 presents some parameterizations that allow answers to that question.

Table 5.1   A comparison of the Zeuthen wage rate and the labour monopoly wage rate

	Quasi-Cobb–Douglas	Quadratic	CES ($\sigma = 0.5$)
e(w)	$\dfrac{w}{[w + \phi]}\dfrac{1}{1 - \beta}$	$\dfrac{w}{\beta - w}$	$\dfrac{1}{2 - 2\sqrt{\beta w}}$
W/Π	$\dfrac{w}{[w + \phi]}\dfrac{\beta}{1 - \beta}$	$\dfrac{2w}{\beta - w}$	$\dfrac{\sqrt{\beta w}}{1 - \sqrt{\beta w}}$
w_{ZEUTHEN}	$\dfrac{1 - \beta}{2\beta}\phi$	$\dfrac{\beta}{4}$	$\dfrac{1}{16\beta}$
w_{MON}	$\dfrac{1 - \beta}{\beta}\phi$	$\dfrac{\beta}{2}$	$\dfrac{1}{4\beta}$

It will be seen that in the case of quasi-Cobb–Douglas and quadratic technologies, the Zeuthen floor is one just half of the labour monopoly floor. In the case of CES technology (with $\sigma = 0.5$) the Zeuthen floor is just one-quarter of the labour monopoly floor. This raises the question: might not the wage floor be less than the competitive wage? Indeed, it may. Figures 5.6 and 5.7 illustrate the possibility of a below-competitive wage in the Zeuthen and Hicks models.

In fact, if the Hicks bargain wage is to generate an unemployment wage, the wage bill in competitive equilibrium must be less than half the maximum wage bill.[14] In other words, there must be big opportunities to increase the wage if the Hicks bargain is ever to create the incentive to force the wage above full employment. Overall, like the Zeuthen, the Hicks bargain seems to shift away greatly the explanation of unemployment. For example, if $\sigma = 0.5$, the wage bill maximizing rate would have to imply an unemployment rate of 80 per cent before the Hicks bargain would yield any unemployment.[15]

The downward pressure on the wage rates under these bargaining models is underlined by the implausibly low wage shares these theories imply. To see this, note that, as $W/\Pi = 1 - e < 1$, the wage bill must

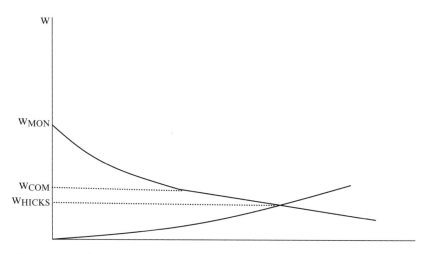

Figure 5.7   The Hicks wage may be beneath the competitive wage

be smaller than the profit bill under the Zeuthen bargain wage. The Hicks theory also implausibly predicts that the wage share is less than the profit share.[16] This prediction is, of course, inconsistent with the experience of developed economies. In order to obtain a wage share as low as these bargaining theories predict, an economy would need to be starved of capital to a degree never observed in developed economies.

These awkward implications need not thwart consideration of these models too badly. We could suppose that the supply of labour vanishes below a certain wage. Then the Zeuthen maximand will not necessitate the wage bill to be less than the profit bill. Similarly in the Hicks bargain, if the supply of labour vanishes below a certain wage then victory to the Confederation does not involve a zero wage, and the wage bill need not be less than the profit bill. Alternatively, in the Hicks bargain we may abandon the wholly arbitrary assumption of equal price of struggle resources; or – which comes down to the same thing – the assumption that the effectiveness of $1 of struggle resources is the same for both sides. This too will imply a higher wage share if the price of struggle resources is higher for the Confederation than for the Union.[17]

CONCLUDING COMMENT

This chapter asked what difference was made for wage setting when the political process requires that the concerned interests reach a bargain on the wage. The investigation is encumbered by the problematic character of bargaining models, which impelled a consideration of bargaining theory, which is not itself a concern of this work.

The chapter took up two of the earliest strands in bargaining theory, but without simply reproducing them. In particular we did not deploy Hicks's assumption that 'the weapon' of the adversaries consists of boycotting the production process, by means of either strikes or lock-outs. On the face of it, there may be some difficulty in assimilating Hicks's conception of the strike/lock-out as the weapon to the present analysis. For while you may physically subjugate an opponent by spending more on bullets than they spend on bullets, you cannot be said to subjugate your opponent physically by staying on the picket line for longer than they lock the factory gates. But we have stressed before that the struggle need not be of a kind that it destroys one protagonist's capability; it is enough that the outcome destroys one protagonist's will, and induces an involuntary 'submission response' on their part. The struggle could be an arm wrestle, or a staring contest. Or a strike. In my understanding the strike/lock-out is one such staring contest. The one that lasts the longest has broken the other's will.

Neither have we simply adopted the post-war profusion of bargaining models. Yet the models we have explored are congruent with some of the landmarks of that profusion. Thus the Zeuthen solution replicates the Nash bargaining maximand; and the outcome of the Hicks bargain when the stoppage is the weapon can be shown to coincide with the Kalai Smorodinsky bargaining solution (Upmann and Gerber 2003).[18]

The problematic character of bargaining theory accounts for the multiplicity of bargaining models, which in turn produces a variety of conclusions. Thus in our analysis the wage is rigid in some models, but malleable in others. Either way, competitive equilibrium and its comparative statics are not restored.

NOTES

1. 'The agreement materialized into the social democratic class compromise, the so-called "Saltsjöbaden spirit", marked by willingness to co-operate and a cross-class, collective sense of responsibility for developments in the national labour market and in the Swedish economy generally' (http://en.wikipedia.org/wiki/Saltsjobaden).
2. Zeuthen's theory has been expounded and critically appraised by a former pupil (Brems 1976), and Harsanyi (1956).
3. As in Chapter 3, we are implicitly assuming that the employment–capital ratio of each firm is not observable by the labour monopoly, and so the 'efficient' strategy of making full employment part of the bargain is not feasible.
4. This incoherence can also be put this way. The actual probability of concession cannot be greater than both the critical concession probabilities, because then both would

refuse; and so the actually probability of concession would be zero. And the actual probability of concession cannot be less than both the critical concession probabilities, or both would concede; and so the probability of concession is one.

5.　　　　$\dfrac{W}{K} = l(w)w$ and $\rho \equiv \dfrac{\Pi}{K} = q(l(w) - wl(w))$. Thus $\dfrac{\partial W/K}{\partial w} = wl' + l$

and　　　　$\dfrac{\partial \dfrac{\Pi}{K}}{\partial w} = q'l' - [wl' + l] = -l$. Thus $\dfrac{\partial W}{\partial \Pi} = e - 1$.

Thus e must be <1 over the 'relevant range' of the wage rate. For if elasticity of demand exceeds one then any increase in the wage rate would reduce both the profit bill and the wage bill, and so would be against the interest of both parties. Bargaining is plainly restricted to those contexts where interest diverge, which here is a situation of the inelastic demand for labour.

6. Some discussion of Hicks's theory occurs in Harsanyi (1956), Rothschild (1994) and Shackle (1957).
7. It is plausible that Hicks's sensitivity to this choice between accord and affray was fostered by the shadow cast by the First World War. Throughout that war, both sides felt they had a choice to make between fighting for victory or, instead, negotiating peace. The war ended, of course, on both Eastern and Western fronts, with peace treaties. The significance of the First World War can be underlined by contrasting it with the Second. In the later war there was no possibility of concluding the war through a negotiated peace. The credibility of such negotiations had been destroyed by the spread of the war through the spectacular repudiation of various non-aggression pacts and Hague treaties. Consequently, the conflict soon became a quasi-exterminatory 'total' war, a war of 'unconditional surrender'; a war that could only end with the conquest of one side by the other. For each belligerent, the only option was victory. The belligerents of the First World War, by contrast, were confronted with a genuine choice, between victory or peace. And that is the choice Hicks was concerned to understand.
8. It simplifies to suppose that the territory's value is not reduced by struggle; it is not damaged by war. This simplification can be relaxed without changing qualitative conclusions. Notice also that victory is treated as purely a means to an end: it is not 'its own reward' in any way. There is no value that is attached to victory as such.
9. That is, the value of victory exceeds the cost of victory. The value of victory to Δ can be measured as the horizontal axis intercept of Δ's concession curve, as that intercept indicates the price of peace to Δ when the peace terms offer Δ nothing; that is, the value of getting everything.
10. To illustrate numerically: suppose there is one unit of territory to be divided ($\Omega = 1$), the value of territory is proportional to territory, but whereas Δ gets \$1 from any square kilometre of ground, D gets \$2 on account of D being a more efficient exploiter. Then:

$$P_D(\iota) = 2[1 - \iota] \qquad P_\Delta(\iota) = \iota$$

$$V_D = 2 \qquad V_\Delta = 1$$

Thus the solution is:

$$2 - 2[1 - \iota] = 1 - \iota$$

or

$$\iota = 1/3$$

D gets 2/3 of the territory, and Δ gets 1/3 of the territory.

11. We allow the 'struggle' to be more than literal physical combat. It could be physically peaceful. It could be a struggle in court, in which case the side that spends more on lawyers wins. It could be a political contest, and so the party wins that spends more on the campaign. In each of these cases there is not physical subjugation, but there is an acceptance of defeat: the losing side accepts the court's decision; the losing party accepts the vote. We could, of course, make an optimizing decision out of that acceptance, but we are not doing so; we are assuming that the involuntary unchosen response of the loser is to accept. Thus we are not necessarily supposing that struggle solves the difference of wills by destroying one adversary's capability; it destroys their capability or destroys their will.

12.
$$q\left(\frac{\Sigma}{K}\right) + 2wl(w) - q(l(w)) = w_{MON}l(w_{MON})$$

$$\frac{\Sigma\partial w}{w\partial\Sigma} = \frac{\Sigma}{K\left[q'l' - 2\dfrac{\partial W/K}{\partial w}\right]} = \frac{1 + \upsilon}{-2 + e} < 0 \text{ and } \frac{\partial L}{\partial\Sigma} = l'K\frac{\partial w}{\partial\Sigma} = \frac{e}{2 - e} < 1.$$

13.
$$q\left(\frac{\Sigma}{K}\right) + 2wl(w) - q(l(w)) = w_{MON}l(w_{MON})$$

Thus:

$$\frac{K\partial w}{w\partial K} = \frac{\Sigma/K}{-q'l' + 2\dfrac{\partial W/K}{\partial w}} = \frac{1 + \upsilon}{2 - e} > 0 \text{ and } \frac{K\partial L}{L\partial K} = 1 - e\frac{K\partial w}{w\partial K} = 1 - \frac{e[1 + \upsilon]}{2 - e}.$$

Even though $e < 1$, $\dfrac{K\partial L}{L\partial K}$ is necessarily positive only when $\upsilon = 0$.

14. The proof turns on the comparison of the Hicks wage bill with the maximum wage bill when the Hicks wage coincides with the competitive wage. Equation (5.17) states:

$$w_{MON}l(w_{MON}) - wl(w_{HICKS}) = q\left(\frac{\Sigma}{K}\right) - [q(l(w_{HICKS})) - wl(w_{HICKS})]$$

So if $w_{HICKS} = w_{COM}$ then

$$w_{MON}l(w_{MON}) - wl(w_{COM}) = q\left(\frac{\Sigma}{K}\right) - [q(l(w_{COM})) - wl(w_{COM})].$$

But $q\left(\dfrac{\Sigma}{K}\right) - q(l(w_{COM})) = 0$, so if $w_{HICKS} = w_{COM}$ then

$$w_{MON}l(w_{MON}) = 2w_{HICKS}l(w_{HICKS}).$$

15.
$$\frac{W_{MON}}{K} = \frac{1}{4} \text{ and } \frac{W_{COM}}{K} = \frac{\dfrac{\beta}{\Sigma/K}}{\left[\dfrac{\beta}{\Sigma/K} + 1\right]^2} = \frac{\dfrac{l_{MON}}{\Sigma/K}}{\left[\dfrac{l_{MON}}{\Sigma/K} + 1\right]^2}.$$

So if $W_{COM}/K = W_{MON}/2K$ (and therefore the Hicks wage coincides with the competitive wage) then

$$\frac{\dfrac{l_{MON}}{\Sigma/K}}{\left[\dfrac{l_{MON}}{\Sigma/K} + 1\right]^2} = \frac{1}{8}, \text{ and } \frac{l_{MON}}{\Sigma/K} \approx 0.2.$$

16.
$$\frac{W}{\Pi} = \frac{wl(w)}{q(l(w)) - wl(w)} = \frac{w_{MON}l(w_{MON})}{q\left(\dfrac{\Sigma}{K}\right)} < 1.$$

17. If resources cost ω more for D than Δ, then D will believe that to win it must spend on struggle resources in excess of ω times what Δ spends; so in equilibrium $X_D = \omega X_\Delta$. Combined with the optimization conditions $X_D = V_D - P_D(\Omega - \iota)$ and $X_D = V_\Delta - P_\Delta(\iota)$ this yields $V_D - P_D(\Omega - \iota) = \omega[V_\Delta - P_\Delta(\iota)]$, and so

$$\frac{\partial \iota}{\partial \omega} = \frac{V_\Delta - P_\Delta(\iota)}{P_D' + \omega P_\Delta'} > 0.$$

The terms of peace move against the party with more expensive resources.

18. Let s be the length of the strike/lockout, where the length of the period in question is unit. The length of strike or lockout that leaves the Confederation and Union indifferent between strike or lockout and agreement:

$$sl(w_{MON})w_{MON} = l(w_{MON})w_{MON} - wl(w)$$

$$q\left(\frac{\Sigma}{K}\right)s = q\left(\frac{\Sigma}{K}\right) - [q(l(w)) - wl(w)]$$

The twist here is that a contest would be decided not by its cost but by its length. Since in equilibrium neither side triumphs over the other, the equilibrium wage is such that both sides concur on the length of stoppage that would be just worth agreeing on the wage.

$$\frac{wl(w)}{w_{MON}l(w_{MON})} = \frac{q(l(w)) - wl(w)}{q\left(\dfrac{\Sigma}{K}\right)}$$

It amounts to each party contracting from its 'bliss point' by the same proportion. Instead of an equilibrium of equal absolute concessions, it is an equilibrium of equal proportionate concessions.

6. How foresight may (and may not) defeat the floor

The analysis of earlier chapters has been wholly short run; wholly within the framework of a single period. Such a framework amounts to supposing that the future is completely neglected by the workforce. This chapter seeks to correct that plainly inadequate assumption. It investigates how foresight would shape the future consequences of the maximization of current wage income, and to what extent allowing for the foresight of these future consequences would recommend to the workforce revision of a strategy of current wage bill maximization. We conclude that in some circumstances the tenet of wage bill maximization will require revision. And yet in other certain circumstances the suitability of the tenet survives the allowance for the foresight. The chapter amounts, then, to a modest rebuttal of any readiness to dispose of wage bill maximization by a pat reference to the 'long run'; and a defence of wage rigidity against the (admittedly) plausible suggestion that foresight will undermine the floor and its rigidity.

The analysis proceeds by recognizing that the linkage between foresight and the longer-run consequences of wage bill maximization is provided by saving. Foresight will shape how much is saved, and consequently how much capital will grow, and as a result how much employment will grow in the future. The chapter identifies what wage bill maximization would spell for the future path of employment once we allow for saving made in the light of that future. It is especially concerned to see whether saving made in the light of that future permits more definite conclusions about the future tendency of unemployment. For we have concluded earlier that a wage floor may, or may not, be implied by wage bill maximization, depending on whether capital is 'small' or 'large'. Is it possible to conclude that rational saving will make capital in the long run 'large', or 'small'? Can we, perhaps, count on saving to surmount the floor? We conclude that the answer is 'not always'; not in the face of a 'large' rate of labour-improving technical progress.

Foresight also makes for a more spacious appreciation by decision-makers of the costs and benefits of wage bill maximization. In the absence of foresight, wage-makers neglect the possibility that, by reducing the profit rate in the present period, 'wage bill maximization' reduces saving, and thereby reduces wage incomes in future periods. In other words, wage-makers neglect the possibility that maximizing current wage incomes is short-sighted, and counterproductive. The last sections of this chapter rectify this neglect of the later wage impacts of present wage actions, and inquire into what extent the recognition of those later effects of present actions would moderate the wage claims of the labour monopolist. To what extent does allowing for the negative impact of high wage levels on saving blunt the labour monopolist's incentive to raise the wage rate? Might that negative impact, in fact, eliminate that incentive altogether, so that the labour interest is actually best served by a competitive wage? In other words, might the allowance for a long-sighted pursuit of labour's self-interest yield a 'harmony' thesis, where the labour interest has no incentive to reduce the profit rate below what the competitive market delivers?

The chapter concludes that the negative impact of higher wage levels on saving will, in the context of infinite horizons models, certainly blunt the labour monopolist's incentive to raise the wage rate. It does not, however, remove it. Further, with sufficiently contracted horizons the recognition of the impact of high wage levels on the return for saving will not have any effect on optimizing wage rates.[1]

THE LONG-RUN CONSEQUENCES OF WAGE BILL MAXIMIZATION

The preceding chapters have concluded that one consequence of wage bill maximization today is the possibility of unemployment today. But what will be the consequences of wage bill maximization today for unemployment in the future, supposing that households save in light of that future? We begin investigating this question by an analytical device that combines a maximum of tractability with a maximum of foresight and futurity: the Ramsey–Solow model. In this model all who live today will live forever; and all who will ever live, live today. It will be seen that wage bill maximization in the context of the model implies that the tendency of unemployment over time becomes a contest between the accumulation of capital and the economization of labour by technical progress. Saving presses down on unemployment, and technical progress presses up. Depending on their strength, either force could predominate, and so the possibility of unemployment in a one-period model is converted, over time, into a necessity or impossibility of unemployment; for over time unemployment will either fall to zero, or rise to 100 per cent.

Consider the familiar Ramsey–Solow model, where, critically, the population consists of a single generation of infinitely lived persons, each maximizing an identical homothetic and separable utility function:

$$U_t = \frac{C_t^\alpha}{\alpha} + \frac{C_{t+1}^\alpha}{\alpha}\frac{1}{1+\delta} + \frac{C_{t+1}^\alpha}{\alpha}\frac{1}{[1+\delta]^2} + \dots \qquad (6.1)$$

The rate of time preference is parametric and positive; the population of workers is exogenous, and (at least initially) owns no capital; unemployment is a matter of job lotteries, augmented by unemployment insurance.

In this simple economy, flukes aside, the unemployment rate will over time either move downwards to 0 per cent, or upwards to 100 per cent. Thus wage bill maximization is inconsistent with a long-run coexistence in the economy of both employed and unemployed. The situation where some are employed and some are unemployed is a passing phenomenon.

The argument for this contention begins with the observation that when labour markets are competitive, the evolution of capital and consumption can be expressed by two differential equations:

$$\frac{dk^*}{dt} = q(k^*)k^* - c^* \qquad (6.2)$$

$$\frac{dc^*}{dt} = \varsigma[\rho(k^*) - \delta]c^* \qquad (6.3)$$

$$k^* \equiv \frac{K}{\Sigma}, \, c^* \equiv \frac{C}{\Sigma}$$

By ruling out $k^* = 0$ and $c^* = 0$ in the long run as inconsistent with utility maximization, we can conclude that capital converges to a steady state value satisfying $\rho(k_{SS}^*) = \delta$.[2]

But (6.2) and (6.3) need amendment in the face of wage bill maximization. For under wage bill maximization the capital–labour ratio cannot be less than the magnitude that makes the elasticity of labour demand equal to one, a magnitude we denote k_{MIN}. For any magnitude of k^* less than k_{MIN} then the capital–labour ratio remains equal to k_{MIN}. Concomitantly, for any magnitude of k^* less than k_{MIN} the profit rate remains equal to $\rho(k_{MIN})$, which is the rate of profit implied by wage bill maximization, ρ_{MON}, that constitutes a ceiling on the rate of profit. Correspondingly, there is now a ceiling on the average product of capital, $q = q(k_{MIN}) = q_{MON}$. Figure 6.1 illustrates.

Thus for all k^* less than k_{MIN}, k^* grows according to:

$$\frac{dk^*}{dt} = q_{MON}k^* - c^* \qquad (6.4)$$

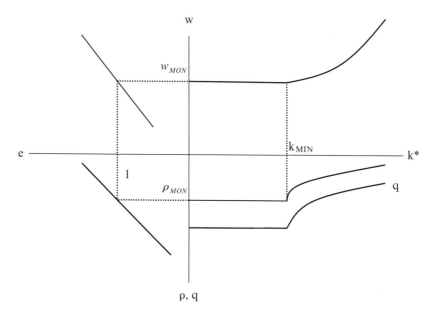

Figure 6.1   The wage rate and the profit rate and capital per head under wage bill maximization

The consumption dynamics may also require revision for $k^* < k_{MIN}$. For insofar as an excess supply of labour produces probabilistic incomes, consumption behaviour alters. But if that excess supply of labour comes in the shape of work rationing, or overmanning, or job lotteries augmented by complete unemployment insurance, then wage income remains deterministic despite the excess supply of labour. And so the deterministic, perfect foresight theory of consumption applies under $k^* < k_{MIN}$. The only difference is that $\rho = \rho(k_{MIN}) = \rho_{MON}$, so consumption grows according to:

$$\frac{dc^*}{dt} = \varsigma[\rho_{MON} - \delta]c^* \qquad (6.5)$$

The long-run destination of consumption and capital turn upon whether steady state capital k_{SS} is greater or less than k_{MIN}. Equivalently, the long-run destination of consumption and capital turns upon whether the ceiling profit rate is either greater or less than the rate of time preference.

Suppose for now that the ceiling profit exceeds the rate of time preference. For all $k > k_{SS}$ (6.2) and (6.3) will apply, as the wage floor does not bind. But for all $k < k_{SS}$ (6.4) and (6.5) apply, as the wage floor does bind. This system is illustrated in Figure 6.2.

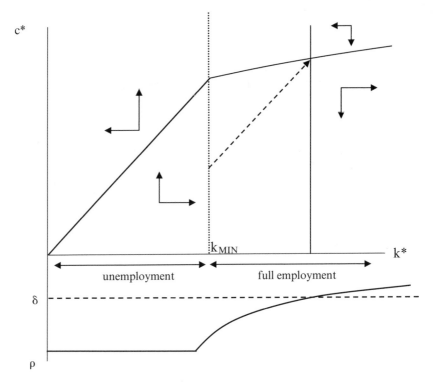

Figure 6.2   The path of capital and consumption per head under wage bill maximization

Suppose the initial capital stock is so small that there is unemployment, $k^*(0) < k_{MIN}$ To avoid long-run zero values c^* or k^*, the plotting of consumption and capital stock will move in a 'north-east' direction, to coincide, at some point in the future, with the 'saddle path' shown in Figure 6.2. That is, capital (and consumption) increases; and increases until full employment is reached. Thence the passage to the long-run steady state is the same as that under equilibrium labour markets.

The upshot, it appears, is that any unemployment created by wage bill maximization will not endure. The growth in capital eventually reduces unemployment to zero. Saving saves the day. In the long run we are all employed.[3]

But there is a menace to this hopeful scenario of inevitable full employment.

It was noted in Chapter 4 that labour augmentation will increase the inelasticity of labour demand. Thus even if the elasticity initially exceeds one at full employment, any persisting trend to augment labour will ultimately reduce the elasticity of labour demand at the full employment below one, thereby creating unemployment. But it is also true that the preceding paragraphs have argued that such unemployment will be eventually 'grown away' by saving. Can saving also save the day in the face of a persisting trend to augment labour? To sharpen the question, recall that any continual augmentation of labour will (by the logic explained in Chapter 4) continually reduce employment per unit of capital. Thus the direction that unemployment takes over time appears to be the outcome of a race between saving (reducing unemployment) and labour-augmenting technical progress (increasing unemployment). Who will win that race?

Saving may win; a perpetual labour-augmenting technical progress need not defy the ultimate triumph of capital accumulation over unemployment. To see this, note that previous modelling, (6.2) to (6.5), can be repeated with barely any revision, simply by replacing K/Σ with capital per unit of 'effective workforce' $K/\lambda\Sigma \equiv \tilde{k}$; and C/Σ consumption per unit of 'effective workforce' $C/\lambda\Sigma$.

$\tilde{k} > \tilde{k}_{MIN}$:

$$\frac{d\tilde{k}}{dt} = q(\tilde{k})\tilde{k} - \tilde{c} - \dot{\lambda}\tilde{k} \qquad (6.6)^4$$

$$\frac{d\tilde{c}}{dt} = \varsigma[\rho(\tilde{k}) - \delta]\tilde{c} - \dot{\lambda}\tilde{c} \qquad (6.7)$$

$\tilde{k} < \tilde{k}_{MIN}$:

$$\frac{d\tilde{k}}{dt} = q_{MON}\tilde{k} - \tilde{c} - \dot{\lambda}\tilde{k}$$

$$\frac{d\tilde{c}}{dt} = \varsigma[\rho_{MON} - \delta]\tilde{c} - \dot{\lambda}\tilde{c}$$

$$\tilde{k} \equiv \frac{K}{\lambda\Sigma}, \tilde{c} \equiv \frac{C}{\lambda\Sigma}$$

By exactly the same logic used to analyse (6.2), we can conclude that full employment can be reached.

But there is a second menace to the conclusion that 'in the long run we are all employed'. This second menace does not itself turn on technical progress, although it does make the threat that technical progress poses to long-run full employment more serious. This second menace lies in the second possible relativity between ρ_{MON} and δ. For we have assumed that $\rho_{MON} > \delta$, allowing the actual rate of profit to match the time preference.

But it may be that $\rho_{MON} < \delta$; the ceiling profit rate is smaller than the rate of time preference. In this circumstance, as wage bill maximization makes the actual rate of profit necessarily less than the rate of time preference, wage bill maximization makes it impossible for the reward for saving ever to be high enough to induce households to maintain capital, rather than consume it. The steady state solution is impossible. Consumption and capital must fall, forever.

What is the equilibrium path? The equilibrium path will avoid the violation of intertemporal optimization implied by any eventually zero-level consumption, which is the consequence of too high a level of initial consumption, a 'north-west' path, and the ultimate consumption of all capital. The equilibrium path also avoids the absurdity of near zero consumption in the face of an ever-burgeoning investment, which is the consequence of too low a level of initial consumption, and a consequent 'south-east' path. The optimizing path chooses that ratio of C to K that ensures K declines at the same rate as C, and so preserving the relativity between C and K:[5]

$$\frac{c^*}{k^*} = q_{MON} - \varsigma[\rho_{MON} - \delta] \tag{6.8}$$

Thus consumption and capital contract at the same parametric rate (see Figure 6.3):

$$\frac{dc^*}{c^*dt} = \frac{dk^*}{k^*dt} = \varsigma[\rho_{MON} - \delta] \tag{6.9}$$

and, in consequence, output and the wages bill contract at the same parametric rate:

$$\frac{dy^*}{y^*dt} = \frac{dw^*}{w^*dt} = \varsigma[\rho_{MON} - \delta] \tag{6.10}$$

$$y^* \equiv \frac{W}{\Sigma} \qquad w^* \equiv \frac{W}{\Sigma}$$

Assuming workers own no capital, budget constraint considerations imply that the consumption of workers each period exactly equals the wage bill each period:

$$c_L^* = w^* \tag{6.11}$$

Consequently all the disinvestment is done by capitalists, and given $c^*/k^* = q_{MON} - \varsigma[\rho_{MON} - \delta]$, their consumption follows:

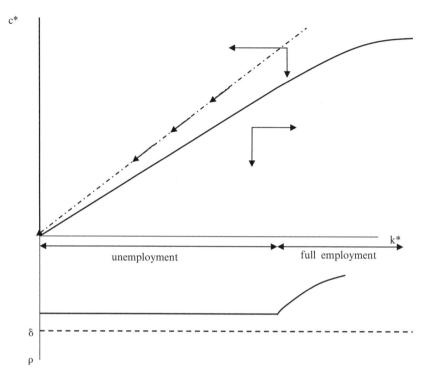

Figure 6.3   *The path of capital and consumption per head under wage bill maximization when the ceiling rate of profit is less than the rate of time preference*

$$c_K^* = [\rho_{MON} + \varsigma[\delta - \rho_{MON}]]k^* \tag{6.12}$$

The remarks above only describe the economy when $\rho_{MON} < \delta$ if there is actually unemployment. For unemployment is not actually inevitable when $\rho_{MON} < \delta$: a sufficiently large endowment of capital would eliminate all unemployment even if $\rho_{MON} < \delta$. But such full employment is passing, because by assumption the profit rate at full employment is below the rate of time preference, and so capital is always decumulating, so the elasticity of demand for labour is always falling. So if the elasticity is not smaller than one at the present endowment of capital, it will sooner or later fall below one, and unemployment will appear. The economy commences the steady state rate of decline described in preceding paragraphs, and unemployment will ultimately approach 100 per cent. In the long run we are all employed. Or unemployed.

The analysis begs the question of: how 'likely' is it that $\rho_{MON} < \delta$?

There are palpable grounds for not taking the 100 per cent unemployment possibility seriously, for it involves a secular fall in per capita consumption and capital, which is grossly at variance with widespread historical experience.

However, the falling employment equilibrium does not necessitate disinvestment and falling living standards once we allow for labour-augmenting technical progress. Under labour-augmenting technical progress it remains the case that the declining employment equilibrium occurs if the steady state rate of profit exceeds the maximum rate of profit:

$$\rho_{SS} > \rho_{MON}$$

However, the expression for the steady state rate of profit is altered by labour-augmenting technical progress. It is now $\rho_{SS} = \delta + \dot{\lambda}/\varsigma$, and so the condition for the declining employment equilibrium is now:

$$\dot{\lambda} > \varsigma[\rho_{MON} - \delta] \tag{6.13}$$

If this inequality holds then consumption per unit of effective labour force, $C/\lambda\Sigma$, will 'grow' at the negative rate $\varsigma[\rho_{MON} - \delta] - \dot{\lambda}$, and capital per unit of effective labour force will 'grow' at the same negative rate. Evidently, a sufficiently large magnitude of technical progress will always make (6.13) true, and induce falling employment. Thus, regardless of the magnitude of ρ_{MON} or δ, a sufficiently large rate of technical progress will always win the contest with capital accumulation.

But this prospect is not as dismal as might be thought. For consumption per unit of workforce, C/Σ, and capital per unit of workforce, K/Σ, need not decline in the 'declining employment economy' that is induced by rapid labour augmentation. If $\dot{\lambda} > \varsigma[\rho_{MON} - \delta]$ but $\rho_{MON} - \delta > 0$ then C/Σ and K/Σ will rise over time at rate $\varsigma[\rho_{MON} - \delta]$, despite $C/\lambda\Sigma$ and $K/\lambda\Sigma$ falling over time. And W/Σ will rise over time at the same rate as K/Σ, as (from Chapter 4) wage bill maximization implies that the wage bill per unit of capital is invariant to labour augmentation.[6] The upshot is steadily rising capital per head and consumption per head, and wages income per head, in spite of perpetually falling employment per head.[7]

If the economy is capable of growing to full employment in the absence of technical progress (that is, if $\rho_{MON} > \delta$), then any rate of technical progress sufficiently large to induce declining employment, will leave C/Σ and K/Σ still growing. Thus the long-run prospect that is opened by the conjunction of labour-augmenting technical progress and capital accumulation is not a really dismal one; it is one of rising wages, consumption and capital per head. And one in which work is heading towards extinction.

THE LONG-RUN IMPOLICY OF WAGE BILL MAXIMIZATION

The previous section has not confronted the full sting of foresight for wage bill maximization. For the previous section simply traced the consequences of wage bill maximization if saving was made in the light of those consequences. But it did not, in the light of those consequences, question the rationality of wage bill maximization.

But must not the incentive for the labour monopoly to increase the current wage bill be blunted by the consequent reduction in capital accumulation? Is it even possible that the incentive is removed altogether? Is it possible that we are left with a 'market harmony' thesis whereby the competitive market wage is in the best interest of both labour and the capital owners?

Any presumption of the 'market harmony thesis' can be disposed of by the consideration of an economy in which $\rho_{MON} < \delta$. As has been explained, in these circumstances wage bill maximization implies that employment tends to zero. This case may, therefore, be considered anomalous, but it is not a case which is biased in favour of the wisdom of raising the wage rate. On the contrary, the gloomy implications of wage bill maximization makes it unpromising terrain for the rationality of raising wages above their competitive level. Nevertheless, even here it can be demonstrated quite easily that, in the eye of a rational labour monopolist, the competitive wage rate may be inferior to an above-competitive wage rate. To see this, suppose, as we may, that in the initial period the economy has the quantity of capital found in the competitive steady state. In this circumstance the comparison of the consumption path for workers under labour monopoly with that under competition amounts to the comparison of a 'middling' but unchanging magnitude of consumption (under competition), with a magnitude that is initially higher than under competition but declines over time to a lower one. The comparison does not yield unambiguous conclusions. Workers' utility will be increased by raising the wage above the full employment wage if:

$$1 - \varsigma\frac{1 - \pi}{\pi} > e \qquad (6.14)^8$$

(where π and e are evaluated at the competitive wage at the steady state), and reduced otherwise.

Thus the market harmony thesis may or may not hold. But it is the latter possibility that is surely the more significant. The message of this example is: even when raising wage rates has such apparently dire consequences, it may still be superior to raise the wage rate above its competitive level.

Of course, it remains moot how real the possibility is. Evidently, $e < 1$ will not constitute a sufficient condition for the expediency of a wage floor. So merely labour demand being inelastic is no longer enough to make it rational to raise the wage above its competitive level; there has to be a degree of inelasticity. It is also clear that the elasticity of intertemporal substitution must be sufficiently small if the possibility is to hold. It must be that $\varsigma < \pi/[1 - \pi]$. The larger the size of ς the less likely the possibility will hold. This makes sense; the larger the value of ς the more severe the rate of contraction induced by any wage rise ($dw^*/w^*dt = \varsigma[\rho_{MAX} - \delta]$) and so the larger the future costs of present wage rises.

But allowing for the later consequences of current wage rises does not necessarily remove the incentive to raise wages above the competitive level.

It is true that although labour monopolist may rationally raise w above the competitive level, it would never be optimal to raise it as much as under wage bill maximization. For the optimal elasticity is now certainly less than 1:

$$e = 1 - \varsigma\left[\frac{1 - \pi}{\pi}\right]\frac{\rho}{\delta} \qquad (6.15)^9$$

Nevertheless, it may be that wage bill maximization ($e = 1$) yields higher utility to capital-less workers than the competitive solution for sufficiently high values of δ.[10] As δ approaches one, the myopic wage bill maximization solution is superior to the competitive steady state. This is quite a strong result; even naive static (goose-killing) labour monopoly may be better than no labour monopoly at all.

THE POTENTIAL RATIONALITY OF WAGE BILL MAXIMIZATION

Up to this point we have given futurity a chance – more than a chance – by assuming a single, infinitely long-lived generation, Ramsey–Solow style. We now turn to the opposite extreme of supposing that the current generation has the briefest future that still constitutes a future. We turn to an overlapping generations model, in which each generation lives two periods, and interrogate it on the extent to which foresight blunts the incentive to raise the wage rate. And the answer is, not at all.

We will suppose positive population growth, and so the young outnumber the old, and are electorally decisive. Despite the apparent complexities of this situation, it is apparent that a Nash-style equilibrium is that each generation chooses the wage rate to maximize the present wage bill; $e(w_t) = 1$.[11] For, in the manner of Nash, this is the 'rule' that is self-enforcing. For if every generation chooses $e(w_t) = 1$ there would be no benefit of any single generation deviating. Consider the budget constraint of the generation that is young in t:

$$C_t^Y + \frac{C_t^0}{1 + \dfrac{\partial Y_{t+1}}{\partial K_{t+1}}} = W_t(w_t) \tag{6.16}$$

Whatever wage in t is chosen by the young, the marginal product of capital in $t + 1$ is chosen by the young of $t + 1$ and so is unchanged at ρ_{MAX} by the logic of the Nash thought experiment (that is, the scrutiny of the benefit of unilateral deviations). Thus the budget constraint is:

$$C_t^Y + \frac{C_t^0}{1 + \rho_{MON}} = W_t(w_t) \tag{6.17}$$

The only thing for the young to do is to choose the wage rate to make the wage bill as large as possible. And so wage bill maximization is restored, and every generation chooses $e(w_t) = 1$.

As in the Ramsey–Solow model, we can trace out the future consequences:

$$K_{T+1} - K_t = q(l(w))K_t - C_t^0 - C_t^Y$$

$$C_t^0 = q(l(w_{MON}))K_t - w_{MON}l(w_{MON})K_t + K_t$$

$$C_t^Y = \frac{w_{MON}l(w_{MON})K_t}{1 + \dfrac{[1 + \rho]^{\frac{1}{1-\alpha}-1}}{[1 + \delta]^{\frac{1}{1-\alpha}}}} \tag{6.18}$$

Therefore:

$$K_{t+1} = wl(w_{MON})\left[1 - \frac{1}{1 + \dfrac{[1 + \rho]^{\frac{1}{1-\alpha}-1}}{[1 + \delta]^{\frac{1}{1-\alpha}}}}\right]K_t \tag{6.19}$$

Assuming that the coefficient on K_t exceeds one, the capital stock grows over time, thereby increasing the elasticity of demand for labour until it is unitary at full employment, and full employment takes hold. We are back with the 'myopic' story of the first sections.

CONCLUDING COMMENT

This chapter opened up the question to what extent the labour monopolist's recognition of the future consequences of its present actions may blunt its incentive to raise wages. A conclusive answer will traverse analytically difficult terrain, and this chapter provides no more than a reconnaissance of that territory. Nevertheless, it identifies some landmarks. The degree of blunting depends on how much futurity the given working generation faces. With a minimum degree (the overlapping generations model) the incentive is completely undulled; with a maximum degree (the Ramsey–Solow model) the incentive is diminished, but not eliminated.

NOTES

1. The model of the chapter's first sections is kindred to the literature of 'dual economy' models of surplus labour (see Dixit 1968, 1973; Robertson 1999). More specific examinations of wage rigidity in a growing economy are supplied by Sgro and Takayama (1981) and Coleman (1998).
2. We are assuming there exists a k^* that satisfies $\rho(k^*) = \delta$. But with a sufficiently large quantity of capital per unit of labour the profit rate either falls to zero, or approaches zero under the quasi-Cobb–Douglas, quadratic and CES functions. Thus for these functions the existence of a steady state is assured under full employment.
3. We can equally infer that work rationing and overmanning will not persist. Both are transient symptoms of capital poverty that, like unemployment, will eventually be overcome by capital accumulation.
4. To explicate (6.6): it is necessarily true that

$$\frac{d\left(\frac{K}{\lambda\Sigma}\right)}{dt} = \frac{dK}{\lambda\Sigma dt} - \frac{K}{\lambda\Sigma}\frac{d\lambda}{\lambda dt}.$$

The national income identity and the production function imply:

$$\frac{dK}{dt\Sigma} = q\left(\frac{K}{\lambda\Sigma}\right)\frac{K}{\Sigma} - \frac{C}{\Sigma}.$$ Equation (6.6) follows.

5. $\dfrac{dk^*}{k^*dt} = q_{MON} - \dfrac{c^*}{k^*}$ and $\dfrac{dc^*}{c^*dt} = \varsigma[\rho_{MON} - \delta]$. If $\dfrac{dc^*}{c^*dt} = \dfrac{dk^*}{k^*dt}$,

   and so c^*/k^* is unchanging over time, then $c^*/k^* = q_{MON} - \varsigma[\rho_{MON} - \delta]$. If $c^*/k^* > q_{MON} - \varsigma[\rho_{MON} - \delta]$ then c^* grows faster than k^*, at an ever accelerating rate, and eventually the capital stock is exhausted. If $c^*/k^* < q_{MON} - \varsigma[\rho_{MON} - \delta]$ then k^* grows faster than $\varsigma[\rho_{MAX} - \delta]$, at an ever accelerating rate, and eventually all output is invested.
6. Equivalently, wage bill maximization ensures that the wage rate rises at $\dot{\lambda}$ but L per unit of K falls at $\dot{\lambda}$.
7. As in the absence of technical progress, workers neither save nor dissave, $\tilde{c}_L = \tilde{w}_L$. All saving is done by capital owners:

$$\tilde{c}_K = [\rho_{MON} + \varsigma[\delta - \rho_{MON}]]\tilde{k} < \rho_{MON}\tilde{k}$$

8. Using discrete time for convenience, the utility of a workforce that owns no capital is:

$$U = \frac{W^\alpha}{\alpha} + \frac{W_1^\alpha}{\alpha}\frac{1}{1 + \delta} + \frac{W_2^\alpha}{\alpha}\frac{1}{[1 + \delta]^2} + \cdots$$

Under the assumed circumstances the wages bill for any wage rate above (or equal to) the steady state competitive wage will, in keeping with with (6.10), 'grow' according to:

$$W_{t+1} = \left[\frac{1 + \rho(w)}{1 + \delta}\right]^{\frac{1}{1-\alpha}} W_t$$

Thus:

$$U = \frac{W(w)^\alpha}{\alpha} + \frac{W(w)^\alpha}{\alpha}\frac{\left[\dfrac{1 + \rho(w)}{1 + \delta}\right]^{\frac{\alpha}{1-\alpha}}}{1 + \delta} + \cdots = \frac{1 + \delta}{\alpha}\frac{W(w)^\alpha}{\left[1 + \delta - \left[\dfrac{1 + \rho(w)}{1 + \delta}\right]^{\frac{\alpha}{1-\alpha}}\right]}$$

Using the magnitude of w at the steady state under competition, this expression will also yield utility under the steady state under competition. Thus deriving the expression with respect to w, and evaluating the derivative at the steady state wage (so that $\rho = \delta$), will yield the condition under which raising the wage above the competitive steady state wage increases utility.

9. This expression seems to provide a sufficient condition for the market harmony thesis. For as δ approaches zero this optimal elasticity must fall so far as necessary to equal the competitive elasticity. This is simply understood; as δ approaches zero, there is no discounting the future. And the wage bill of the steady state will exceed the wage bill for a declining economy for an indefinitely long period of time. Thus the cost of forgoing the competitive outcome becomes infinitely large. The upshot is that there is a harmony thesis if the rate of time preference is sufficiently low. An alternative interpretation if the annihilation of the advantage of monopolization if δ is sufficiently low would refer to the fact that the lower rate of time preference, the higher the competitive steady state wage, so the advantage of the monopoly wage is smaller. To put it another way: the lower δ, the higher K_{ss}, and so the more elastic labour demand, the less the advantage of monopoly wages.

10. We wish to compare utility of a capital-less worker under labour market competition with their utility when the wage rate is set so that e = 1. Suppose the initial endowment of capital is the steady state one. If $q = l/[l + \beta]$ (and so σ parametrically equals 0.5), then $W/K = \beta k/[1 + \beta k]^2$. But under labour market competition $L = \Sigma$, so in the steady state: $k = K_{SS}/\Sigma$. So

$$\frac{W_{COM}}{K_{SS}} = \frac{\dfrac{\beta K_{SS}}{\Sigma}}{\left[1 + \dfrac{\beta K_{SS}}{\Sigma}\right]^2}.$$

But as $\rho = 1/[1 + \beta k]^2$, we may say $\delta = 1/[1 + \beta K_{SS}/\Sigma]^2$, and so

$$\frac{W_{COM(SS)}}{\Sigma} = \frac{W_{COM}}{K_{SS}}\frac{K_{SS}}{\Sigma} = \frac{[1 - \sqrt{\delta}]^2}{\beta}.$$

Under wage bill maximization k = 1/β, and so

$$\frac{W_{MON}}{K_{SS}} = \frac{1}{4}. \text{ Thus } \frac{W_{MON(SS)}}{\Sigma} = \frac{W_{MON}}{K_{SS}} \frac{K_{SS}}{\Sigma} = \frac{[1 - \sqrt{\delta}]}{4\beta\sqrt{\delta}}.$$

Under competition the wage bill is constant over time, but under wage bill maximization the wage bill 'grows' at the (negative) rate of

$$\left[\frac{1 + \rho_{MAX}}{1 + \delta}\right]^{\frac{\alpha}{1-\alpha}}.$$

Thus a comparison of utility is a comparison of:

$$\frac{1 + \delta}{\delta} \frac{\left[\frac{[1 - \sqrt{\delta}]^2}{\beta}\right]^\alpha}{\alpha} \quad vs \quad \frac{1 + \delta}{1 + \delta - \left[\frac{1 + \rho_{MON}}{1 + \delta}\right]^{\frac{\alpha}{1-\alpha}}} \frac{\left[\frac{[1 - \sqrt{\delta}]}{4\beta\sqrt{\delta}}\right]^\alpha}{\alpha}$$

11.   Or $w_t = w_{COM}$ if $e(w_t) = 1$ implies an excess demand for labour.

7. Why the 'property-owning democracy' may nationalize capital rather than regulate labour

Chapter 6 brought to the centre of the analysis the accumulation capital. But so far the analysis has assumed that the workforce has accumulated no capital. This chapter relaxes that seemingly incongruent assumption, and asks: 'Does the ownership of capital by the workforce dull, or even remove, the incentive for the electorate to "vote for unemployment" by favouring a legal minimum on wage rates?'

The chapter argues that the answer to this question will depend critically on how the workforce's capital is managed. If the workforce's capital is managed on standard profit-maximizing lines then the incentive to 'vote for unemployment' by means of an above-market wage rate is, indeed, reduced, and perhaps to extinction. However, if the workforce's capital is managed, not on profit-maximizing lines, but in a way so as to maximize the total wage and profit incomes of the workforce, then the wage rate is not reduced relative to the wage bill maximizing rate, and may be higher. Further, under such 'maximizing management' of the workforce's capital, employment will be actually increased relative to employment under wage bill maximization, and perhaps to the point of full employment.

It appears, therefore, that the 'property-owning democracy' threatens the ruin of the 'labour monopoly' explanation of unemployment. For it appears that the management of the workforce's capital in the way that maximizes the labour interest actually increases the wage rate relative to competition, and without necessarily any cost to unemployment.

These implications obtain greater resonance if the management of worker-owned capital is (plausibly) seen as a publicly owned enterprise; managed, not on profit-maximizing lines, but in the interests of the median voter. Thus in this chapter the consideration of workforce-owned capital moves the analysis from electorally managed minimum wage rates, and towards electorally managed 'government-owned corporations', 'state-owned enterprises' or 'government business enterprises'.

But the economic logic of 'electorally managed' public enterprises impels the analysis further onwards to encounter the issue of privatization. For in our analysis the 'electorally managed' public enterprise will face the menace that many 'cooperative' solutions to optimization face: being undermined by defection. Insofar as any worker can exclude their own capital from being managed on non-profit-maximizing lines by the public enterprise, and instead manage it themselves according to standard profit-maximizing precepts, they will do so, and public enterprises will shrivel. The chapter concludes, consequently, with the prospect of an unstable dialectic between wage regulation, nationalization and privatization; whereby nationalization dominates regulation of privately owned capital, but privatization restores privately owned capital.[1]

WORKER PLAYING CAPITALIST

The chapter's analysis turns on a contrast between two ways in which a worker-as-median-voter may pursue their interest when they own some capital: a wage-setting strategy, and a capital management strategy.

In the wage-setting strategy each member of the workforce manages their capital as a profit-making capitalist would; employing labour until the marginal product of labour equals the real wage. The wage rate is, accordingly, set by the majoritarian process so as to maximize the median voter's wage plus profit on their capital.

To make these ideas precise, suppose each worker has the same certain endowment of capital, k_W. Since (we suppose for now) each worker manages their capital on profit-maximizing lines, the demand for labour remains the neoclassical one, with the plotting of L against w coincident with the plotting of L against the marginal productivity. The maximand for the labour monopolist consequently is:

$$\max_{w}: \frac{l(w)K}{\Sigma}w + \rho k_W \qquad (7.1)$$

This implies an expression for the optimal elasticity of the demand for labour:

$$e = 1 - \frac{k_W}{K/\Sigma} \equiv s_C \qquad (7.2)^2$$

Thus the optimal elasticity no longer equals unity; it equals the 'pure' capital owners' share of the capital stock, s_C, which is less than one. Therefore in order to secure that optimal elasticity the wage floor will be reduced relative to the case where the workforce owned no capital. Table

Table 7.1   Wage rates and employment under 'wage-setting'

	Quasi-Cobb–Douglas	Quadratic	CES ($\sigma = 0.5$)
w_{SET}	$\dfrac{\phi[1 - \beta]s_C}{1 - [1 - \beta]s_C}$	$\dfrac{\beta s_C}{[1 + s_C]}$	$\dfrac{[2s_C - 1]^2}{4\beta s_C^2}$
l_{SET}	$\left[\dfrac{\beta - s_C\beta[1 - \beta]}{\phi}\right]^{\frac{1}{1-\beta}}$	$\dfrac{\beta}{[1 + s_C]2\phi}$	$\dfrac{\beta}{2s_C - 1}$

Note: s_C = share of total capital owned by pure capital owners.

7.1 provides parametric illustrations of the effect on w and employment per unit of capital for three production functions.

Two points about this 'moderation' in the wage rate are worth noting. Firstly, there will always be some reduction compared to the wage bill maximizing wage rate, no matter how small is the workers' ownership of capital. Secondly, the wage rate may be so moderated that the optimal wage is reduced to the competitive wage, and full employment is restored.[3]

An Employment Representation of Wage-Setting Equilibrium

Congruent with the phrase 'wage-setting' the previous section identified its equilibrium by means of the choice of a wage rate. But the wage-setting equilibrium can also be represented in terms of terms of employment choices, and that representation will prove useful later. To do so we suppose that the capital owned by capital owners and that owned by the workforce operate in two different 'sectors': a capitalist-owned sector, and a workforce-owned sector. Given this, we can imagine attempting to isolate the wage-setting optimum by incremental adjustments to employment. Consider: the benefit to the labour interest of an extra unit of labour employed in the capitalist-owned sector is $\partial W_C/\partial L_C$. But every increase in L_C must be accompanied by a fall in the wage rate (to match the fall in $\partial Y_C/\partial L_C$), and therefore, to keep the marginal product in line with the wage, must be accompanied by an increase in L_W, and that obviously adds its own benefit to the labour interest. The benefit to the labour interest of an extra unit of L_W is not $\partial W_W/\partial L_W$ but $\partial Y_W/\partial L_W$; for all of the increment in output in the workforce-owned sector (wages and profits) accrues to the labour interest. But how large is the increase in L_W that must accompany an increase in L_C? Profit maximization necessitates that $L_W/K_W = L_C/K_C$,

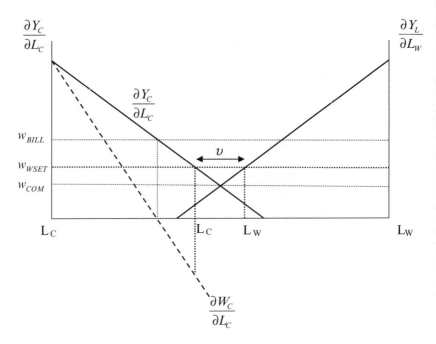

Figure 7.1   The 'wage-setting' solution when the workforce owns half the capital

so $\Delta L_W = \Delta L_C K_W / K_C$. Thus for every unit expansion in L_C the total benefit to the labour interest is:

$$\frac{\partial W_C}{\partial L_C} + \frac{\partial Y_W}{\partial L_W}\frac{K_W}{K_C} = 0 \qquad (7.3)^4$$

This wage-setting optimization condition in terms of employment can also be represented to good purpose diagrammatically (Figure 7.1). And, to help clarity, we specifically suppose in Figure 7.1 that the production function is quadratic, and that $K_W = K_C$. The competitive wage corresponds to the intersection of the marginal products schedules of the two sectors. The wage bill maximizing wage – that makes the marginal wages bill in each sector zero – is also indicated. The wage-setting equilibrium is also isolable in Figure 7.1. Invoking the particular assumption $K_W = K_C$ permits the rewriting of the optimizing condition (7.3) as $\partial W_C / \partial L_C + \partial Y_W / \partial L_W = 0$. But given the common wage $\partial Y_W / \partial L_W = \partial Y_C / \partial L_C$ we infer that optimal wage-setting is secured by $\partial W_C / \partial L_C + \partial Y_C / \partial L_C = 0$. The magnitude of L_C that achieves that is shown in Figure 7.1.

The upshot is that under wage-setting the wage rate, and the unemployment rate, is reduced relative to the wage bill maximizing rate.

Two qualifications should be noted.

A workforce with a negative endowment of capital

Workers' ownership of capital may be negative. For while the presumption is that workers will accumulate as the economy accumulates, there is the possibility that workers will (rationally) acquire debt, not capital, during the growth process.[5] If the labour interest was in debt, then the right-hand side of equation (7.3) would exceed one, the elasticity that maximizes the workforce's net income would exceed one, and the wage rate would be higher than under wage bill maximization. The incentive now is to drive the wage up so as to push down the interest burden on workers' debt.

A workforce with heterogeneous endowments of capital

We have assumed that all workers own the same amount of capital. If they do not, the simplicity of the previous conclusion regarding the optimal elasticity disappears, but the qualitative conclusion endures: the optimizing wage rate is lower than under a capital-less workforce, at least under the assumption that the median voter owns some capital.[6] Who is the median voter depends on, amongst other things, the number of capitalists, who would vote against any wage rise above the competitive level. The more numerous such capitalists, then the location of the median voter shifts towards a worker endowed with more capital, and the wage will be still lower. (Notice that if capital is concentrated, then for a given amount of capital, capitalists will be numerically fewer, and so the electorally optimal wage rate will be higher.)

WORKERS PLAYING CAPITAL AGAINST THE CAPITALIST

The wage-setting strategy dealt with in the preceding section supposed that workers' capital is operated on classic profit-maximizing lines. For that reason treatment of workers' capital may seem incoherent. For classic profit maximization obviously permits the possibility of unemployment. And does not any unemployment mean the labour interest forgoing a benefit? Since all of the product from workers' capital accrues to workers, why not employ some of the unemployed to increase the product of workers' capital, and so increase the income derived from workers' capital (wages plus workers' profits)? Granted, it could not be optimizing for a

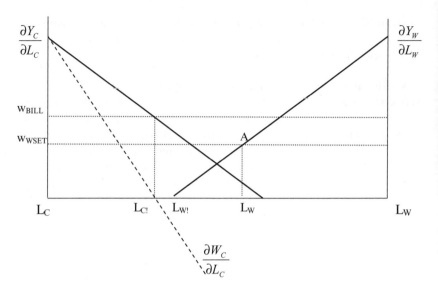

Figure 7.2   The suboptimality of 'wage-setting'

single worker operating alone to employ the unemployed, for in hiring the
unemployed this single worker would be reducing their own profit income,
even if increasing all other workers' incomes. However, if all the workforce
agreed to take on an equal share of the unemployed, all the workforce all
would benefit.

The 'incoherence' of the wage-setting labour monopoly of the previous
section may be brought out by Figure 7.2. Figure 7.2 repeats Figure 7.1 in
depicting wage-setting rate, w, but the focus is now on the implied amount
of labour employed by workers' owned capital, L_W. The figure brings out
that a greater volume of employment would improve the workers' interest. Suppose employment by workers' capital was increased to $L_{W!}$. The
sum of wages earned from employment by workers' capital plus profits
of workers' capital increases by the triangle $AL_WL_{W!}$. And it could do still
better than that. It could also reduce employment in the capitalist sector to
$L_{C!}$, and thereby increase the wage bill in the capitalist sector.

To put the point more formally, if labour monopoly is able to choose
different magnitudes for L_C and L_W, then the labour interest would be
optimized by ensuring:

$$\frac{\partial W_C}{\partial L_C} = \frac{\partial Y_W}{\partial L_W} \qquad (7.4)$$

which is obviously different from the wage-setting equilibrium condition (7.3). And the labour monopoly *can* choose L_C and L_W to be different from each other. L_C can be chosen indirectly by the labour monopolist setting the wage rate appropriately. And L_W can be chosen directly by the labour monopolist under a strategy of capital management. In this schema all workers receive the same wage rate regardless of what sector they work in. Workers additionally whatever profits they earn on their own capital.

To sum up, we have established that workers' ownership of capital gives the greatest incentive not simply to raise wage rates, but to 'overemploy' labour; to employ on their capital more labour than profit maximization would warrant.[7] Table 7.2 illustrates this for three production functions, under the assumption of some unemployment.

Table 7.2   Employment by sector under 'capital management' (per unit of capital)

	Quasi-Cobb–Douglas	Quadratic	CES ($\sigma = 0.5$)
l_C	$\left[\dfrac{\phi}{\beta^2}\right]^{\frac{1}{\beta-1}}$	$\dfrac{\beta}{4\phi}$	β
l_W	$\left[\dfrac{\phi}{\beta}\right]^{\frac{1}{\beta-1}}$	$\dfrac{\beta}{2\phi}$	3β

Note: Row 1 indicates the wage bill maximizing rate of labour per unit of capital in the profit-maximizing sector ($q'(l_C) + l_C q''(l_C) = 0$). Row 2 indicates the zero marginal product rate of labour per unit of capital in the employment-maximizing sector, except for CES case where it indicates the labour–capital ratio that yields zero profits in the employment-maximizing sector.

The upshot of workers' ownership of capital is the emergence of two sectors distinguished not only by their owners but also by their behaviours: a profit-maximizing sector, and an 'employment-maximizing' sector. In the model's 'employment-maximizing sector' we see a picture of the commonplace 'state sector' (composed of 'government-owned corporations', 'state-owned enterprises', 'government business enterprises', 'public enterprises' and so on). The sector has been financed by the population at large (its capital is the capital of the workforce), and it is managed not in a manner to maximize its income, but in the interests of the electorate. Prominent elements in these state sectors include state-owned oil sectors, state forests, state hydroelectricity schemes, government schools and, of course, public transport systems; all labour-intensive, and managed to a considerable degree for the sake of 'jobs'.

What will be the implications of such capital management for variables of interest?

THE POSSIBILITY OF THE FULL EMPLOYMENT UNDER A CAPITAL MANAGING LABOUR MONOPOLY

Capital management has two significant implications for unemployment. The capital management equilibrium invoked by Figure 7.2 involves some unemployment, but capital management may also yield full employment. So capital management has two equilibria: an unemployment equilibrium and a full employment equilibrium.

Under the capital management unemployment equilibrium:

$$\frac{\partial W_C}{\partial L_C} = \frac{\partial Y_W}{\partial L_W} = 0 \qquad (7.5)$$

Employment has been expanded in each sector such that the benefit from an extra employment is zero. Any more labour would be redundant to the purpose of the labour monopoly. If an extra unit of labour was to appear it would be left unemployed (see Figure 7.3).

In this capital management equilibrium the wage rate is, in fact, 'set'; set

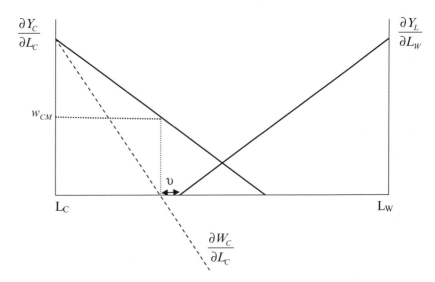

Figure 7.3   An unemployment equilibrium under capital management

at that rate which maximizes the wage bill paid by the profit-maximizing sector. The employment-maximizing sector absorbs labour until its marginal product is zero. Any labour still not employed remains unemployed.

The second capital management equilibrium is:

$$\frac{\partial W_C}{\partial L_C} = \frac{\partial Y_W}{\partial L_W} > 0 \tag{7.6}$$

This is an equilibrium of full employment. In both sectors there is obviously a benefit from an extra unit of employment. So if an extra unit of labour supply was to appear, it would not be left idle but would be employed in the two sectors. Figure 7.4 illustrates.[8]

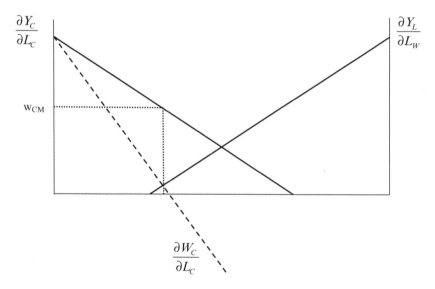

Figure 7.4   A full employment equilibrium under capital management

In this full-employment equilibrium the wage rate is not directly set by the labour monopoly. Rather, it is left to be determined by competition between the capitalists over the supply of labour 'left over' after the employment of the optimum amount of labour in the employment-maximizing sector.

Which equilibrium shall occur?

As full employment requires a positive marginal product of capital in the employment-maximizing sector, it would appear that the prospect of this equilibrium diminishes as the amount of capital owned by the workforce shrinks, on account of the greater pressure on marginal productivity if the employment-maximizing sector is to soak up all labour supply not employed in the profit-maximizing sector. To put this point by a hypothetical case: what if there was only a single dollar of workers' capital, and in its absence wage bill maximization would spell a million unemployed? How could one dollar employ a million without reducing the marginal product of labour to zero? Thus it would appear there is some minimum amount of capital owned by the workforce that will secure full employment under a capital managing labour monopoly. However, this plausible contention appears undermined by the observation that for some technologies the marginal product of labour is positive no matter how high the labour–capital ratio: the CES technology is one example. Since under CES $\partial Y_W/\partial L_W$ must always exceed zero, it would seem that under CES the full employment equilibrium always occurs. But that leaves us with a paradox. Suppose there is just one dollar of workers' capital, and (otherwise) a million unemployed? By what strange magic can one dollar employ a million? Seemingly another consideration has been neglected: the imperative that the employment-maximizing sector be 'financially viable', and not make losses.

Non-Negative Profits in the Employment-Maximizing Sector

Suppose that the employment-maximizing sector is constrained from making losses.[9] In other words, suppose the average product of labour in the employment-maximizing sector is constrained from being lower than the wage:

$$\frac{q\left(\dfrac{L_W}{K_W}\right)}{L_W/K_W} \geq w = q'\left(\frac{L_C}{K_C}\right) \tag{7.7}$$

Will this constraint be 'binding', or will it be satisfied by the equilibrium already described: $\partial W_C/\partial L_C = \partial Y_W/\partial L_W > 0$?

For the quadratic production functions and the quasi-Cobb–Douglas production the non-negative profit constraint is not binding: the semi-inequality of (7.7) is satisfied by both the production functions as a strict equality.[10] For those two technologies there are exactly zero profits in the employment-maximizing sector under capital management equilibrium, described by: $\partial W_C/\partial L_C = \partial Y_W/\partial L_W > 0$.

But for the CES function the constraint is binding; the semi-inequality will not be satisfied by the CES function if $\sigma = 0.5$. The capital management 'optimum' $\partial W_C/\partial L_C = \partial Y_W/\partial L_W > 0$ would produce losses in the employment-maximizing sector. The constrained optimum must differ.

In what way? It might appear that the transition from the unconstrained optimum to the constrained optimum would require an expansion in employment in the profit-maximizing sector equal to a contraction in employment in the employment-maximizing sector. For such a reallocation in employment will reduce losses in the employment-maximizing sector by simultaneously raising its average productivity (by reducing employment in the employment-maximizing sector) and reducing the wage it pays (by expanding the profit-maximizing sector's employment). The expansion in employment in the profit-maximizing sector also attenuates the loss in total product from the employment-maximizing sector by increasing the wages bill in the profit-making sector ($\partial W_C/\partial L_C = \partial Y_W/\partial L_W > 0$). It would appear, then, that this matching contraction (in the employment-maximizing sector) and expansion (in the profit-maximizing sector) could be magnified sufficiently so that financial losses in the employment-maximizing sector are eliminated, without any reduction in employment below full employment. This agreeable scenario is, however, illusory. For it may be that before that losses in the employment-maximizing sector are eliminated, the marginal wage bill in the profit-making sector falls to zero, $\partial W/\partial L_C = 0$. In that circumstance, any further expansion in L_C to match reductions in L_W will not attenuate the loss in workers' income, but only add to it, and therefore will not be pursued. Thus further required reduction in the financial losses of the employment-maximizing sector will be secured solely by a reduction in employment in that sector, without a matching increase in employment in the profit sector. Unemployment consequently appears.

To summarize: a requirement that the employment-maximizing sector not make losses means that CES technology does not necessitate full employment under CES ($\sigma = 0.5$) technology regardless of the size of workers' capital. The requirement that the employment-maximizing sector not make losses means that unemployment is possible under capital management with CES technology. Thus with CES technology, as with the quasi-Cobb–Douglas or quadratic technologies, capital management only assures full employment if the workforce's capital is sufficiently large.[11]

CAPITAL MANAGEMENT STRATEGY COMPARED WITH THE WAGE-SETTING STRATEGY

We know capital management will secure greater overall incomes for workers than wage-setting would achieve, as capital management always has the option of duplicating the labour allocation under wage-setting.[12]

But how will capital management differ from wage-setting with respect to other outcomes?

The Wage Rate

The wage rate under capital management will exceed the wage rate under wage-setting. Thus workers' ownership of capital will by itself drive down the wage; but that ownership combined with a management that optimizes the labour interest will drive up the wage.

Proof: The wage-setting optimization condition (7.3) implies:

$$\frac{\partial W_C}{\partial L_C} < 0$$

while the alternative capital management optimizing conditions imply:

$$\frac{\partial W_C}{\partial L_C} \geq 0$$

Thus employment in the profit-maximizing sector is always lower under capital management than under wage-setting, so the wage rate is always higher under capital management than under wage-setting. This reflects the fact that under capital management the elasticity of labour demand is greater than or equal to one, whereas under wage-setting the elasticity of labour demand is below one.

Sectoral Employment

Employment in the profit-maximizing sector

As the wage rate under capital management is always higher than that under wage-setting, employment in the profit-making sector is always lower under capital management than under wage-setting. In intuitive terms, relative to the wage-setting outcome, as the workforce has no interest in profits earned by capital owners, the wage rate is increased to at least the wage bill maximizing level in the profit-making sector. The negative impact of employment in the profit-making sector is underlined by this observation: even if employment in the employment-maximizing sector could not, for some reason, be increased beyond its wage-setting level, there remains a reward for reducing employment in the profit-making sector from its wage-setting level, since in the wage-setting equilibrium, $\partial W_C/\partial L_C < 0$.

Employment in the employment-maximizing sector
Employment in the employment-maximizing sector is always higher under capital management than under wage-setting. To underline this point: it will be rewarding to the labour interest to increase employment in the employment-maximizing sector relative to the wage-setting outcome even if, for some reason, employment in the profit-maximizing sector cannot be changed (see Figure 7.2).

The Total Demand for Labour

We see above that capital management has a negative effect on employment in one sector, but a positive effect on employment in the other. Will one effect predominate? With both quadratic and quasi-Cobb–Douglas production functions, the positive effect predominates, and total employment is increased relative to wage-setting. Capital management secures, for any amount of aggregate capital, either more employment for the given wage, or a higher wage for a fully employed labour force. This 'over-employment' does not eliminate a negative relation between observed wage and employment: the 'demand curve'. Under capital management, for a given stock of capital, the real wage will decline with a greater supply of labour, and consequent greater employment.[13] It is just that the capital managing labour monopoly shifts the 'labour demand curve' to the right.

However, under CES, total employment is reduced under capital management compared to wage-setting. This might be understood as follows: the unemployment solution of CES occurs where there is little workers' capital; so little workers' capital, that the size of the positive stimulus in the employment-maximizing sector is no compensation for the shedding of labour in the profit-maximizing sector.

Labour Productivity

Under capital management both the marginal (and average) productivity of labour is lower in the employment-maximizing sector than in the profit-maximizing sector.[14]

Social Inefficiency

The capital management strategy cannot be socially efficient, as it reduces the marginal productivity of labour in the employment-maximizing sector below that of the profit-maximizing sector. It will also be inefficient on account of any unemployment it may produce. But is it more or less socially inefficient than wage-setting? There are two conflicting effects.

Under CES there is both lower employment and misallocation, and output is lower. Table 7.3 gives details.[15]

Table 7.3   The relative outcomes of capital management to wage setting

	Total employment	Total output
Quasi-Cobb–Douglas	$\dfrac{1 - s_C + s_C\beta^{\frac{1}{1-\beta}}}{[1 - s_C[1 - \beta]]^{\frac{1}{1-\beta}}} > 1$	$\dfrac{[1 - s_C[1 - \beta]]^{\frac{\beta}{1-\beta}}[1 - \beta][1 + s_C\beta]}{[1 - s_C][1 - \beta] + s_C\beta^{\frac{\beta}{1-\beta}}[1 - \beta^2]} > 1$
Quadratic	$\dfrac{[2 - s_C][1 + s_C]}{2} > 1$	$\dfrac{[1 + s_C]^2}{1 + 2s_C}[2 - 1.25s_C] > 1$
CES	$[3 - 2s_C][2s_C - 1] < 1$	$\left[\dfrac{3 - s_C}{2}\right]s_C < 1$

On one hand, as we have noted, total employment will be higher under capital management with quadratic and quasi-Cobb–Douglas technology. On the other hand, any higher level of employment is inefficiently allocated, as the marginal product of labour in the employment-maximizing sector is lower than in the profit-maximizing sector. It turns out that for the quadratic and quasi-Cobb–Douglas production functions the total employment effect dominates the misallocation effect, and output is higher under capital management. Not only does the workforce benefit, but society does, too.

STATE SECTORS AND PRIVATIZATION

We have argued that capital management, implemented through a state sector, is superior as far as the labour interest is concerned to wage-setting. Thus, the electorate (assuming workers are in a majority) would always vote to nationalize their own capital. The 'property-owning democracy' will prefer nationalization to wage regulation.

But two qualifications should be borne in mind.

Heterogeneous Capital Endowments

The superiority of capital management over wage-setting was established on the assumption that all the workforce had the same endowment of capital. Could the existence of different endowments create a fracture in the interests of the workforce? The existence of a contingent of capital-less workers will not diminish support for capital management; as the only interest of such a contingent is in the wage, and capital management increases the wage relative to wage-setting. However, it is on account of this wage premium that a sufficiently capital-rich worker might object to capital management. As all capitalists suffer from capital management relative to wage-setting, so a worker with a sufficiently 'large' endowment of capital would prefer wage-setting to capital management. The worker with a lot of capital would not favour nationalization. This constituency might be large enough to join with capitalists to favour wage-setting over capital management.

Defection

The strategy of capital management suffers from the perennial threat to all 'cooperative' optimization: defection. To explicate this proposition, the profit rate on capital in the employment-maximizing sector is zero, but positive in the profit-maximizing sector. Thus any given worker would be better off if they (alone) could withdraw some portion of capital from 'management' and operate it, as the beneficiary, on profit-maximizing lines. Such transferral to profit-maximizing ownership ('privatization') will according to the model reduce the demand for labour and wages. The constituents of the labour interest therefore face a Prisoner's Dilemma: if every worker gets what they want for themselves, every worker is worse off. The consequence of this is perhaps a perpetually fluctuating border between the private sector and the state sector, as privatization is followed by renationalization, and further privatization. A confident answer would require a greater articulation of political decision-making processes.[16] Whatever the answer, each wants privatization for themselves, but not for others. The model, then, suggests that we should not be surprised to see that privatization is prevalent but controversial.

CONCLUSION

The chapter is concerned to identify the consequences of the workforce owning capital. There is wide presumption, known as the 'embourgeoisement thesis', which plausibly suggests that this ownership will make 'capitalists' of the workforce, and undermine the foundation of labour monopoly, and efface the impact of labour interest on wages and unemployment. This chapter's opening section demonstrates that this vision can be analytically articulated.

However, the chapter also calls attention to a different possible consequence of the workforce owning capital: that the labour interest would
optimize by constituting the workforce's capital into an 'employment-
maximizing' sector, which is collectively managed so that the rate of profit
is zero.

Rather than the wage being driven down, the wage is driven up; and
rather than the profit rate being increased, it is reduced. At the same time,
this strategy shares with wage-setting the conclusion that ownership of
capital by the workforce will reduce unemployment, and perhaps to zero.
Thus ownership of capital does strain the labour monopoly explanation of
unemployment, but by no means eliminates it.

The possibility of an 'employment-maximizing' strategy means that labour
monopoly remains socially significant even in the face of the 'embourgeoisement' of the workforce. The social cost is not a matter of unemployment,
but of overemployment. The upshot is that 'employment maximization'
allows an integral theory of both private sector and state employment, and
an integral theory of unemployment and overemployment.

NOTES

1. The subject of this chapter recalls the literature on 'cooperatives' and 'worker-managed firms' (see Horvat 1986).

2.
$$\frac{\partial EU_i}{\partial w} = \frac{l(w)K + wl'(w)K}{\Sigma} + \frac{\partial \rho}{\partial w}k_w = 0$$

Invoking the neoclassical factor price frontier, $\frac{\partial \rho w}{\partial w \rho} = -\frac{[1 - \pi]}{\pi}$:

$$l(w)K + wl'(w)K - \frac{\rho[1 - \pi]}{w\pi}k_w^*\Sigma = 0$$

The second-order condition is again ensured by assuming $\partial e/\partial w > 0$.

3. This raises the question: if workers' ownership of capital reduces wage claims and increases profits, could capital owners benefit by giving their capital away? As $\Pi_C = \rho s_C K$, we may infer

$$d\Pi_C = K\left[\frac{\partial \rho}{\partial s_C}s_C + \rho\right]ds_C. \text{ But } \frac{\partial \rho}{\partial s_C} = \frac{\partial \rho}{\partial w}\frac{\partial w}{\partial s_C} = -\left[\frac{1 - \pi}{\pi}\right]\frac{\rho}{w}\frac{1}{e'},$$

using $e(w) = s_C$. And, from Chapter 3, $\frac{1}{e'} = \frac{w}{e}\left[\frac{\pi}{1 - \pi}\right]\frac{1}{1 - \sigma}$.

Thus $d\Pi_C = \left[-\frac{\rho}{1 - \sigma} + \rho\right]Kds_C < 0.$

Conclusion: given a parametrical elasticity of technical substitution, it would be improving for capital owners to give their capital away, at least until full employment is reached. It is not, of course, improving for a solitary capital owner to give their capital away; the action must be collective.

4. More formally, the wage-setting equilibrium can be described by:

$$0 = \frac{\partial W_C}{\partial w} + \frac{\partial Y_W}{\partial w} = \frac{\partial W_C}{\partial L_C}\frac{\partial L_C}{\partial w} + \frac{\partial Y_W}{\partial L_W}\frac{\partial L_W}{\partial w} = \left[\frac{\partial W_C}{\partial L_C} + \frac{\partial Y_W}{\partial L_W}\frac{\partial L_W}{\partial w}\frac{\partial w}{\partial L_C}\right]\frac{\partial L_C}{\partial w}$$

Thus:

$$0 = \frac{\partial W_C}{\partial L_C} + \frac{\partial Y_W}{\partial L_W}\frac{K_W}{q''(l_w)}q''(l_C)\frac{1}{K_C}$$

The equality in labour–capital ratios in the two sectors, flowing from the common wage rate, allows this to be simplified to (7.3).

5. In the Ramsey–Solow model workers necessarily accumulate during the approach to the steady state if $\sigma > 1$. For if $\sigma > 1$ then the labour share falls with capital accumulation, and the wage bill grows slower than output. But as consumption necessarily grows faster than output during the approach to the steady state, it follows that the workforce's consumption grows faster than its wage income throughout the approach to the steady state. And this can only mean that initially capital-less workers choose $C_W(0) < W(0)$, and workers become capital owners, for otherwise they would violate their budget constraint. But if $\sigma > 1$ then labour demand is elastic, and consequently labour monopoly is irrelevant.

6. If different workers own different amounts of capital then different workers will be most advantaged by different rates of wages. Assuming the expected utility of worker is:

$$EU_i = \frac{l(w)K}{\Sigma}w + \rho k_i$$

then, the optimal elasticity for i, e_i, satisfies:

$$e_i = 1 - \frac{k_i}{K/\Sigma} \equiv s_K$$

Rank these elasticities by size; there will be some elasticity such that half want a higher elasticity (higher wage) and some want a lower elasticity (lower wage). That is the median voter elasticity.

7. The capital management equilibrium will be altered by the existence of workers' capital located beyond the sway of special management, and (therefore) operated on orthodox profit-maximizing lines. Not surprisingly, the wage rate is reduced. Employment in the employment-maximizing sector remains at the level that drives the marginal product to zero. But in the profit-maximizing sector – some of which is now owned by workers – the wage rate will be reduced in proportion to the share of capital in that sector owned by workers, in accordance with a logic already explored under wage-setting.

8. The full employment capital management equilibrium is more formally described as $q'(l_C) + l_C q''(l_C) = q'(l_W)$ and $l_C s_C + l_W[1 - s_C] = \Sigma/K$, where $s_C =$ share of total capital owned by pure capital owners.

9. Of course, profits must also be non-negative in the profit-making sector. That additional constraint may prevent the allocation of labour described by $\partial W_C/\partial L_C = \partial Y_W/\partial L_W$. For example, if $q = 1 - \varphi/l$ then the marginal wages bill is always negative, and the marginal product is always positive; and the two can never be equal. In this production function, the maximization of the wage bill in the profit-making sector dictates that employment in that sector be reduced until the profit rate falls to zero. Since $\partial Y/\partial L$

     is always positive under this production function, all labour left not employed by the profit-maximizing sector will be absorbed in the employment-maximizing sector.

10. If either $l^\beta - \phi l$ or $l\beta - l^2\phi$ then $q'(l_W) = q'(l_C) + q''(l_C)l_C$ implies $q(l_W)/l_W = q'(l_C)$. As for CES, we begin by observing that it is a mathematical necessity $[l_C + \beta][\beta - l_C] < \beta^2$. But if (CES style) $q = l/[l + \beta]$ then $q'(l_W) = q'(l_C) + q''(l_C)l_C$ implies $\beta - l_C = [l_C + \beta]^3/[l_W + \beta]^2$. Therefore $[l_C + \beta]^4/[l_W + \beta]^2 < \beta^2$, and so $1/l_W + \beta < \beta/[l_C + \beta]^2$, and so $q(l_W)/l_W < q'(l_C)$.

11. But why should the majority workforce not impose taxes on capital owners to meet all losses? Indeed, why should the majority workforce not impose a 100 per cent tax on capital income? For that matter, why should the majority workforce not simply expropriate all capital? The answer would lie in the fact these actions are not electoral equilibria. For a subset of capital owners could form a majority coalition with a subset of the workforce to direct the proceeds of any expropriation solely to that subset of the workforce, in return for that subset of capital owners being allowed to retain some capital. Of course, the capital owners outside the subset would reply with a coalition proposal of their own . . . and the construction of rival coalitions would continue ad infinitum.

12. By a parallel logic we can be sure that capital managing labour monopoly must secure a better overall outcome for workers than pure competition would achieve.

13. $q'(l_C) + l_C q''(l_C) = q'\left(\dfrac{\dfrac{\Sigma}{K} - l_C s_C}{1 - s_C}\right)$. Therefore, $\dfrac{\partial l_C}{\partial \Sigma/K} = \dfrac{q''}{[1 - s_C]\dfrac{\partial W_C}{\partial l_C} + s_C q''} > 0$.

Therefore w falls if $S_C \approx 1$.

14. The theory is suggestive that this inferiority may be significant: $\dfrac{MPL_{L\,\max}}{MPL_{\Pi\,\max}} - 1 = -\dfrac{1}{e}$
and $\dfrac{1}{e} = -\dfrac{\pi}{\sigma} \approx -2/3$

15. Total employment: Table 7.1 indicates total employment per unit of capital under wage-setting. Table 7.2 indicates employment per unit of capital under capital management in the two sectors. The expressions for l_W and l_C can be substituted into $L = K_w l_w + K_C l_C = K[[1 - s_C]l_w + s_C l_C]$ to derive total employment per unit of capital for each strategy.
   Total output: under wage-setting, employment per unit of capital (see Table 7.1) is substituted back into the production function. Under capital management, employment per unit of capital (see Table 7.2) yields an average product of capital in each sector, which is weighted by the capital in each sector to yield total output: $Y = K_w q(l_w) + K_C q(l_C) = K[[1 - s_C]q(l_w) + s_C(l_C)]$.

16. If each voter voted as if their vote was decisive then the workforce would reject a privatization that would allocate to each member of the workforce an equal share of the capital of the employment-maximizing sector. But the adequacy of the 'direct democracy' modelling is particularly questionable in Prisoner's Dilemma situations: everyone has an incentive to cheat the choice of the 'direct democracy'. Everyone is a special interest whose will is contrary to the choice of the 'direct democracy'.

8. Unemployment as a benefit of unemployment benefits

Until this point it has been assumed that the only incentive to restrict employment lies in the greater wage incomes that a restriction would yield. But restricting employment will also provide a reward in terms of increasing the amount of what economists call 'leisure'; the various uses of time that are unpaid, but valued all the same. To ignore a valuation that seem powerful in shaping labour market outcomes is untenable. The present chapter investigates what the recognition the value of leisure will signify for the shape of electorally optimal labour market regulation.

Unsurprisingly, the analysis concludes that allowing for this second, additional, incentive to restrict employment extends the impact of labour monopoly to circumstances previously beyond its reach. But it also modifies the character of the impact of labour monopoly, and not just its range. Once leisure is allowed to be valuable, the strong wage rigidity results of simple wage bill maximization are diluted. It is no longer the case that the wage rate has a zero elasticity to the capital stock. It is possible the wage rate may be just as sensitive to the capital stock as it would be under a wholly competitive labour market. However, it can be shown that under the most plausible conditions the elasticity of the wage rate to capital is smaller than under competitive labour markets, and employment correspondingly has a greater elasticity. So, to attempt a summary, it might be said that in allowing for the value of leisure the impact of labour monopoly becomes broader, but shallower.

The allowance for the value of leisure also warrants a differentiation between two instruments of the labour monopolist that were hitherto judged equivalent: 'work rationing' and 'job lotteries'. The analysis suggests that the 'rationing' of work produces a better outcome for the labour monopolist than a minimum on wages. This apparent superiority provides a rationale for the ubiquity of 'leisure rights' in modern democracies: mandatory annual leave, maxima on the length of a working week, minimum 'sick leave' entitlements; as well as the recurrent murmur of 'work–life balance' by representatives of the labour interest. However, it will be argued that the difficulties in enforcing work rationing give space for a scheme of wage regulation, secured by a scheme of unemployment benefits, to triumph in a 'second-best' sense. The analysis therefore makes stronger the nexus between unemployment benefits and unemployment. It is not simply that unemployment benefits make (apparent) unemployment voluntary; rather, they allow the division of the workforce, into those who have work and those who do not, to be a better strategy than curtailing the work of all.

THE LABOUR MONOPOLY OPTIMUM IF LEISURE IS REWARDING

To allow for the utility of leisure we write the utility function as:

$$U_i = u(c_i) + v(j_i) \qquad (8.1)$$

$1 = h + j; c = $ consumption; $j = $ leisure

As before, we suppose the electorate is made up of Σ persons with identical utility functions, who collectively select a 'work ration' implemented, perhaps, by way of a legal maximum on hours worked. Thus the electorate chooses $l^* \equiv L/\Sigma$ to solve:

$$\underset{l^*}{Max\,U} = u\left(l^*w\left(\frac{l^*}{k^*}\right)\right) + v(1 - l^*) \qquad (8.2)$$

The solution to this maximization problem is presented in Figure 8.1 by means of a wage bill hill and indifference curves between work per person, l^*, and wages per person, w^*. It is contrasted there with the competitive equilibrium.

The optimum may be represented algebraically,[1]

$$w - m = w\left[\frac{1}{e}\right] \qquad (8.3)$$

$$m \equiv \frac{v'}{u'}$$

Equation (8.3) can be interpreted as saying that the sellers of leisure (the labour interest) mark up the price of leisure, w, over its subjective cost, m (the consumption at which they value a unit of leisure) according to the size of the elasticity of demand for labour; the more inelastic the demand the higher the mark-up.

Rewriting (8.3) as:

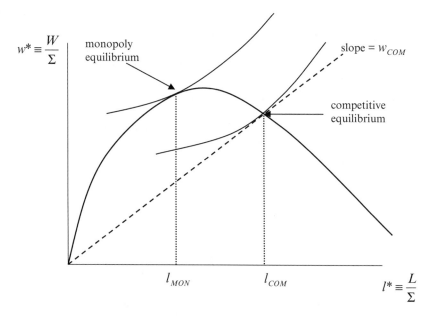

$$w^* \equiv \frac{W}{\Sigma}$$

monopoly equilibrium

slope $= w_{COM}$

competitive equilibrium

l_{MON} l_{COM}

$$l^* \equiv \frac{L}{\Sigma}$$

Figure 8.1   The labour monopoly equilibrium with leisure

$$e = \frac{w}{w - m} \tag{8.4}$$

makes plain that the optimal elasticity of labour demand must now exceed one. Thus the wage rate is higher than under simple wage bill maximization, and employment is lower. The higher wage reflects the additional benefit to restricting hours worked that is now present; not only does the restriction add to wage incomes, but it now also adds directly to utility, through increased leisure. Concomitant with $e > 1$ – and as is evident from Figure 8.1 – the wage bill is no longer maximized.[2] The wage bill may, indeed, be lower than under competition, and must be so whenever the demand for labour is elastic at the full employment outcome. The wage bill is not maximized because wage income is now being sacrificed for the sake of more leisure. It is on account of the leisure incentive to forgo wage income that the size of the contraction in employment, relative to the competitive equilibrium, is larger the more slowly the marginal utility of leisure ebbs in the face of the increased quantity of leisure. In other words, how substitutable is consumption for leisure? The more substitutable, the greater the contraction, as leisure maintains its equivalence in spite of its increased quantity. At the opposite extreme, when J and C are perfect complements there may be no contraction at all.

It is because wage income is intentionally forgone to obtain more leisure that the labour monopoly equilibrium no longer requires the existence of a 'wage bill hill'. For W to rise with employment without limit, as is the case if $\sigma \geq 1$, is now consistent with a labour monopoly equilibrium being distinct from the competitive equilibrium.[3]

Indeed, putting aside extreme cases, it seems impossible for labour monopoly equilibrium to coincide with competitive equilibrium. For the monopoly optimization $e = w/[w - m]$ can only coincide with competitive condition, $w = m$, when $e = \text{infinity}$. It seems impossible for full employment (that is, the competitive equilibrium) to occur under labour monopoly. This conclusion contrasts with our earlier conclusion that under wage bill maximization there was always some sufficient large quantity of capital that would drive the wage bill maximizing outcome to coincide with the competitive one.

As the present conclusion of the apparent necessity of an excess supply of labour is plainly inconsistent with the historical record, it is worth noting that the result does not extend to certain extremities of substitution in production and consumption.

Firstly, an excess supply of labour is not necessary if capital and labour are perfectly substitutable, and the marginal product of labour is consequently parametric.[4] Over any range of employment where the marginal product of labour is constant, the locus of the wage bill and employment is linear, and so the labour monopolist maximizes by setting m = w, just as in perfect competition.

Secondly, an excess supply of labour is not necessary when consumption and leisure have zero substitutability, and the two are perfect complements. In that case labour monopoly coincides with the competitive equilibrium whenever the demand for labour is elastic in the competitive equilibrium. For in that circumstance a higher wage must reduce the wage bill and so reduce consumption, and under perfect complements that must reduce utility, so the labour monopolist has no incentive to increase the wage above competitive levels (Figure 8.2).[5]

Thirdly, an excess supply of labour is not necessary if the utility function is not continuously differentiable. Of course the optimization condition (8.3), does assume continuously differentiabilty. But if there is a point where the marginal utility of leisure discontinuously jumps, perhaps at some 'customary' length of working day, then the labour monopoly outcome can coincide with the competitive outcome (Figure 8.3).

These three exceptions do rest on anomalies. Anomalies aside, an excess supply of labour is a necessity once leisure is allowed for. The upshot of allowing for leisure is that an excess supply of labour is now a much more ubiquitous phenomenon. The fact that leisure now has a direct benefit has

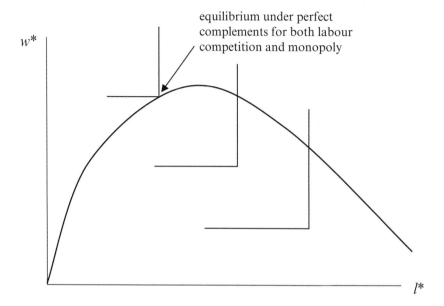

Figure 8.2   Labour monopoly may have a zero impact if leisure and consumption are perfect complements

spread the reach of labour monopoly: 'large' elasticities of technical substitution that previously made labour monopoly outcome coincide with the competitive outcome no longer do so; 'large' capital stocks that made Lm equivalent no longer do so.[6]

But how large is the size of the distortion necessitated by labour monopoly? How serious is this excess supply of labour? Two considerations suggest that it is large: firstly, 'direct' measurement resting on assumptions about functional forms and parameters; and secondly, 'indirect measurement' that rests on an equivalence between labour monopoly distortion and other distortions.

To pursue first 'direct' measurement, suppose $U = \ln C + \ln J$, that is, the elasticity of substitution between consumption and leisure, χ, is 1. Then the proportionate contraction in employment brought by labour monopoly can be solely related to the elasticity of labour demand. More precisely, as it can be shown:[7]

$$l^*_{COM} = \frac{1}{2} \text{ and } l^*_{MON} = \frac{e-1}{e+e-1},$$

we infer:

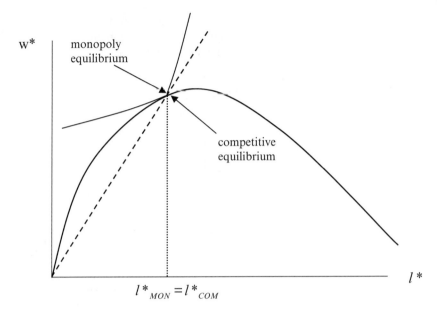

*Figure 8.3   Labour monopoly may have a zero impact if the marginal
            rate of substitution between leisure and consumption changes
            discontinuously*

$$\frac{l^*_{MON} - l^*_{COM}}{l^*_{COM}} = \frac{1}{e + e - 1} \tag{8.5}$$

If $e = 2$ then the proportionate contraction is 1/3. Evidently, for even a 'high' elasticity of labour demand the distortion is substantial.

The distortion is also significant if we instead suppose $U = C + J^\alpha$, that is, the marginal utility of consumption is constant, and the elasticity of leisure choice to the wage is parametric. We can obtain an expression for the 'rate of excess leisure'; that is, the fraction of leisure that is unwanted by the wage-taking utility-maximizing household:

$$\text{rate of excess leisure} = 1 - \left[\frac{e-1}{e}\right]^\Gamma \tag{8.6}^8$$

If $e = 2$ and $\Gamma = 2$ then the rate of excess supply is 75 per cent. This exercise does, however, beg many questions about the justice of the parameters and the functional form.

The second means of gauging the distortion created by the labour monopoly is to benchmark it by reference to other distortions. To do this we need to rewrite the optimization condition (8.3) as:

$$w\left[1 - \frac{1}{e}\right] = m \qquad (8.7)$$

This is analogous with the optimization condition under perfect labour market competition in the presence of an income tax:

$$w[1 - t] = m \qquad (8.8)$$

Thus the labour monopoly with leisure (without an income tax) is equivalent to a perfectly competitive economy with an income tax rate equal to the inverse of the elasticity of the demand for labour. To illustrate, if the elasticity was 1.5 (reflecting a profit share of ⅓ and an elasticity of technical substitution of ½), then the equivalent income tax rate would be ⅔; a very significant income tax.

VOLATILITY AND RIGIDITY

Earlier chapters have stressed that if the utility of leisure is disregarded, then labour monopoly implies extreme wage rigidity: the wage rate will have zero elasticity to fluctuations in labour demand brought by changes in the capital stock. But once leisure is allowed for, perfect wage rigidity retreats to polar cases. Nevertheless, under plausible conditions the real wage rate will have a smaller elasticity to the capital stock under labour monopoly than under labour competition. Thus a measure of wage rigidity remains.

The key point is that the allowance for the utility of leisure imparts to the comparative statics of the labour monopoly the strong flavour of the comparative statics of competitive labour markets, and this flavour is only weakened to the extent that the elasticity of technical substitution sinks below unity.

The distinct tincture of labour monopoly comparative statics by those of labour competition arises from the essential similarity of the optimization conditions for labour competition and labour monopoly:

$$w = m \qquad \text{Competition}$$

$$w = m\frac{e}{e - 1} \qquad \text{Monopoly}$$

If $\sigma = 1$ the correspondence in comparative statics becomes very close, and sometimes exact. For if $\sigma = 1$ then e is parametrical, and we may conclude from the above equalities that under both regimes the critical comparative static, $\partial l^*/\partial k^*$, is inferred from an expression of the type, $w(l^*/k^*) = m(l^*, l^*/k^*) \times$ constant. Thus labour competition and labour monopoly will share identical expressions for comparative statics.[9]

An illustrative implication of the correspondence in comparative statics if $\sigma = 1$ lies in the case where the elasticity of substitution between consumption and leisure, χ, is one (for example U = CJ). Then the labour supply schedule of a capital-less workforce will have zero elasticity to w. And consequently under a competitive labour market an increase in the capital stock will have zero impact on employment, and increase only the wage.

However, exactly the same flexibility in the wage will be found under labour monopoly if we assume $\sigma = 1$. If $\sigma = 1$ then e is a parametrical, and by the argument of the previous paragraph the comparative statics are coincident. Thus under labour monopoly an increase in the capital stock will only increase the wage rate, with zero effect on employment.[10] And a decrease in the capital stock will only decrease the wage, with zero effect on employment. Thus the wage rate is, in effect, adjusted by the labour monopolist to cancel all the employment impact of any shock to capital, both positive and negative; a phenomenon we previously encountered under wage bill maximization, and dubbed wage volatility. But under wage bill maximization, wage volatility was restricted to certain shocks (for example Hicks-neutral change). Now under the specified circumstances the labour monopoly adopts a wage volatility strategy with respect to all shocks, producing a wage response that completely immunizes employment against shocks. This is exactly how the wage acts under competition, under the specified circumstances. The upshot is that if $\chi = \sigma = 1$ then the quantity of employment under labour monopoly is as resistant to the state of labour demand as under perfect competition, and is wholly explained by fluctuations in the supply of labour.

This mimicry of competitive comparative statics when $\sigma = 1$ does not require $\chi = 1$. If $\chi > 1$ then under competition there will be a positively sloped labour supply schedule, and so a positive relationship between both the wage and capital stock, and employment and capital stock. But, assuming $\sigma = 1$, then by the earlier argument, labour monopoly also produces a positive relationship between both the wage and capital stock, and employment and capital stock. If $\chi < 1$ then under competition there will be a negative between relation employment and the capital stock, reflecting the now backward-bending labour supply (and an even more positive relationship between the wage and capital stock also reflecting the now backward-bending labour supply). But, assuming $\sigma = 1$, then there will also be a negative relationship between employment and the capital stock under labour monopoly. The increase in capital induces the wage to rise so much that employment is reduced, reflecting the very same income effect pressures that produce the same reduction under competition.

Thus we might say that if $\sigma = 1$ then the difference between competition and monopoly lies not at all in the comparative statics, but purely in the equilibrium states. For the equilibrium level of employment is lower under labour monopoly than under competition; but how that equilibrium shifts to shocks is not appreciably different if $\sigma = 1$.

So it might seem that the easily won victory of labour monopoly in predicting real wage rigidity in the context of wage bill maximization dissolves once the labour monopolist allows for the value of leisure. But recall that if $\sigma = 1$ there was never any wage rigidity under simple wage bill maximization, anyway; the comparative statics of labour monopoly there, too, were the same as under labour competition. Thus the identicality of comparative statics if $\sigma = 1$ is common to both wage bill maximization and utility maximization.

Only once $\sigma < 1$ does there emerge a comparative statics of labour monopoly distinct from labour competition. The explanation is that if $\sigma < 1$ then e is no longer parametrical. When e was parametrical then an increase in capital necessitated an equal proportionate increase in w and m under both monopoly and competition. But now an equiproportionate increase in w and m will not preserve an equilibrium under monopoly; for the increase in w will now increase e, and so reduce the optimal excess ('mark-up') of w over m. Thus w must not rise as much as m. The rise in w is restrained. And that restraint reinforces equilibration by a second channel; for by magnifying the employment response, the wage restraint enlarges the increase in m,[11] and that too contributes to achieving a reduced 'mark-up' of w over m.

To illustrate the divergence of monopoly wage behaviour from competitive wage behaviour we can again use the case where $\chi = 1$. The supply of labour is absolutely inelastic to the wage, so under competition employment is absolutely inelastic to the capital stock, but under labour monopoly employment now rises in face of the higher w secured by an increased K: $L/\Sigma = [e(w) - 1]/[e(w) + e(w) - 1]$. And (concomitantly) the wage rises not so much; the responsiveness of e to w has moderated the responsiveness of wages, and increased the responsiveness of employment to a labour demand shock.[12]

The magnitude of the moderation of the wage response depends on the sensitivity of the elasticity of the demand for labour to w. It is easy to see that the greater the increase in e in response to w, the greater the required moderation in the wage rate rise, and the greater the employment increase.

As $\partial e/\partial w$ approaches infinity, the admissible increase in w becomes infinitely small. Similarly, as $\partial e/\partial k$ approaches infinity the admissible increase in w becomes infinitely small

But what determines the elasticity of e? We know from Chapter 3 that the sensitivity of e, to both w and k, is a negative function of σ. Thus the smaller σ, the larger the sensitivity of e to w, and so the smaller admissible increase in w. Wage 'stickiness' goes with a low degree of substitutability between capital and labour.

As the degree of substitutability of capital and labour approaches zero, a strict wage rigidity appears.[13] Thus under labour monopoly as σ approaches zero, the elasticity of w to K approaches zero, and employment is unit elastic to the capital stock. Strict wage rigidity, it seems, pertains to the most extreme measure of non-substitutability between capital and labour.

Strict wage rigidity also characterizes the situation of the most extreme substitutability between consumption and leisure, $\chi = \propto$. But this is simply the case where there is no 'rise in the wage rate' for labour monopoly to moderate. For when leisure and consumption are perfect substitutes, the marginal rate of substitution is parametric at m!, and under competition the wage rate remains unchanged at the m! regardless of the capital stock, and employment is unit elastic to capital under competition. Under labour monopoly, the solution is $w = m!e(w)/[e(w) - 1]$, and the wage is also evidently wholly determined by technology and completely invariant to the capital stock, and employment unit elastic to capital.[14]

But barring the polar cases of $\sigma = 0$ and $\chi = \propto$, the wage rate does increase in response to K, and does fall in response to Σ.[15] So wage rates have neither the complete inflexibility of wage bill maximization, nor the complete flexibility of labour competition.

The conclusion that labour monopoly moderates the rise in the wage rate that is produced by extra capital finds a counterpart in the conclusion that under labour monopoly an increase in capital reduces the excess supply of labour. A rise in K, by increasing w, necessitates from optimization an increase in m/w. That is, the valuation of leisure, m, rises towards the opportunity cost of leisure, w. This excess of the opportunity cost of leisure over its valuation is reduced, and this may be interpreted as a reduction in the pressure of excess supply.

WHAT STRATEGIES CAN REACH THE OPTIMUM?

The preceding section assumes the labour monopoly uses a strategy of work rationing.

A difficulty with this assumption is that, taken literally, a work ration-ing scheme would consist of coupons that would need to be 'paid' every time anyone wished to work. This, as an economy-wide proposition, seems unreal (although the union membership card has sometimes performed the function of such a 'coupon'). Are there other instruments that could achieve the same effect as work coupons?

Overmanning

Recall, from Chapter 3, that when the maximand was simply wage income, there existed a degree of overmanning that could achieve anything that work rationing could achieve. This is not the case now, at least not as long as leisure 'on the job' is not a perfect substitute for leisure off the job. Overmanning would still improve the labour interest as long as e < 1 at the competitive equilibrium, as overmanning under that circumstance would increase the demand for labour. Therefore if overmanning was the only instrument available to the labour monopoly it would still adjust θ until e = 1. But such a maximum will be inferior to the work-rationing maximum. Because whatever amount of effective labour is done under the overman-ning optimum, work rationing could have secured the same quantity com-bined with increased leisure, as part of the time endowment previously used by doing nothing at work can now be spent as genuine leisure.[16]

Taxation

Taxation might be a means of securing optimal work rationing. Imagine a workforce-controlled legislature imposing an income tax or consumption tax, such that all its proceeds are returned to the workforce in terms of flat grants (perhaps in the form of subsidized health, schools or transport). To secure the labour supply that is equal to the optimal work ration the legislature simply chooses *t* to satisfy:

$$t = \frac{1}{e} \tag{8.9}$$

t = rate of tax

Such a rate secures the utility that secures the best a labour monopoly can do under work rationing without invoking an unreal scheme of universal work ration coupons.

This scenario casts a new aspect on taxation, as the electorate is will-ingly imposing a 'tax burden' upon itself, not to fund public goods, but to discourage itself from working so much. The scenario may rationalize the phenomenon of the 'churning' of revenues, whereby the electorate taxes itself merely to return the revenues to itself; something completely useless in the absence of utility of leisure. The scenario also provides a new theory of movements in the tax rate, as the chosen tax rate moves inversely with the optimal e. A larger K must raise optimal w, and so e; therefore the tax rate falls.

Yet this logic may seem all too ingenious. It also begs questions about the political control of revenue, the evasion of taxes, and the possibility that the tax rate necessary to finance the genuine functions of government may exceed the tax rate that would optimize the labour supply.

An Hours Maximum

A more plausible means of rationing work would be to impose a universal maximum on hours $= L^*/\Sigma$, while the wage rate is kept flexible. If the employee is liable for punishment for working more than x hours then a maximum would work if enforced. But this is not the maximum of hours of the kind commonly seen. Typically, a maximum forbids an employer from offering (or requiring of) an employee a contract for more than x hours. This prohibition will not have the effect as coupons; indeed it would have no effect at all, as the worker could work as many hours as they like simply by having several employers. The wage rate would adjust so that all would work as long they liked, but possibly with several different employers. The intention of the prohibition can be avoided.

It is true that if there is a fixed cost to employment decisions (a transaction cost) then profit maximization would induce firms to require all employees to work up to the maximum; the firm minimizes its number of employees for a given amount of work, and it becomes more difficult to evade the maximum by having several part-time jobs. So a maximum might work. But historical experience indicates that maxima remain unchanged for long periods. Its hard to such see such unchanging restrictions as constituting the optimum described earlier in the chapter.

THE WAGES–BENEFITS NEXUS

Can the control of the wage rate secure the work ration optimum?

Control of the wage rate could do so if employment is dispensed randomly to workers in tiny packets ('days'). In this schema everyone is merely guaranteed a wage rate; no one is guaranteed a work ration. But by the law of large numbers everyone gets pretty much the same quantity of work, that which equals the optimum work ration.

However, employers may not wish to conjure with such tiny packets of work. If there are 'transaction costs' (a cost in the number of employment contracts) they will wish to reduce the number of employees to the minimum; and so those employed will work until w = m, and those unemployed will not work at all. The work rationing arrangement has vanished.

To summarize, we are left with the thought that the work ration optimum described earlier is not a credible account of labour monopoly behaviour. For coupons are unreal, and schemes that replicate coupons are not convincing; the tax rate necessary to finance government spending might exceed the optimum-ration-replicating tax rate; an hours maximum seems too rigid; a wage minimum requires a presence of probabalistic allocation of tiny packets of work.

So we are led to analyse how the impact of labour monopoly is altered by leisure when the instrument is 'job lotteries'; where, owing to transaction costs, work comes in large randomly allocated packets (jobs), of length h. Assuming complete unemployment insurance, the maximand under job lotteries is:

$$EU = p[u(wh - zZ) + v(1 - h)] + [1 - p][u(Z - zZ) + v(1)]$$
$$(8.10)$$

Z = the quantity of unemployment insurance

z = the price of one unit of unemployment insurance

h = the length of 'a job' as a fraction of each person's time endowment.

The utility-maximizing choice of insurance implies that the maximand reduces to:

$$EU = u(wl^*(w)) + pv(1 - h) + [1 - p]v(1) \qquad (8.11)[17]$$

But to explore such a maximand would be to ignore the fact that such job lotteries have a serious evasion problem. For the analysis above has assumed complete unemployment insurance. But complete unemployment insurance implies that the utility outcome of being jobless will exceed the utility outcome of being in work (as income is the same, but the jobless have greater leisure). Therefore, complete insurance is unviable if workers can refuse jobs; or, to be more precise, can refuse (or avoid) job offers without the insurer being aware that they are doing so.

Instead of complete insurance, we might analyse the maximand pertaining to the complete absence of insurance:

$$EU = p[u(wh) + v(1 - h)] + [1 - p]v(1)$$

Or using $p = lK/h\Sigma$,

$$EU = \frac{l(w)K}{h\Sigma}[u(wh) + v(1 - h) - v(1)] + v(1) \qquad (8.12)$$

Clearly the maximizing value of w is independent of the magnitude of K, and Σ. So complete rigidity of the wage rate with respect to movements in K, and Σ, returns in the absence of any job insurance.

But to assume a total absence of job insurance seems an inappropriate response to the difficulties of job assurance. For job lotteries have their own internal (part) remedy to asymmetric information. We can imagine a job lottery insurance scheme sufficiently ungenerous in its pay-out so that it leaves those unemployed no better or worse off than the employed:

$$u(hw - \tau) + v(1 - h) = u\left(\tau\frac{L(w)/h}{\Sigma - L(w)/h}\right) + v(1) \qquad (8.13)$$

In this situation the employed do not envy the unemployed, and vice versa. The employed cannot be working shorter hours than they would judge utility-maximizing; that is in neither their interest nor that of their employers, who seek to minimize the number they employ for the given amount of work. The employed cannot be working longer hours than they would judge utility-maximizing; they would wish to reduce their hours, and employers would need to pay an inducement to the indifferent unemployed to accept working longer hours. Thus:

$$h = h(w, \tau) \qquad (8.14)$$

and so:

$$u(h(w, \tau)w - \tau) + v(1 - h(w, \tau)) = u\left(\tau\frac{L(w)/h(w, \tau)}{\Sigma - L(w)/h(w, \tau)}\right) + v(1) \qquad (8.15)$$

τ = unemployment benefit levy (paid by only by the employed).

The labour monopolist maximizes:

$$\underset{w,\tau}{Max}\, u(h(w, \tau)w - \tau) + v(1 - h(w, \tau))$$

subject to (8.15).

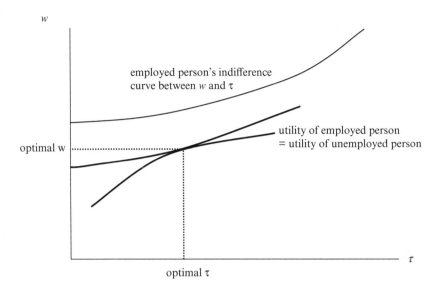

Figure 8.4   The optimum wage rate and unemployment benefit contribution

Figure 8.4 presents the optimization by means of indifference curves between w and τ, and the constraint that w and τ must be so that the utility of being unemployed is the same as being employed.

In mathematical terms, the optimization yields:

$$\frac{\tau}{wh} = \frac{1 - \dfrac{lK}{h\Sigma} - e_S^\tau}{e + e_S} \tag{8.17}$$

This optimization condition can be understood as expressing the proportion of the wage contributed to insurance ('the wedge') as a function of the unemployment rate:

$$wedge = \frac{\upsilon - e_S^\tau}{e + e_S} \tag{8.18}$$

$$wedge \equiv \frac{\tau}{hw} \qquad \upsilon \equiv 1 - \frac{lk^*}{h}$$

$$e_S \equiv \frac{\partial h}{\partial w}\frac{w}{h} \qquad e_S^\tau \equiv -\frac{\partial h}{\partial \tau}\frac{\tau}{h}$$

But this is an expression of one equation in two variables, w and τ. The full statement of equilibrium requires the satisfaction of both:

$$\frac{\tau}{wh(w,\tau)} = \frac{1 - \dfrac{l(w)k^*}{h(w,\tau)} - e_S^\tau}{e(w) + e_S(w,\tau)} \tag{8.19}$$

$$u(h(w,\tau)w - \tau) + v(1 - h(w,\tau)) = u\left(\tau\frac{\dfrac{l(w)k^*}{h(w,\tau)}}{1 - \dfrac{l(w)k^*}{h(w,\tau)}}\right) + v(1) \tag{8.20}$$

These two equalities determine w and τ. And they determine the unemployment rate υ. They also determine the size of the unemployment benefit, $\tau[1 + \upsilon]/\upsilon$. Thus the schema captures the labour monopolist making an optimizing choice not only for the wage rate, but also for the 'social insurance' contribution, τ, the size of unemployment benefits and the unemployment rate.

The exogenous variable that governs the choices of these variables is $k^* \equiv K/\Sigma$. One can infer that w and τ (and so υ and the unemployment benefit) are invariant to 'balanced' changes in Σ and K that leave K/Σ unchanged. But how changes in K/Σ change w and τ is a more intricate matter. The simplest case to analyse is constant marginal utility of consumption, with no income effects in the supply of labour, and risk neutrality over risks in consumption:

$$\text{Max} \quad wh - \tau + v(1 - h) \tag{8.21}$$

$$\text{st} \quad wh - \tau + v(1 - h) = \tau\frac{L/h}{\Sigma - L/h} + v(1)$$

The constraint can be solved for τ, and substituted back into the expression to yield the maximand solely in w:

$$\underset{w}{Max} \quad \frac{W}{\Sigma} + v(1 - h)\frac{L/h}{\Sigma} + v(1)\frac{[\Sigma - L/h]}{\Sigma} \tag{8.22}$$

or:

$$\underset{w}{Max} \quad \frac{K}{\Sigma}\frac{l(w)}{h(w)}[h(w)w + v(1 - h(w)) - v(1)] + v(1) \tag{8.23}$$

Clearly the maximizing value of w is independent of the magnitude of K/Σ. Thus both K and Σ are completely irrelevant to w. We again encounter complete wage rigidity.[18] To explicate the result, the maximand is the sum of expected wage income per person plus the expectation of the loss of utility from getting work. Both these expectations are unit elastic to the capital stock per head, so changes in capital stock per head will not change the maximizing wage rate. Of course, the case of constant marginal utility of consumption is an extreme one, in which there is no benefit from having the unemployment insurance anyway.

The case with more general preferences can be illustrated by Figure 8.4. An increase in K/Σ will shift the constraint in Figure 8.4 upwards and yield an increase in w, and a reduction in υ.

The preceding analysis leaves us with the thought that unemployment benefits are integrally tied up with the regulation of real wages for the benefit of labour monopoly. They are not merely an ad hoc picking-up-the-pieces consequence of regulation, but a precondition for their best use. Neither are they a leisure subsidy of indistinct provenance as they must be in a competitive model labour market (how could competitive model generate any unemployment benefit? there is no unemployment[19]).

It might be objected that the apparent nexus between unemployment benefits and unemployment under labour monopoly is critically damaged by the fact that even the most favourably blessed job lottery scheme is inferior to an effectively enforced schema of work rationing. This is because, for any wage rate, expected utility under job lotteries must be less than utility under work rationing, even under complete insurance.[20] This is simply because a job lottery must also be a leisure lottery; some (the unemployed) get the prize of large leisure. By contrast under work-sharing, whatever the wage rate, the resulting total of leisure is shared out equally and with complete predictability for any worker. This loss from the riskiness of the leisure allocation means that the optimum job lottery outcome must be inferior to the optimum work ration.

But the inferiority of job lotteries to work rations does presume that work rations are effectively enforced. And the effective enforcement is doubtful. No one wants to be rationed. If a literal coupon scheme is used, people will offer to work without coupons, and cut their wage to induce employers to give them that work. If a maximum hours worked scheme is used, people will offer to work in defiance of the maximum, and will cut their wage to induce employers to give them that work. The point is that job lotteries, augmented by the unemployment benefit, are evasion-proofed in that people are content to be unemployed. They are content to contribute to the scarcity of labour.[21] The most robust scheme for maximizing workforce interests seems to be a wage minimum buttressed by unemployment benefits.

CONCLUDING COMMENTS

The household's optimizing choice of the labour supply has been a key part of much macroeconomics since the 1980s. It does not function, however, as an 'essential assumption', a *sine qua non*. Neither does it function as a 'fighting assumption', to reduce adversaries to concession. Rather its contribution is as an assisting and facilitating assumption; to help equilibrium macroeconomics make sense of the observed world. For if 'demand' explains nothing, then 'supply' must explain all. Hence the emphasis on labour supply choice.

In the labour monopoly approach to employment the household's optimizing choice of the labour supply cannot be said to have any of these functions. It is not an essential, fighting or assisting assumption. In fact, the allowance for an optimizing choice of the labour supply weakens the implication of wage rigidity, which is not to the advantage of the approach; and seems to make inevitable an excess supply, which certainly does it no credit. Finally, it makes 'job lotteries' unambiguously inferior to work rationing, and thereby withers the promise of labour monopoly theory.

But once we allow that it may be harder to enforce work rationing than wage minima then the allowance for the value of leisure allows us to paint a more integral picture of the optimization of the labour monopolist; a picture in which the labour monopolist chooses not only the wage rate but also the unemployment rate, the size of social insurance contributions and the unemployment benefit.

NOTES

1. $\dfrac{\partial U}{\partial l^*} = u'\left[\dfrac{l^*}{k^*}w' + w\right] - v' = 0$, and so on.

2. The conclusion that wages income is not maximized does rest upon the *marginal* utility of leisure being positive. If total utility from leisure is positive but the marginal utility of leisure is zero, wage bill maximization returns.

3.
$$\frac{\partial U}{\partial l^*} = u'\frac{\partial w^*}{\partial l^*} - v' = 0$$

$$\frac{\partial^2 U}{\partial l^{*2}} = \frac{\partial^2 w^*}{\partial l^{*2}}u' + \left[\frac{\partial w^*}{\partial l^*}\right]^2 u'' + v'' < 0$$

Given $u'', v'' < 0$, the satisfaction of the SOC of the maximum no longer requires $\partial^2 w^*/\partial l^{*2} < 0$.

4. That circumstance means the demand for labour is infinitely elastic, and so is considered anomalous; but the coexistence of distinct 'technologies' may generate an infinitely elastic demand for labour over certain range of employment, while preserv-

ing a finite elasticity at employment levels outside that range. (See Wicksell 1934 and Coleman 1985).

5. Under perfect complements, if the demand for labour is inelastic at the competitive equilibrium then the labour monopoly will raise wage rates until the wage bill is maximized. Any further increase would only reduce consumption, and so utility. With perfect complements labour monopoly either produces the identical outcome to the perfectly competitive outcome, and full employment, or produces wage bill maximization and an excess supply of labour.

6. The ownership of capital by workers does not make the excess supply of labour any less necessary. The optimization condition becomes $- e + 1 - k_W^*/k^* = -em/w$. Thus m = w only if $k_W^*/k^* = 1$. Thus m = w only when entire capital stock is owned by workers.

7. Under labour market competition the optimization condition, when $\chi = 1$, is $w = C/J$. Combined with the time constraint $\Sigma = J + L$ and the expenditure constraint $C = wL$, it yields $L/\Sigma = 1/2$. Under labour monopoly the optimization condition when $\chi = 1$ is $w(e - 1)J = eC$. Combined with the time constraint and the expenditure constraint it yields $L/\Sigma = [e - 1]/[e + e - 1]$, where $e > 1$.

8. Letting J be the amount of leisure that would maximize the utility of the wage-taking households; $J^{\alpha-1} = w$. Let J_{MON} be the amount of leisure chosen by the labour monopolist; from (8.2) $J_{MON}^{\alpha-1} = w[[e - 1]/e]$. Thus $[J_{MON} - J]/J_{MON} = 1 - [[e - 1]/e]^{1/1-\alpha}$.

9. This is not to say that the magnitude of $\partial l^*/\partial k^*$ is necessarily the same for competition and monopoly, as the identical expression $\partial l^*/\partial k^*$ will be evaluated at different magnitudes of l*.

10. Recall from our previous analysis of this case that $L/\Sigma = [e - 1]/[e + e - 1]$. But e is parametrical when $\sigma = 1$. Thus employment per unit of population is parametric, and invariant to the capital stock.

11. By increasing v'. And – given the elastic demand for labour – by increasing W, and so reducing u'.

12. If $\chi > 1$ then under competition there is a positively sloped labour supply schedule and so a positive relationship between both the wage and capital stock, and employment and capital stock. But as long as $\sigma < 1$ then under labour monopoly the relationship between the wage and capital stock will not be so positive, and correspondingly employment will be more elastic to the capital stock.

13. The optimization condition (8.2) may be written:

$$e\left[1 - \frac{m}{w}\right] = 1$$

$$e\left(\frac{k^*}{l^*}\right)[1 - n(k^*, l^*)] = 1, \qquad n \equiv \frac{m}{w}$$

Thus:

$$\frac{l^*dk^*}{dl^*k^*} = \frac{\dfrac{e'[k^*/l^*]}{e} + l^*en_{l^*}}{\dfrac{e'[k^*/l^*]}{e} - k^*en_{k^*}}$$

As $e'[k^*/l^*]/e = [[1 - \sigma]/\sigma][1 - \pi]$ it would seem that as σ approaches zero, $e'[k^*/l^*]/e$ approaches infinity and l^*dk^*/dl^*k^* approaches one (unless π approaches one as σ goes to zero, but the opposite seems more likely).

14. We might be tempted to say in summary: perfect substitutability between consumption and leisure maximizes the difference between the equilibrium states, but minimizes the differences in comparative statics; zero substitutability between consumption and leisure minimizes the difference between the equilibrium states, but maximizes the differences in comparative statics. In all, a distinct labour monopoly statics is fostered by low substitutability between K and L, and C and J.

15. $\sigma < 1$ is a sufficient condition for $\partial w/\partial k^* > 0$. Proof.

$$e(w) = \cfrac{1}{1 - \cfrac{v'}{u'w}}$$

Suppose, contrary to the contention, an increase in k* reduces w. Then the left hand side falls as K rises, assuming $\sigma < 1$. And so the right hand side must fall. That necessitates a fall in $v'/u'w$. But v' increases, as the supposed reduction in w increases l(w), thereby reducing J. And u' falls, as the supposed reduction in w increases w l(w), owing to the elasticity of labour demand being in excess of 1. Thus v'/wu' rises, and so the right hand side rises. Contradiction.

16. The inferiority of the overmanning instrument is underlined by the fact that if work rationing is available, the labour monopolist will ignore an overmanning instrument even if it is available:

$$U = u(\theta q'(\theta l^*)l^*) + v(1 - l^*)$$

$$\frac{\partial U}{\partial \theta} = l^*[\theta l^* q'' + q']u'$$

But if the labour monopolist can choose l*:

$$\frac{\partial U}{\partial l^*} = \theta[q' + l^*\theta q'']u' - v' = 0$$

and so:

$$\frac{\partial U}{\partial \theta} = \frac{v'}{\theta}l^* > 0$$

Thus the labour monopoly only wants always to increase θ, and so labour monopoly leaves θ at its assumed maximum at one. In fact, labour augmentation is always to the advantage of the labour interest under work rationing. Because when labour demand is elastic the labour interest is always benefited by labour augmentation, and labour demand at its optimum is now always elastic. The labour monopoly is now a friend of labour-augmenting technical change.

17. Maximizing with respect to Z:

$$zpu'(wh - zZ) = [1 - p][1 - z]u'(Z - zZ)$$

From z = 1 − p:

$$[1 - p]pu'(wh - zZ) = [1 - p]pu'(Z - zZ)$$

Therefore, $wh = Z$, and so $u(wh - zZ) = u(pwh) = u(l^*w)$.

18. There is no 'rigidity' in τ. $\tau = [1 - lK/h\Sigma][wh + v(1 - h) - v(1)]$, and τ consequently falls as K rises.

19. Obviously a competitive market might supply wage rate insurance. But that is not 'unemployment insurance'. And if the shocks to the wage rate are common across the labour force then the only feasible wage rate insurance is self-insurance.

20. Given $p = l^*/h$, $1 - l^*$ equals the mathematical expectation of leisure hours; $1 - l^* = p[1 - h] + [1 - p]1$. Therefore, supposing the marginal utility of leisure diminishes, it is necessarily true:

$$pv(1 - h) + [1 - p]v(1) < v(1 - l^*).$$

Consequently, expected utility under job lotteries with complete insurance = $u(wl^*) + pv(1 - h) + [1 - p]v(1)$, is less than $u(wl^*) + v(1 - l^*)$, utility under work-sharing. This argument for the inferiority of job lotteries to work rations does depend upon the marginal utility of leisure diminishing. If marginal utility is constant, job lotteries will, in the above framework, be just as effective as work rationing. If marginal utility is constant then in an unconstrained labour market there is a zero marginal propensity to consume out of non-wage income, which seems doubtful. Of course, if leisure choice (and labour supply) is constrained, then the propensity to consume out of non-wage income is one.

21.   Of course there is an evasion issue concerning the extraction of the tax for the finance of the unemployment benefit.

APPENDIX

Define an indirect utility function for being in employment:

$$\psi(w, \tau) \equiv u(hw - \tau) + v(1 - h) \qquad (A8.1)$$

and an unemployment 'benefit function':

$$b(w, \tau) \equiv \tau \frac{L/h}{\Sigma - L/h} \qquad (A8.2)$$

The labour monopolist chooses to maximize the indirect utility function subject to the utility of being employed equalling that of being unemployed,

$$\text{Max} \quad \psi(w, \tau) + \phi[\psi(w, \tau) - u(b(w, \tau)) - v(1)] \qquad (A8.3)$$

The manipulation of the first-order conditions implies:

$$\frac{\psi_w}{\psi_\tau} = \frac{b_w}{b_\tau} \qquad (A8.4)$$

But as:

$$b(w, \tau) \equiv \tau \frac{L(w)/h(w, \tau)}{\Sigma - L(w)/h(w, \tau)} \qquad (A8.5)$$

we infer:

$$b_\tau = \frac{[\Sigma h - L]L - \tau L \Sigma h_\tau}{[\Sigma h - L]^2}$$

and:

$$b_w = \tau \frac{[\Sigma h - L]L' - L[\Sigma h_w - L']}{[\Sigma h - L]^2} = \tau \frac{\Sigma[hL' - Lh_w]}{[\Sigma h - L]^2} \qquad (A8.6)$$

So:

$$-\frac{\psi_w}{\psi_\tau} = \frac{\tau \dfrac{\Sigma[hL' - Lh_w]}{[\Sigma h - L]^2}}{\dfrac{[\Sigma h - L]L - \tau L \Sigma h_\tau}{[\Sigma h - L]^2}} = -\tau \frac{\Sigma\left[h\dfrac{L'}{L} - h_w\right]}{\Sigma h - L - \tau \Sigma h_\tau} \qquad (A8.7)$$

Roy's identity, that relates optimally chosen quantity (here, h) to the ratio of the positivized marginal utility cost of a higher price to the marginal utility benefit of a higher income, implies:

$$h = -\frac{\Psi_w}{\Psi_\tau} \tag{A8.8}$$

Thus:

$$h = \frac{\tau \, \Sigma h \left[-\dfrac{wL'}{L} + w\dfrac{h_w}{h} \right]}{w \;\; \Sigma h - L - \tau \Sigma h_\tau} \tag{A8.9}$$

Equation (8.9) follows.

9. Why the majority may choose the wage of the minority

It might be questioned whether the analyses of the previous chapters have much relevance to the contemporary world. For the previous chapters deal with restrictions on competition that intend to embrace the whole workforce. But in the present-day world restrictions on competition infrequently have such a universal aspiration. Much more commonly, such restrictions are imposed only on small and marginal sections of the labour force, with the wage rates of the great bulk of the labour force left to competitive forces. It seems that for only a minority of the poorly paid is regulation of the labour market a palpable reality.

This chapter confronts the challenge that the relative marginality of labour market regulation poses to the standpoint of this book, and investigates whether it is possible for the moral of the preceding chapters to apply even in the situation where only a minority face wage regulation.

To undertake this investigation the modelling of labour's contribution to production needs to be developed. Up till now the labour force has been assumed to be homogeneous, and so there could be only one wage rate; there could be no 'minimum wage' distinct from the wage rate paid to all. This chapter therefore shifts away from the assumption of homogeneous labour to embrace the heterogeneity of labour, and is thereby able to answer various questions regarding the 'electorally optimal' wage regulation in the context of many different types of labour. Might it ever be to the advantage of a majority of purely self-interested voters to establish a minimum wage for (a minority) of low-paid employees? Under what circumstances would it be advantageous? What will the consequences be of the establishment of a minimum wage by a self-interested majority? And more generally: to what extent can the system of minimum wages be assimilated into the approach of this work? To what extent will the median voter model outlined in previous chapters remain relevant to the real world?

This chapter expounds a simple, tractable, aggregative, neoclassical model to answer those questions. The model implies that a majority of purely self-interested voters will find it optimizing to establish a minimum wage in the presence of: (1) a 'sufficiently large' supply of labour; or (2) a 'sufficiently small quantity of capital'; or (3) a 'sufficiently large' degree of substitutability between the different types of labour; or (4) a 'sufficiently small' degree of substitutability between capital and labour. Thus a minimum wage will arise in an economy 'glutted with labour', or 'stinted of capital', or one in which labour is relatively homogeneous.

In the chapter's model the 'wage rigidity' conclusions of earlier chapters reappear, refashioned. For despite a degree of wage flexibility sectorally, the model exhibits a rigidity in wage rates in the aggregate. While the model implies, unsurprisingly, that the wage rates of labour types set competitively will fall with any reduction in the capital stock, it also shows the majority-chosen minimum wage moves 'perversely' with respect to capital shocks, as the minimum will *rise* in the face of a reduced capital stock. These divergent movements in sectoral wage rates (some up, some down) raise the question of the response of the average of wage rates to capital stock shocks, and underpins a further conclusion of the model: heterogeneous labour mimics the wage rigidity of the previous chapters, in that a certain index of the average wage rate is perfectly inelastic to the capital stock. Thus the analysis concludes that the 'rigidity message' of preceding chapters is not literally beholden to an assumption of a homogeneous workforce paid some universal wage rate; the phenomenon of a rigidity on average may be produced by the regulation of only one small part of the labour market.

The chapter adds a new dimension to the analysis of earlier chapters by embracing a conflict of interests beyond the opposition of 'capital' and 'labour'. In the present analysis the key conflict is between low- and high-wage earners. Perhaps the model's most arresting aspect is the potentially inequitable character of wage regulation born of that conflict. In the earlier chapters the cost of labour monopoly was borne by capital owners, and by each member of the labour force with an equal chance, as unemployment was a gamble that every member of the workforce was equally exposed to. In the present model it is possible for the majority to risklessly advance their own wage incomes by imposing a wage regulation that reduces employment and wage incomes of the least-well-paid.[1]

AN AGGREGATE PRODUCTION FUNCTION WITH HETEROGENEOUS LABOUR

The model maintains the assumptions of the maximally simple model of Chapter 3, but supposes that output is produced by M distinct 'types' of labour, rather than one, each with their own wage rate. As before, the electorate is composed of a capital-less workforce, the majority of which may impose a wage minimum.[2] The problem at hand is: what minimum wage rate (if any) will be the electoral equilibrium?

In order to make headway in solving this problem we will adopt a specific modelling of technology. We assume output is produced by K, capital, and Λ, according to:

$$Y = Kq\left(\frac{\Lambda}{K}\right) \qquad q' > 0, q'' < 0 \qquad (9.1)$$

Λ is not 'the quantity of labour', but an input, itself produced by an array of M heterogeneous labour types, according to a CES-style production function:

$$\Lambda = [\sum L_j^\beta]^{1/\beta} \qquad \beta < 1$$

$$\frac{\partial \Lambda}{\partial L_j} > 0, \frac{\partial^2 \Lambda}{\partial L_j} < 0 \text{ all } j \qquad (9.2)$$

To illustrate concretely, we might suppose a pastoral economy in which Y is 'wool', K is 'sheep', and Λ is 'fences'. The L_js are the various types of labour that make the fences. Although Λ is not labour , it is worth noting that Λ amounts to an index of aggregate labour inputs, on account of the fact that Λ is produced solely by types of labour under constant returns to scale.

The upshot is that output may be expressed:

$$\frac{Y}{K} = q\left(\frac{[\sum L_j^\beta]^{1/\beta}}{K}\right) \qquad \frac{\partial Y}{\partial L_j} > 0, \frac{\partial^2 Y}{\partial L_j^2} < 0 \text{ all } j \qquad (9.3)$$

This technology will determine the factor demands and factor prices that will shape the interests of the M labour types.

The wage rate for any labour type j plainly equals the marginal productivity of type j, which will depend negatively on its own employment level, L_j, and positively upon capital, K, as (9.4) makes evident:

$$w_j = \left[\frac{\Lambda}{L_j}\right]^{1-\beta} q'\left(\frac{\Lambda}{K}\right) \text{ all } j \qquad (9.4)$$

Three further remarks about the labour technology are worth making.

First, the marginal productivity of any L_j in producing Λ is increased by a larger amount of any L_k. Thus all labour types are 'complementary' in a physical sense.

Second, in a price sense all labour types are substitutes for one another. For we can always obtain the choices of L_1, L_2 L_3, . . . that will minimize the cost of producing a specified amount of Λ, given a series of wage rates w_1, w_2, w_3, . . ., and the technical constraint $\Lambda = [\sum L_j^\beta]^{1/\beta}$. Such a cost minimization exercise implies for any two labour types j and k:

$$\frac{L_j}{L_k} = \left[\frac{w_k}{w_j}\right]^{1/(1-\beta)} \tag{9.5}$$

The higher the relative size of wage j, the lower the relative employment of labour type j. The labour types are always substitutes in relative terms. Thus 'the elasticity of substitution between any two labour types' is:

$$^L\sigma = \frac{1}{1-\beta} \tag{9.6}$$

Clearly, this elasticity may vary from the infinite ($\beta = 1$), indicating perfect substitutability between the labour types, to zero ($\beta = -\infty$), indicating perfect complementarity between the labour types. As $^L\sigma$ is a positive function of β, we can additionally infer that the elasticity of substitution between any two labour types is also an indicator of the degree of complementarity between Lj's productivity at the margin in producing Λ. As $^L\sigma$ rises, β rises, and the degree of complementarity falls.

Thirdly, in the model all the M labour types are 'symmetrical' to each other with respect to their contribution to production, and (therefore) they all have exactly the same demand functions. Thus there is no 'hierarchy' of labour types in terms of some 'inherent productivity'; for given supplies of other labour types, each labour type has the same marginal productivity as any other labour type in equal supply. Neither are there subgroups within the M types in terms of substitutability; it is not as if there are chefs and cooks in one corner, and rugby league and rugby union players in the other.

What the labour types do differ in, in the model, is in the magnitude of their supply; some are in greater supply than others. We will index each type's supply from 1 to M, going from the smallest to the largest. So:

$$\Sigma_1 < \Sigma_2 < \Sigma_3 < \ldots \Sigma_M \tag{9.7}$$

Given our assumed technology, this implies that in a competitive equilibrium,

$$w_1 > w_2 > w_3 > \ldots w_M \tag{9.8}[3]$$

Turning from wages to profits, the marginal product of capital is solely a function of Λ/K, and so the profit rate and profit share depend solely on Λ/K:

$$\rho = q\left(\frac{\Lambda}{K}\right) - \frac{\Lambda}{K}q'\left(\frac{\Lambda}{K}\right) \tag{9.9}$$

$$\pi = 1 - \frac{\frac{\Lambda}{K}q'(\Lambda/K)}{q(\Lambda/K)} \tag{9.10}$$

The magnitude of Λ/K is, evidently, significant. And it is variable; Λ and K will be substituted for one another depending of their relative prices. The 'price of capital' here is the rate of profit, that equals the marginal product of capital. The price of Λ, denoted ξ, is the marginal product of Λ:

$$\xi \equiv q'(\Lambda/K) \tag{9.11}$$

Since Λ is wholly produced by labour it is not surprising that ξ, the price of Λ, can be shown to equal to a certain index of wage rates, ω:

$$\omega \equiv \sum \frac{L_j}{\Lambda}w_j \tag{9.12}[4]$$

Evidently, ω is an index that weights each wage rate by its labour type's average input requirement, and so ω amounts to an index of the labour cost of producing one unit of Λ. And so from a cost of production perspective, the price of Λ, ξ, will inevitably equal ω.

The degree of substitutability between Λ and K can be gauged by borrowing the ordinary 'elasticity of technical substitution' between labour and capital:[5]

$$^\Lambda\sigma \equiv \frac{\partial\frac{\Lambda}{K}\frac{\rho}{\xi}}{\partial\frac{\rho}{\xi}\frac{\Lambda}{K}} = \frac{q'\pi}{-[\Lambda/K]q''} \tag{9.13}$$

Borrowing again from the theory of two factor production functions, we can say that the profit share will be a positive (negative) function of the Λ/K according as to whether the elasticity of substitution between Λ and K is less than (greater than) one. As will be seen, the chapter's theory of the minimum wage rate produces extreme results if $^\Lambda\sigma > 1$. So we will assume henceforth that $^{\Lambda}\sigma < 1$. So, for a given K, there is a positive relation between π and Λ, and this relation proves to be significant.

Given this framework, is there some minimum wage rate, w_{MIN}, that will be preferred by a majority over all other minimum wage rates? If so, what is that minimum wage?

THE LOGIC OF THE INTERESTS

This section argues that a minimum wage will be favoured by the majority if the full employment of labour makes the output of Λ 'large' relative to K. In more economic terms: a minimum wage will characterize those economies with an abundance of labour, or a shortage of capital.

To introduce the argument, consider the electorate choosing a minimum wage just a scintilla above the competitive equilibrium wage rate of the most abundantly supplied labour type. Such a minimum wage will reduce employment amongst that labour type, M, while all other labour types remain fully employed. If we were to imagine the minimum wage rate rising further, employment of labour type M, L_M, will fall further, until employment of type M equals in size the supply of next most abundantly supplied labour, Σ_{M-1}. Any further rise in w_{MIN} will reduce the magnitude of both L_{M-1} and L_M, but with all other labour types still fully employed. Further rises in w_{MIN} will reduce L_{M-1} and L_M (and only L_{M-1} and L_M) until the common magnitude of L_{M-1} and L_M has shrunk to the supply of labour of Σ_{M-2}. A further wage rise will reduce L_M, L_{M-1} and L_{M-2} to some common magnitude. And so on.[6]

So the rising minimum wage yields a picture of unemployment 'spreading upward' from the most abundantly supplied (and lowest-paid) labour type to the less and less abundantly supplied (and better-paid) types.[7]

As the minimum wage rate rises we can say that the labour supply falls into to two categories. Firstly, there exist some types that, at the given minimum wage, are fully employed; we will call them inframarginal types. Secondly, there will exist m types of labour, each experiencing unemployment, and with a common magnitude of employment, $L_M = L_{M-1} = \ldots L_{M-m+'1}$. These types of labour we will call marginal labour.

Evidently, an increase in the minimum wage affects the marginal and inframarginal types in different ways.

For any marginal labour type a higher w_{MIN} increases their wage rate (trivially), but also reduces their employment. What is the net impact of a higher w_{MIN} on the welfare of that marginal labour type? If the employment of a given labour type is randomly allocated across the supply of the given labour type, then the evaluation of the welfare impact of a higher w_{MIN} requires only the evaluation of the elasticity of demand for that labour type to w_{MIN}, e_M^{MIN}. For that elasticity will tell whether the wage bill of the labour type has risen or fallen in the face of a higher w_{MIN} and, therefore, whether the expected wage income of the labour type has risen or fallen:[8]

> If $e_M^{MIN} > 1$ then the wage bill of marginal labour is reduced by a higher minimum wage.

> If $e_M^{MIN} < 1$ then the wage bill of marginal labour is increased by a higher minimum wage.

$$e_M^{MIN} \equiv - \frac{\partial L_M}{\partial w_{MIN}} \frac{w_{MIN}}{L_M}$$

For any inframarginal labour type, a higher w_{MIN} has no impact on their employment, but nevertheless (in general) affects their wage. The critical thing requiring evaluation is the cross-elasticity of the wage rate of the inframarginal types to w_{MIN}, as that will tell us whether the wage bill of the inframarginal marginal labour type has risen or fallen:

> If $\varepsilon_I^{MIN} > 0$ then the wage bill of the inframarginal labour type 'I' increased by a higher minimum wage.

> If $\varepsilon_I^{MIN} < 0$ then the wage bill of inframarginal labour type 'I' is reduced by a higher minimum wage.

$$\varepsilon_I^{MIN} \equiv \frac{\partial w_I}{\partial w_{MIN}} \frac{w_{MIN}}{w_I}$$

What factors determine these two elasticities?

The Elasticity of L_M to w_{MIN}

It can be shown (see Appendix) that the positivized elasticity of the demand for marginal labour[9] conforms to:

$$e_M^{MIN} = \frac{{}^L\sigma \dfrac{{}^{\wedge}\sigma}{\pi}}{s^L\sigma + [1-s]\dfrac{{}^{\wedge}\sigma}{\pi}} \tag{9.14}$$

where:

$$s \equiv \frac{mL_M^\beta}{L_1^\beta + L_2^\beta + \ldots mL_M^\beta} \tag{9.15}$$

s equals the share of the total wages bill accounted for by the wages bill of marginal labour types, and varies between zero and one.[10]

Evidently, e_M^{MIN} is a kind of average of $^L\sigma$ and $^\Lambda\sigma/\pi$. More precisely e_M^{MIN} is a 'weighted harmonic mean' of $^L\sigma$ and $^\Lambda\sigma/\pi$. Consequently $^L\sigma$ and $^\Lambda\sigma/\pi$ place an upper and lower bound on the magnitude of e_M^{MIN}, so that e_M^{MIN} is always smaller than the larger of the two, and always larger than the smaller of the two.

An important implication of e_M^{MIN} being an average of $^L\sigma$ and $^\Lambda\sigma/\pi$ is that, as $^L\sigma$ and $^\Lambda\sigma/\pi$ can both be greater (or both smaller) than one, the elasticity of marginal labour to the minimum wage rate may be either greater (or smaller) than one.

It will also prove useful to note that $^L\sigma$ and $^\Lambda\sigma/\pi$ can be interpreted as measures of two different elasticities of labour demand: one very 'narrow' and the other 'wide'. First, consider a 'narrow' elasticity: the proportionate reduction in employment of type j to the proportionate increase in wage of type j, holding all other wage rates constant, e_j^j. Supposing type j accounts for only a very small contribution to the production of Λ, and that Λ is essentially invariant to w_j, we can infer from $w_j = [\Lambda/L_j]^{1-\beta}q'(\Lambda/K)$ that:

$$e_j^j = \frac{1}{1-\beta} = {}^L\sigma \tag{9.16}$$

Now consider the proportionate decline in total employment to an equiproportionate increase in the wage rates of all labour types. This 'wide' elasticity equals $^\Lambda\sigma/\pi$.[11] Evidently, the elasticity of demand for marginal labour is the harmonic mean of these two elasticities. As s rises from zero to one, the elasticity moves from equality to the 'narrow' elasticity to an equality with the 'wide' elasticity.[12]

Finally, the elasticity of the demand for marginal labour is increasing in both $^L\sigma$ – the substitutability of labour types for each other – and $^\Lambda\sigma$ – the substitutability of 'fences' for capital. The presence of $^L\sigma$ gauges, of course, how much marginal labour is substitutable for inframarginal labour. The presence of $^\Lambda\sigma$ reflects the fact that the demand for any type of labour is a demand derived from the demand for Λ; the more sensitive the demand for Λ to its cost, the more sensitive will be the demand for any labour type to its cost.

The Cross-Elasticity of w_I to w_{MIN}

It can be shown (see Appendix) that for any inframarginal labour type the cross-elasticity of the wage of the inframarginal to the minimum wage is:

$$\varepsilon_I^{MIN} = e_M^{MIN}\frac{\partial \Lambda}{\partial L_M}\frac{L_M}{\Lambda}\frac{\left[{}^L\sigma - \dfrac{{}^\Lambda\sigma}{\pi}\right]}{{}^L\sigma\dfrac{{}^\Lambda\sigma}{\pi}} \qquad (9.17)$$

Evidently, the cross-elasticity may be either positive or negative. And this ambiguity is critical. If the cross-elasticity is positive then a rise in the minimum wage will raise the inframarginal wage, and that creates the incentive for the inframarginal types to raise the minimum wage, even though the minimum wage does not apply to them. But if it is negative, a rise in the minimum wage will reduce the inframarginal wage, and there is no incentive for the inframarginal to raise the minimum wage. Both these possibilities turn out to be important. The first explains why a minimum wage exists; the second explains why the minimum wage does not rise so high as to include everyone.

The cross-elasticity will be either positive or negative according as to whether ${}^L\sigma > {}^\Lambda\sigma/\pi$ (positive) or ${}^L\sigma < {}^\Lambda\sigma/\pi$ (negative).[13]

This conclusion can be understood as follows. An increase in w_{MIN} will reduce the employment of marginal labour, and that will have both a benefit, and cost, to the inframarginal labour types. On the one hand, the reduction in marginal labour reduces the output of Λ, thereby increases the marginal productivity of fences, and so makes inframarginal labour more valuable. This tends, obviously, to make for a positive cross-elasticity. On the other hand, a reduction in marginal labour also makes inframarginal labour less productive in making fences, because of the physical complementarity between marginal labour and inframarginal labour. This makes for a negative cross-elasticity. How the contrary effects net out will depend on the relative strength of these two effects: the sensitivity of the price of Λ to a reduction in its supply, and the degree of physical complementarity between marginal labour and inframarginal labour. These two strengths are measured by ${}^\Lambda\sigma$ and ${}^L\sigma$, respectively.

The smaller ${}^\Lambda\sigma$, the stronger the positive impact on the cross-elasticity, as the change in price of Λ associated with any change in the quantity of Λ will be larger. And the smaller ${}^L\sigma$, the stronger the negative effect, as the complementarity between labour types is larger. Thus we conclude that the cross-elasticity nets out positive the smaller ${}^\Lambda\sigma$, and the larger ${}^L\sigma$.

The differing impacts of ${}^L\sigma$ and ${}^\Lambda\sigma$ on the magnitude of the cross-elasticity might also be explained as follows: if a rival sells more cheaply than yourself, but is highly substitutable for yourself ($^L\sigma$ is large), then you will be rewarded by a rise in their wage, as that rise destroys their employability. Thus the higher $^L\sigma$ (that is, the more substitutable labour) the more likely a positive cross-elasticity. At the same time, the smaller $^A\sigma$, the less substitutable capital is for 'fences', and an increase in wage rates of marginal labour will be in larger measure 'paid for' by reduced remuneration in capital, rather than other types of labour. Thus a lower $^A\sigma$ tends to a positive cross-elasticity.

But we can see from (9.14) that the sign of the cross-elasticity depends, critically, upon one other variable apart from $^L\sigma$ and $^A\sigma$; and that is the profit share. And the profit share itself varies with ratio of Λ to K. So for a given K, $^L\sigma$ and $^A\sigma$, whether the cross-elasticity is positive or negative comes down to the magnitude of Λ. So whether the inframarginal labour type favours a wage minimum or not depends on the level of Λ.

Finally, the cross-elasticity – be it positive or negative – has the same magnitude for all inframarginal types in the model. It is not possible for one inframarginal type to have a positive cross-elasticity, while another has a negative, and there is (consequently) disagreement as to the desirability of a change in w_{MIN}. No: either all types have a positive cross-elasticity, or all types have a negative cross-elasticity; and so all inframarginal agree types as to whether they do, or do not, favour a minimum wage.

THE EXISTENCE AND CHARACTER OF A WAGE MINIMUM

Under what circumstances, then, will a majority favour the introduction of minimum wage?

The conclusion that the electorate falls into two differently affected groups, the marginal and the inframarginal, suggests weighing the electoral strength of each. However, the contrasting impacts of a minimum on the marginal and the inframarginal groups is not relevant to the circumstances under which a minimum wage will be introduced, simply because in the absence of a minimum there is no marginal group to speak of. Prior to its introduction everyone is fully employed. So the only factor that governs the introduction of a wage minimum is whether ε_I^{MIN}, the cross-elasticity between a (hypothetical) minimum wage and the inframarginal wage, is positive or negative at full employment. So, from (9.14) we may say:

If at full employment $^L\sigma > \dfrac{^A\sigma}{\pi}$ then there will be a minimum wage rate.

Evidently, we cannot relate the existence of a wage minimum unambiguously to the magnitude of any single parameter, or exogenous variable. A wage minimum may be introduced no matter how large or small is $^L\sigma$. A wage minimum may be introduced no matter how large or small is $^\Lambda\sigma$. For any parameters $^L\sigma$ and $^\Lambda\sigma$, the direction of the inequality instead hangs upon the profit share, and so the size of Λ.

Figure 9.1 is a means of conveying how the size of Λ determines the relative size of $^L\sigma$ and $^\Lambda\sigma/\pi$. It plots $^\Lambda\sigma/\pi$ against Λ. It is a negative plotting, reflecting the positive response of π to Λ on the supposition that $^\Lambda\sigma < 1$. Figure 9.1 also permits us to locate the particular magnitude of $^\Lambda\sigma/\pi$ at full employment, for the full employment of the supplies of all the various labour types implies a certain magnitude of Λ, Λ_{FE}, that can also be indicated in Figure 9.1.

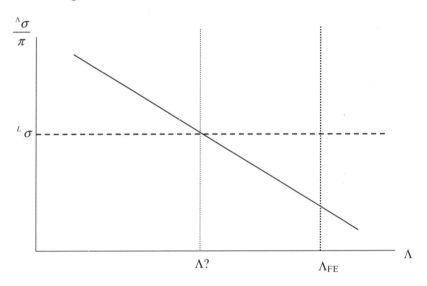

Figure 9.1   The cross-elasticity is zero at less than full employment

If we additionally indicate $^L\sigma$ in Figure 9.1 then we can compare the size of $^L\sigma$ with the size of $^\Lambda\sigma/\pi$ at full employment, and infer the cross-elasticity. Clearly in Figure 9.1, at the full employment output of Λ, the cross-elasticity is positive. Therefore 'everyone' favours some wage minimum above the market wage paid to the most abundant (and least well-paid) labour type. And so a minimum is established.

But how high will the minimum wage be? It might be that thought that the minimum wage will be increased until Λ is so low that $^\Lambda\sigma/\pi = {}^L\sigma$, and the cross-elasticity is zero. This is indicated by Λ? in Figure 9.1. All those types that are fully employed will presumably favour a minimum wage rate this high. However, the types that are fully employed might not constitute a majority. What if that median voter is a member of a labour type that is experiencing unemployment at the minimum wage that generates Λ?, and is therefore 'marginal'? Then the magnitude of the cross-elasticity would be irrelevant to their interest, and we cannot conclude that they (and so the majority) favour that minimum wage. To deal with this possibility we need to identify the employment status of the median voter. The median voter is obviously a member of the labour type 'in the middle' of the workforce. So indexing the labour types in terms of abundance, the median type of labour would be defined by this equality:

$$\Sigma_1 + \Sigma_2 + \dots \Sigma_{MEDIAN} = \Sigma/2 \qquad (9.18)^{14}$$

In order to identify the employment status of the median labour type for any magnitude of Λ, we can think of a minimum wage rate so high that all more abundant types experience unemployment, but supply of the median type is fully employed. Define Λ_{MEDIAN} as the output of Λ at that wage rate. At $\Lambda = \Lambda_{MEDIAN}$ the types of labour that are fully employed account for at least half the workforce. Figure 9.2 plots Λ_{MEDIAN}.

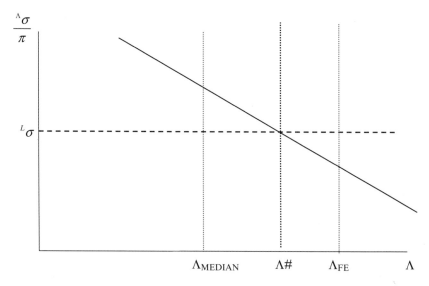

Figure 9.2   The median type is fully employed

At $\Lambda = \Lambda\#$ in Figure 9.2 the median voter is employed, and it would appear that the electoral equilibrium is a minimum wage such that

$\Lambda = \Lambda\#$. More than half the workforce consists of fully employed labour types. Thus more than half the electorate would only have their wage rate reduced by further increases in the minimum wage, and would therefore oppose it. Of course, the marginal types would want a lower minimum wage if the elasticity of marginal labour exceeds one. But they are in an electoral minority. The irrelevance of the wishes of marginal types also applies if the marginals wanted a higher minimum wage rate, as they would if the demand for marginal labour was inelastic.[15]

But the conclusion of the preceding paragraph is too hasty. For the possibility that the demand for marginal labour might be inelastic when the cross-elasticity is zero means we cannot conclude that all fully employed types would oppose a higher minimum wage when the cross-elasticity is zero. It is possible that some of those fully employed types would benefit from the minimum wage being pushed still higher; high enough to transform themselves into a marginal type, since by transforming themselves into a marginal type, they benefit from the rise in expected income that would come from a still higher wage if the demand for marginal labour was inelastic. In order to cope with this possibility we need to map e_M^{MIN} on the figure. Recall e_M^{MIN} is always smaller than the larger of $^L\sigma$ and $^\Lambda\sigma/\pi$, and always larger than the smaller of the two. 'Thus' we have the relation between e_M^{MIN} and Λ depicted in Figure 9.3.

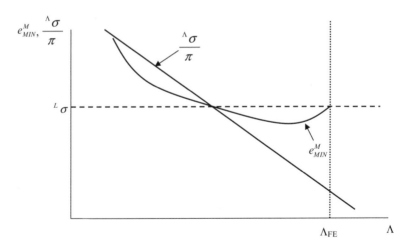

Figure 9.3   The elasticity of the demand for marginal labour is a function of L

Clearly if we suppose that e_M^{MIN} exceeds one, then marginal groups have only lost by the minimum wage and no inframarginal voter would have any incentive to make themselves marginal, and we can confidently

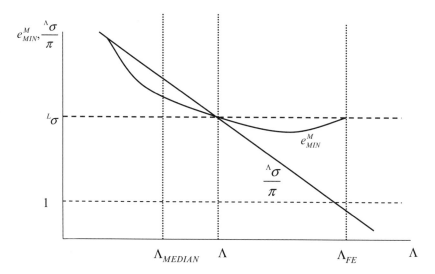

Figure 9.4   A standard equilibrium

conclude that $^{\Lambda}\sigma/\pi = {}^{L}\sigma$. Figure 9.4 depicts this situation, which we will call a standard equilibrium

Figure 9.4 completes 9.2, and helps bring out some features of the equilibrium. It brings out that the imposition of the minimum wage in this case has a distinctly antisocial aspect. For although a majority of workers are benefited by the minimum wage, the expected incomes of the lowly paid are harmed.[16] The wage rates received by the lowly paid rise, but their total wages incomes fall, since in Figure 9.4 the demand for marginal labour is elastic. All those who receive the minimum wage would be benefited by a reduction in the minimum wage. They may be benefited by its complete abolition. And they would make common cause with capital owners, who would also, of course, prefer a lower minimum wage.[17]

Figure 9.4 simply assumes that the demand for marginal labour is elastic. However, if $^{L}\sigma < 1$ then it is entirely possible that the demand for marginal labour be inelastic at the point where the cross-elasticity was zero (see Figure 9.5).[18]

In such situations as that depicted in Figure 9.5, Λ?, corresponding to $^{\Lambda}\sigma/\pi = {}^{L}\sigma$, need not necessarily constitute the equilibrium. For the fully employed types that are paid only a little more than the minimum may favour a further rise in the minimum wage rate, so as to transform themselves into a marginal labour type, and so permit themselves to share in the exploitation of the inelastic demand for marginal labour. Of course, such a wish of few fully employed labour types need not itself reverse the

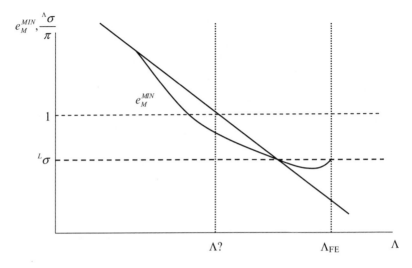

Figure 9.5   When the standard equilibrium might not be an equilibrium

majority in favour of the existing w_{MIN}. But the wish may extend beyond just a few of the worst-paid fully employed labour types; it might encompass even the median type. The median type would compare the loss in income that they would experience while w_{MIN} was being driven up to the point that they start experiencing unemployment, with the gain they would reap from then on as w_{MIN} is driven up so far that the elasticity of demand for marginal labour equals one.[19] It is possible that that this comparison would recommend even the median type wishing to be priced into unemployment.

So the model allows two possible equilibria. It is possible that the electoral equilibrium requires $^\Lambda\sigma/\pi = {}^L\sigma$. In that case the majority is not covered by the minimum wage. But it is also possible that the equilibrium is

$$\frac{{}^L\sigma\dfrac{^\Lambda\sigma}{\pi}}{\dfrac{^\Lambda\sigma}{\pi}[1-s]+s{}^L\sigma} = 1.$$

In this case less than half of the workforce is not covered; less than half make up labour types that experience full employment. But a world in which the median labour type is paid the minimum wage seems peculiar. So henceforth we will assume an equilibrium in which the minimum covers only a minority of the labour: $^\Lambda\sigma/\pi = {}^L\sigma$.

SOME PERVERSE COMPARATIVE STATICS

Supposing the equilibrium is such that $^{\Lambda}\sigma/\pi = {}^{L}\sigma$, and the majority of the labour force are not covered by the wage rate, how will changes in capital and the supply of labour affect: (1) the minimum wage; (2) the wage rates of inframarginal workers; and (3) the employment and unemployment rates of marginal workers?

An Increase in Capital

An increase in capital will increase employment and w_1, but *reduce* w_{MIN}.

This is because an increase in capital requires an equiproportionate increase in Λ in order to maintain a zero cross-elasticity between the minimum wage rate and the inframarginal wage, and so preserve electoral equilibrium. Proof: we know that the condition for a zero cross-elasticity between the minimum wage rate and the inframarginal wage is:

$$\frac{^{\Lambda}\sigma}{\pi\left(\dfrac{\Lambda}{K}\right)} = {}^{L}\sigma$$

Therefore, Λ must increase equiproportionately with K:[20]

$$\frac{\partial\Lambda}{\partial K}\frac{K}{\Lambda} = 1 \qquad (9.19)$$

But Λ can only increase by means of an increase in marginal employment. The response of Λ to marginal employment is represented by an elasticity:

$$\frac{\partial\Lambda}{\partial L_M}\frac{L_M}{\Lambda} = \frac{mL_M^{\beta}}{L_1 + \ldots L_{M-m+1} + mL_M^{\beta}} = s \qquad (9.20)[21]$$

m = number of marginal labour types.

Recall:

$$w_{MIN} = \left[\frac{\Lambda}{L_{MIN}}\right]^{1-\beta} q'\left(\frac{\Lambda}{K}\right) \qquad (9.21)$$

Thus, using equations (9.19), (9.20) and (9.21):

$$\frac{dw_{MIN}}{w_{MIN}} = \frac{d\Lambda/\Lambda - dL_M/L_M}{{}^{L}\sigma} = \frac{dK/K}{{}^{L}\sigma}[1 - 1/s] < 0 \qquad (9.22)$$

Thus the minimum wage falls with capital.[22]

What of the impact of capital growth on inframarginal wage rates? For any type I of inframarginal labour:

$$w_I = \left[\frac{\Lambda}{L_I}\right]^{1-\beta} q'\left(\frac{\Lambda}{K}\right) \qquad (9.23)$$

Given that Λ/K is fixed, and L_I is fixed we may infer:

$$\frac{\partial w_I}{\partial K}\frac{K}{w_I} = \frac{1}{{}^L\sigma} \qquad (9.24)$$

Thus inframarginal wage rates grow when capital grows, and may grow faster than capital.

To summarize, as capital grows, fully employed types experience an increase in their wage rate, and less than fully employed types experience a reduction in their wage rate.[23] How might we try to understand this last unexpected conclusion? We might begin by observing that in the absence of a reduction in w_{MIN}, an increase in K will make the cross-elasticity negative. That is because an increase in K reduces the share of Y accruing to capital. That increases the elasticity of the demand for Λ to its price, ${}^\Lambda\sigma/\pi$, that in accordance with Marshallian–Hicksian propositions rises as the proportion of costs accounted for by Λ rises. But the larger elasticity means a smaller the increase in the price of Λ consequent upon any given reduction in supply. Thus the reward for fully employed types of a higher minimum wage in terms of higher factor prices flowing from the increased price of Λ, consequent upon its reduced supply, is now smaller. Thus as the cross-elasticity was zero before, it will now be less than zero. So a reduction in the minimum wage will increase the inframarginal wage. So the minimum wage is reduced, and the inframarginal wage is increased.

It should be borne in mind that the perverse response of the minimum wage in the face of capital movements may not be contrary to the interests of marginal labour types. For the elasticity of demand for labour in this equilibrium may be elastic.

The consideration of this comparative static introduces a condition as to what circumstances will produce a minimum wage rate. This condition is a shortage of capital. In a situation where the cross-elasticity is negative at full employment (and so there is no minimum wage) a reduction in capital will reduce the wage share, thereby reduce the elasticity of the demand for Λ to its price, and so make larger the increase in the price of Λ consequent upon any reduction in its supply. A sufficiently large reduction in K will reduce the labour share so much that the cross-elasticity becomes positive at full employment, and the inframarginal types now switch to favouring a minimum wage rate. Thus a capital-stinted economy will opt for the institution of a minimum wage rate, while a capital-glutted economy will opt for its abolition. The conclusion of the previous paragraph – that an increase in K will reduce w_{MIN} – is really just a way of repeating this last conclusion.

An Increase in Labour Supplies

The analysis is congruent with the notion of earlier chapters' analyses that wages are rigid with respect to the supply of labour.

The key property is that the magnitude of Λ is strictly invariant to the supply of any type of labour; it is determined solely by the equilibrium condition, $\pi(\Lambda/K) = {}^{\Lambda}\sigma/{}^{L}\sigma$. This allows us to infer that an increase in the supply of marginal labour types has no impact on any wage rate, or employment; 'wage rigidity', in other words.

But we can also infer that an increase in the supply (and therefore the employment) of any type of inframarginal labour must mean a reduction in the employment of marginal labour, in order to leave the magnitude of Λ unchanged. Thus an increased supply of high-wage labour induces a reduction in those high wages, that prices out the employment of minimum-wage labour. By how much is minimum-wage labour displaced? We can infer:

$$m\frac{dL_M}{dL_I} = \left[\frac{L_M}{L_I}\right]^{1-\beta} \qquad (9.25)^{24}$$

As $L_M > L_I$ we conclude that any increase in inframarginal labour supply reduces employment marginal labour by more. That is, any increase in inframarginal labour supply reduces total employment.

What about the impact on wage rates? An increase in L_I must reduce I's wage rate:

$$w_I = \left[\frac{\Lambda}{L_I}\right]^{1-\beta} q'\left(\frac{\Lambda}{K}\right) \qquad (9.26)$$

All other inframarginal wages are unchanged.

And the minimum wage rate? Recall:

$$w_{MIN} = \left[\frac{\Lambda}{L_M}\right]^{1-\beta} q'\left(\frac{\Lambda}{K}\right) \qquad (9.27)$$

We have concluded that an increase in inframarginal labour supply reduces L_M. But that implies that w_{MIN} rises. Thus an increase in the supply of inframarginal labour must increase the minimum wage rate.

Finally, it is easy to appreciate that a 'neutral' increase in 'the supply of labour' – an equiproportionate increase in the supply of all labour types – reduces marginal employment, increases the minimum wage rate, and reduces the wage rates of all inframarginal labour types. Wage rates respond 'perversely' to labour supply shocks.

The consideration of this comparative static introduces a condition as to what circumstances will produce a minimum wage rate in the first place. One of them is a glut of labour. Consider: in a situation of full employment an equiproportionate increase in the supply of all labour types will reduce the labour share, reduce the elasticity of the demand for Λ to its price, and so make larger the increase in the price of Λ consequent upon any reduction in supply of Λ. The positive stimulus to inframarginal wage rates of a rise in the marginal wages would larger. So in a situation where the cross-elasticity was negative at full employment (and so there is no binding minimum wage) it will now be less negative at full employment. A sufficiently large increase in labour supplies will make the cross-elasticity positive at full emploment, and the inframarginal types will favour a minimum wage rate. Thus a labour-glutted economy will opt for the institution of a minimum wage rate, while a labour-scarce economy will opt for its abolition. Our present conclusion – that an increase in labour supplies will reduce w_{MIN} – almost just a way of repeating that previous conclusion.

Wage Rigidity (and Volatility) Again

Chapter 3 stressed how the optimal wage was completely inelastic to increases in K and the labour supply. Does such wage rigidity recur here? In an aggregate sense, yes. We have already noted that an increase in K will cause divergent movements in the wage rates of the marginal and inframarginal. But it is an easy matter to demonstrate that the weighted average of wage rates, ω, will be completely unaffected by K. Recall the index $\omega \equiv \sum L_j/\Lambda w_j = q'(\Lambda/K)$. As we have noted, Λ/K has zero elasticity to K. And Λ/K also has a zero elasticity to the change in the labour supply of any type of labour. Therefore ω has a zero elasticity to both changes in the capital stock, and the supplies of labour.[25]

CONCLUSIONS

The chapters preceding the present one explored models in which a homogeneous workforce found it advantageous to raise the wage rate above its competitive rate and brave the consequent risk of unemployment. That analysis frequently concluded that the most advantageous wage rate was completely inelastic to the supply of labour, and the quantity of capital: wage rigidity.

The present chapter has brought out that the unreal and vulnerable assumption of a completely homogeneous labour force is not necessary for those conclusions. Its simple model of labour heterogeneity demonstrates that the same implications of collective choice by the workforce – unemployment and (average) wage rigidity – occur when the labour force is not homogeneous. And those implications are no longer borne by a regulation of wage rates across the whole workforce that is at obvious variance with present-day realities. The cogency of the labour monopoly approach seems enhanced rather than depleted by allowing for heterogeneity.

NOTES

1. The suggestion that minimum wage laws have been established for the benefit of the majority not covered by them seems first to have been advanced with any tenacity by economists working in a Public Choice framework (for example Steindl 1973). After some broad a priori exploration of the notion (Keech 1977; West 1977; Browning 1978), this literature turned towards empirical investigation of the hypothesis (Sobel 1999; Blais et al. 1989). A recent a priori treatment is Danziger (2009).
2. The wage minimum that the majority chooses is assumed to be a universal minimum, and not an 'occupational' or 'labour-type-specific' minimum wage.
3. We are assuming the elasticity of substitution between labour types is finite but non-zero. If, contrary to assumption, the labour types are perfect substitutes ($^L\sigma = \infty$) then we have no wage dispersion:

$$w_1 = w_2 = w_3 = \ldots w_M$$

If, contrary to assumption, the labour types are perfect complements ($^L\sigma = 0$) then we have maximum wage inequality

$$w_1 > 0 = w_2 = w_3 = \ldots w_M.$$

4. Proof that $\xi = \omega = q'(\Lambda/K)$. Using (9.4) and (9.2):

$$\omega \equiv \sum w_j \frac{L_j}{\Lambda} = \sum \left[\frac{\Lambda}{L_j}\right]^{1-\beta} q'(\Lambda/K)\frac{L_j}{\Lambda} = \sum \frac{L_j^\beta}{\Lambda^\beta} q'(\Lambda/K) = q'(\Lambda/K)\frac{1}{\Lambda^\beta}\sum L_j^\beta$$
$$= q'(\Lambda/K) \equiv \xi.$$

5. The production function can be written $Y/K = q(\Upsilon)$, where $\Upsilon \equiv \Lambda/K$ and the two factor prices are $\rho = q(\Upsilon) - \Upsilon q'(\Upsilon)$ and $\xi = q'(\Upsilon)$ we infer:

$$^\Lambda\sigma \equiv \frac{\partial \Upsilon}{\partial[\rho/\xi]}\frac{\rho/\xi}{\Upsilon} = \frac{q'q - \Upsilon q'^2}{-\Upsilon qq''} = \frac{q'[1 - \Upsilon q'/q]}{-\Upsilon q''} = \frac{q'\pi}{-\Upsilon q''}$$

Consequently the elasticity of the demand for Λ to its price, ξ, equals $^\Lambda\sigma/\pi$.

6. Notice that no labour type is ever completely 'priced out' by the minimum wage: no type ever experiences 100 per cent unemployment.

7. A more formal case for the 'upward spread' thesis would rest on the proposition that the full employment of labour type N is a sufficient condition for the full employment of types 1 to N − 1. Proof. As $\Sigma_1 < \Sigma_2 < \Sigma_3 < \ldots \Sigma_M$ it must be that if the marginal productivity of type N evaluated at $L_N = \Sigma_N$, exceeds w_{MIN} then the marginal productivity (when fully employed) of all types with a supply smaller than Σ_N will exceed w_{MIN}. Thus if $L_N = \Sigma_N$, then $L_1 = \Sigma_1$; $L_2 = \Sigma_2$; $\ldots L_{N-1} = \Sigma_{N-1}$. Conversely, if the marginal productivity of type n, at $L_n = \Sigma_n$, is exceeded by w_{MIN} then marginal productivity of all types (when fully employed) with a supply larger than Σ_N will be exceeded by w_{MIN}. Thus if $L_N < \Sigma_N$, then $L_{N+1} < \Sigma_{N+1}$; $L_{N+2} < \Sigma_{N+2}$; $\ldots L_M < \Sigma_M$. The upshot is that unemployment can only spread consecutively; from type M to M − 1, to M − 2 and so on.

8. In measuring this elasticity there is no need to distinguish which type of marginal labour we are referring to. All marginal labour types (under our assumptions) have the same demand for labour function, and the same quantity of employment, L_M.

9. The 'elasticity' here is a particular one. We are interested in the ratio of the reduction in marginal employment relative to an increase in the minimum wage, holding constant all levels of inframarginal employment.

10. s is necessarily less than the share of total employment accounted for by marginal employment. Clearly, we would expect s to be a small magnitude 'realistically'.

11. Let $\dfrac{dw_i}{w_i} = \dfrac{dw}{w}$ for all i. Then $\dfrac{d\omega}{\omega} = \dfrac{dw}{w}$. So $\dfrac{d\Lambda}{d\Lambda} = -\dfrac{^\Lambda \sigma}{\pi} \dfrac{dw}{w}$. But given $\dfrac{dw_i}{w_i} = \dfrac{dw}{w}$ for all i, we can also say

$$\frac{dL}{L} = \frac{d\Lambda}{\Lambda},$$

    where $L \equiv \Sigma L_i$, as there will be no change in the relativities between the L_i's. Thus

$$\frac{dL}{L} = -\frac{^\Lambda \sigma}{\pi} \frac{dw}{w}.$$

12. If s = 0 then $e_{MIN}^M = {}^L \sigma$. This makes sense: when marginal employment is indistinguishable from zero, any increase must have an impact on Λ indistinguishable from zero, and so only the substitutability between labour types signifies. As s approaches 1, $e_{MIN}^M = {}^\Lambda \sigma / \pi$. This also makes sense: when all employment is marginal (and paid the same wage, w_{MIN}) there is now no possibility of substituting between labour, and only the possibility of substituting between K and Λ remains.

13. Evidently, the cross-elasticity is zero if the 'narrow' elasticity equals the 'wide elasticity'. This makes sense: if these two are equal then the decline in demand for labour j in response to an x per cent increase in wj is the same regardless of whether other labour types increase their wage rate or not. And that amounts to saying that what happens to other wage rates is irrelevant to demand for j. And that amounts to saying that the cross-elasticity is zero.

14. More exactly, the median type is defined by the two conditions $\Sigma_1 + \Sigma_2 + \ldots \Sigma_{MEDIAN} > \Sigma/2$ and $\Sigma_1 + \Sigma_2 + \ldots \Sigma_{MEDIAN-1} < \Sigma/2$.

15. Figure 9.2 brings out why the model would produce extreme results if $^\Lambda \sigma > 1$. It remains the case that if $^L \sigma > {}^\Lambda \sigma / \pi$ at full employment then the minimum wage would be imposed. But if $^\Lambda \sigma > 1$ then increasing the minimum wage would only increase $^\Lambda \sigma / \pi$, and so make the cross-elasticity still more positive, and so only increase the incentive to raise the minimum still higher. The incentive would only disappear when $\Lambda = \Lambda_{MEDIAN}$, the median type is on the verge of becoming marginal, and half the workforce is made up of types that are experiencing unemployment.

16. Note the two elasticities of the demand for labour: the 'narrow' elasticity of the demand

for type N to w_N, and the 'broad' elasticity of the total demand for labour to a rise in all wage rates, both $= {}^L\sigma$.

17. It is not necessarily true that all marginal labour types would prefer no minimum wage at all. For some may have been made better off by the chosen minimum wage as compared with the competitive outcome. Consider, for example, a type whose supply is only a tiny amount above the supply of the type that is only 'just' fully employed. They suffer only a tiny unemployment, but have a higher wage than under competition.

18. If $\dfrac{\dfrac{{}^\Lambda\sigma}{\pi}\,{}^L\sigma}{\dfrac{{}^\Lambda\sigma}{\pi}[1-s]+s{}^L\sigma} < 1$ when $\dfrac{{}^\Lambda\sigma}{\pi} = {}^L\sigma$ then ${}^L\sigma < 1$.

19. In fact, it seems possible that all types of labour might find advantage in making themselves marginal, and experiencing unemployment, paid at the 'minimum wage' (which would apply to all).

20. This argument suggests that the elasticity of technical substitution must be parametrical to secure the conclusion. But it need not. Unpacking the elasticity of technical substitution, a zero cross-elasticity requires $-\Lambda q''(\Lambda/K)/[q'(\Lambda/K)K] = 1 - \beta$. Clearly Λ must be unit elastic to K, regardless of whether or not the elasticity of technical substitution is parametrical.

21. $$\frac{\partial\Lambda}{\partial L_M}\frac{L_M}{\Lambda} = mL_M^{\beta-1}[L_1 + \ldots L_{M-m+1} + mL_M^\beta]^{1/\beta-1}\frac{L_M}{[L_1 + \ldots L_{M-m+1} + mL_M^\beta]^{1/\beta}}$$
$$= \frac{mL_M^\beta}{\ldots + mL_M^\beta}$$

22. More precisely:
$$\frac{dw_M}{dK}\frac{K}{w_M} = -\frac{1}{{}^L\sigma}\frac{\text{Average } w_I}{w_{MIN}}\frac{L_{INFRA}}{L_{MARGINAL}} < 0.$$

23. Check: we know the profit rate is unaffected by the increase in K. But the profit rate cannot be unaffected if all wage rates rise (or all wage rates fall). Some wage rates rise (those of the inframarginal), and one wage rate falls (the marginal), leaving the profit rate unaltered.

24. We know:
$$\Lambda = [\sum_j L_j^\beta]^{1/\beta}$$

Thus:

$$[L_I^{\beta-1}dL_I + mL_M^{\beta-1}dL_M][\sum_j L_j^\beta]^{1/\beta-1} = 0$$

25. Chapter 4 stressed that the optimal wage rate would move up and down in tandem with some shocks, such as Hicks-neutral technology shocks, with employment registering no change at all. The same is true in the present model. Hicks-neutral progress amounts to the equal augmentation of K and Λ, and is represented by writing $Y = \eta Kq(\Lambda/K)$, while leaving $\Lambda = [\sum_j L_j^\beta]^{1/\beta}$. The condition ${}^\Lambda\sigma/\pi(\Lambda/K) = {}^L\sigma$ leaves Λ/K unaltered by the shock to η, and therefore Λ unaltered by the shock to η. But $w_j = [\Lambda/L_j]^{1-\beta}\eta q'(\Lambda/K)$. Thus the wage rate for reach type increases by η, and the employment for each type remains exactly unchanged.

APPENDIX

The Elasticity of the Demand for a Marginal Labour Type

$$w_j = \left[\frac{\Lambda}{L_j}\right]^{1-\beta} q'\left(\frac{\Lambda}{K}\right) \tag{A9.1}$$

Substituting out Λ and choosing units so that $K = 1$:

$$w_j = L_j^{\beta-1}[L_1^{\beta} + \ldots L_j^{\beta} + \ldots L_k^{\beta}]^{1/\beta-1} q'([L_1^{\beta} + \ldots L_j^{\beta} + \ldots L_k^{\beta}]^{1/\beta}) \tag{A9.2}$$

As the employment levels of all m marginal labour types is the same, L_M:

$$w_{MIN} = L_M^{\beta-1}[L_1^{\beta} + L_2^{\beta} + \ldots mL_M^{\beta}]^{1/\beta-1} q'([L_1^{\beta} + L_2^{\beta} + \ldots mL_M^{\beta}]^{1/\beta}) \tag{A9.3}$$

Thus:

$$\frac{L_M}{w_{MIN}} \frac{dw_{MIN}}{dL_M}$$

$$= \frac{[\beta - 1]L_M^{\beta-1}\Lambda^{1-\beta}q'(\Lambda) + L_M^{\beta-1}L_M[\Lambda^{1-\beta}q''(\Lambda) + [1 - \beta]\Lambda^{-\beta}q']\dfrac{\partial\Lambda}{\partial L_M}}{L_M^{\beta-1}\Lambda^{1-\beta}q'(\Lambda)} \tag{A9.4}$$

so:

$$\frac{L_M}{w_{MIN}} \frac{dw_{MIN}}{dL_M} = \beta - 1 + \frac{L_M[\Lambda^{1-\beta}q''(\Lambda) + [1 - \beta]\Lambda^{-\beta}q']\dfrac{\partial\Lambda}{\partial L_M}}{\Lambda^{1-\beta}q'(\Lambda)} \tag{A9.5}$$

or:

$$-\frac{L_M}{w_{MIN}} \frac{\partial w_{MIN}}{\partial L_M} = \frac{1}{{}^L\sigma} + \frac{L_M}{\Lambda} \frac{\partial\Lambda}{\partial L_M}\left[\frac{\pi}{{}^\Lambda\sigma} - \frac{1}{{}^L\sigma}\right] \tag{A9.6}$$

As:

$$\Lambda = [L_1^{\beta} + L_2^{\beta} + L_3^{\beta} + mL_M^{\beta}]^{1/\beta} \tag{A9.7}$$

$$\frac{L_M}{\Lambda} \frac{\partial\Lambda}{\partial L_M} = \frac{mL_M^{\beta}}{L_1^{\beta} + L_2^{\beta} + \ldots mL_M^{\beta}} \tag{A9.8}$$

so:

$$-\frac{L_M}{w_{MIN}}\frac{\partial w_{MIN}}{\partial L_M} = \frac{1}{^L\sigma} + \frac{mL_M^\beta}{L_1^\beta + L_2^\beta + \ldots mL_M^\beta}\left[\frac{\pi}{^\Lambda\sigma} - \frac{1}{^L\sigma}\right] \quad (A9.9)$$

The positivized elasticity of demand for marginal labour:

$$-\frac{w_{MIN}}{L_M}\frac{\partial L_M}{\partial w_{MIN}} = \frac{^L\sigma^\Lambda\sigma}{^\Lambda\sigma + s^L\sigma\pi - s\dfrac{^\Lambda\sigma}{\pi}} \quad (A9.10)$$

The Cross-Elasticity of Inframarginal Wage to Minimum Wage

Choosing units so that K = 1:

$$w_I = L_I^{\beta-1}\Lambda^{1-\beta}q'(\Lambda) \quad (A9.11)$$

$$\frac{\partial w_I}{\partial L_M} = L_I^{\beta-1}\left[\frac{\partial \Lambda}{\partial L_M}\right][\Lambda^{1-\beta}q''(\Lambda) + [1-\beta]\Lambda^{-\beta}q'(\Lambda)] \quad (A9.12)$$

$$\frac{\partial w_I}{\partial w_{MIN}} = \frac{\partial w_I}{\partial L_M}\frac{\partial L_M}{\partial w_{MIN}} = \frac{\partial L_M}{\partial w_{MIN}}L_I^{\beta-1}\left[\frac{\partial \Lambda}{\partial L_M}\right][\Lambda^{1-\beta}q''(\Lambda) + [1-\beta]\Lambda^{-\beta}q'(\Lambda)] \quad (A9.13)$$

$$\frac{\partial w_I}{\partial w_{MIN}}\frac{w_{MIN}}{w_I} = \frac{\partial L_M}{\partial w_{MIN}}\frac{w_{MIN}}{L_M}\left[\frac{\partial \Lambda}{\partial L_M}\frac{L_M}{\Lambda}\right]\left[\Lambda\frac{q''(\Lambda)}{q'(\Lambda)} + [1-\beta]\right] \quad (A9.14)$$

$$\frac{\partial w_I}{\partial w_{MIN}}\frac{w_{MIN}}{w_I} = -\frac{\partial L_M}{\partial w_{MIN}}\frac{w_{MIN}}{L_M}\left[\frac{\partial \Lambda}{\partial L_M}\frac{L_M}{\Lambda}\right]\left[-\Lambda\frac{q''(\Lambda)}{q'(\Lambda)} - [1-\beta]\right] \quad (A9.15)$$

$$\frac{\partial w_I}{\partial w_{MIN}}\frac{w_{MIN}}{w_I} = e_M^{MIN}\frac{\partial \Lambda}{\partial L_M}\frac{L_M}{\Lambda}\left[\frac{\pi}{^\Lambda\sigma} - \frac{1}{^L\sigma}\right] = e_M^{MIN}\frac{\partial \Lambda}{\partial L_M}\frac{L_M}{\Lambda}\frac{\left[^L\sigma - \dfrac{^\Lambda\sigma}{\pi}\right]}{^L\sigma\dfrac{^\Lambda\sigma}{\pi}} \quad (A9.16)$$

10.   Rigidity and volatility in the face of the cycle: a neoklassikal[1] analysis

This chapter seeks to give the labour monopoly theory a greater resonance with common appearances by relaxing a certain assumption that has so far been maintained throughout: that the marginal productivity of labour diminishes. This assumption has been key; it is the diminishing marginal productivity of labour that yields the labour demand curve that the labour monopoly exploits. This assumption is also near universal. But its relaxation is, nevertheless, warranted. Considerations of 'realism' suggest that we do not exist in a twice-differentiable world, but one dominated by linearity (constant marginal cost) and zero substitutability (fixed coefficients). Still more importantly, the twice-differentiable aggregate production function sits awkwardly with the observed behaviour of labour demand. For the twice-differentiable aggregate production function makes the labour demand schedule solely a matter of technical knowledge and the size of capital stock; both of which might be thought to change slowly, more slowly than the sudden movements in labour demand observed during the business cycle. To put the point another way: the very real wage rigidity that will predict unemployment under the twice-differentiable production function will also predict a degree of 'employment rigidity' that is not commonly observed. Must the labour monopoly account of unemployment be hostage to such a doubtful model of labour demand?

This chapter therefore investigates whether the labour monopoly account of unemployment can extend to an economy where a marginal productivity theory of wages does hold on account of fixed coefficient technologies: a 'neoklassikal economy'. It asks: will a labour monopolist face a well-defined negative labour demand schedule in spite of fixed coefficients? If so, will demand be inelastic, and so provide the labour monopolist with the incentive to create unemployment by choosing a wage above the competitive level? And if it does have that incentive, will the chosen wage be rigid, or volatile, or something else? The analysis concludes that in many respects the fixed coefficient neoklassikal model reproduces the results of the ordinary neoclassical model.

It will be argued, further, that the neoklassikal model is not merely a replicator of the neoclassical model, but also constitutes a more suitable

184

vehicle for the appraisal of the remedy for unemployment by means of government spending. For not only does the model 'take unemployment seriously' by allowing for its existence; it is also not tied to the 'employment rigidity' of ordinary neoclassical models but instead admits some of the flavour of Keynesian models by predicting that unemployment will be responsive to expectations about the future profitability of investment. All the more interesting, therefore, are the model's anti-Keynesian conclusions concerning the government spending multiplier. In the neoklassikal model an increase in government purchases will reduce total employment.

THE ELEMENTS OF A NEOKLASSIKAL GROWTH MODEL

This section presents the chapter's 'neoklassikal' model; one that makes all the standard neoclassical assumptions (utility maximization, perfect foresight, price-taking firms) save one: instead of the neoclassical twice-differentiable aggregate production function, the model assumes a 'klassikal' fixed coefficient technology operating in two sectors: consumption goods and capital goods.[2]

The economy has two outputs; consumption and capital. The production of a units of consumption requires one unit of capital and b units of labour, to operate the capital. There is no possibility of substituting labour for capital in the production of consumption: the isoquants are L-shaped, and there is no 'marginal product of labour'. Thus as long as capital is not a free good, the production of consumption is:

$$C_t = aK_t \qquad (10.1)$$

The production of one unit of capital requires one unit of labour, and no other input. So we could imagine a labourer fashioning with their hands 'a machine'. A unit of capital evaporates at rate d.[3] Thus the quantity of capital in the next period will equal $1 - d$ of capital in the current period plus the production of capital this period. Since the production of capital equals total employment minus employment in the consumption sector, bK, we have.

$$K_{t+1} = K_t[1 - d] + L_t - bK_t \qquad (10.2)$$

The growth of consumption is determined by maximization of an identical homothetic utility function:

$$U = C_t^\alpha + \frac{C_{t+1}^\alpha}{1 + \delta} + \frac{C_{t+2}^\alpha}{[1 + \delta]^2} + \ldots \tag{10.3}$$

by a given cohort of infinitely lived persons under 'perfect capital markets'. Thus:

$$\frac{C_{t+1}^1}{C_t^1} = \left[\frac{1 + \rho_t}{1 + \delta}\right]^\varsigma \tag{10.4}$$

$$\varsigma \equiv \frac{1}{1 - \alpha}$$

This equality expresses the paradigmatic neoclassical explanation of the valuation of future consumption in terms of current consumption, $1/[1 + \rho]$. The value of future consumption in terms of current consumption falls as future consumption becomes more plentiful, and current consumption scarcer.

The rate of profit also must equal the relativity between the pay-off from producing a machine and the cost of producing it:

$$1 + \rho_t = \frac{\alpha - bw_{t+1} + [1 - d]\xi_{t+1}}{w_t} \tag{10.5}$$

$\xi_t \equiv$ price of unit of capital in terms of consumption in t

As long as some capital is produced in t + 1 then the price of capital must match its cost of production:

$$\xi_{t+1} = w_{t+1} \tag{10.6}$$

thus:

$$1 + \rho_t = \frac{a + [1 - b - d]w_{t+1}}{w_t} \tag{10.7}$$

The model is completed by invoking a wage-setting process.

COMPETITIVE WAGE-SETTING: A FULL-EMPLOYMENT MODEL

Suppose, to begin, that wages instantly adjust to secure full employment. Then we may write:

$$L_t = \Sigma \tag{10.8}$$

and:

$$K_{t+1} = \Sigma + [1 - b - d]K_t \qquad (10.9)$$

Equation (10.9) is the 'equation of motion' in the capital stock. It is a first-order difference equation with the solution:

$$K_t = \left[K(0) - \frac{\Sigma}{b + d}\right][1 - b - d]^t + \frac{\Sigma}{b + d} \qquad (10.10)$$

Evidently, the profile of capital over time is entirely determined by $K(0)$, Σ, b and d, and is entirely independent of preference parameters, δ and σ. As long as $K/\Sigma < 1/b + d$, K will grow over time until a steady state quantity of capital is reached:

$$K_{SS} = \frac{\Sigma}{b + d} \qquad (10.11)$$

Unlike the neoclassical Ramsey–Solow model this steady state is not a matter of an equality between the rate of time preference and the marginal product of capital; for there is no marginal product of capital. And unlike the classical Ricardian model the steady state is not a result of a parity between the marginal product of labour and the wage at which the population growth is zero; for there is no marginal product of labour. Rather, the steady state occurs because so much capital has been produced that the entire workforce is absorbed in either operating the existing capital, or in building machines to replace those that wear out. So there is no labour left over to add to the capital stock.

Since $C_t = aK_t$ the path of consumption exactly tracks the quantity of capital:

$$\frac{C_{t+1}}{C_t} = \frac{K_{t+1}}{K_t} \qquad (10.12)^4$$

But the growth in consumption governs the rate of profit through the equimarginal condition of utility maximization. So by (10.4), (10.9) and (10.12) we can infer:

$$\frac{1 + \rho_t}{1 + \delta} = \left[\frac{\Sigma}{K_t} + 1 - b - d\right]^{1/\varsigma} \qquad (10.13)$$

Equation (10.13) evidently determines the rate of profit in any period t. It indicates that the rate of profit at any period t is a negative function of b; the more labour absorbed in the production of consumption the less there is available to build new machines, and so the smaller the rate of increase in C, and so the smaller ρ. The rate of profit at any period t is also a positive function of the rate of time preference,[5] and a diminishing function of the elasticity of intertemporal substitution (assuming the rate of profit exceeds the rate of time preference).

Critically, (10.13) also indicates that the rate of profit at any period t is a negative function of the quantity of capital per unit of labour supply. Thus as K/Σ rises over time, the profit rate falls over time until the steady state quantity of capital is reached, yielding a steady state rate of profit:

$$\rho_{ss} = \delta \qquad (10.14)^6$$

So although there is no equality in the steady state between the rate of time preference and a (non-existent marginal) product of capital, there is an equality of the rate of profit and the rate of time preference.

The determination of profit allows for the determination of the wage rate. The expression for the actual rate of profit rate (10.7) can be rewritten as an expression for the wage rate:

$$w_t = \frac{a}{1 + \rho_t} + \frac{[1 - b - d]w_{t+1}}{1 + \rho_t} \qquad (10.15)$$

Repeated leading and substitution yields:

$$w_t = \frac{a}{1 + \rho_t} + \frac{[1 - b - d]a}{[1 + \rho_t][1 + \rho_{t+1}]} + \frac{[1 - b - d]^2a}{[1 + \rho_t][1 + \rho_{t+1}][1 + \rho_{t+2}]} + \ldots \qquad (10.16)$$

We see that the wage rate equals a sort of 'discounted' product of capital. Given (10.10) and the expression for the rate of profit in any period $t + i$, $1 + \rho_{t+i} = [\Sigma/K_{t+i} + 1 - b - d]^{1/\varsigma}[1 + \delta]$, the wage in t can be boiled down to an expression composed solely of parameters and the quantity of capital in t.[7,8] And given the monotonic fall in the rate of profit over time as capital rises over time to its steady state, the wage raises over time. It ultimately assumes its own steady state value:

$$w_{ss} = \frac{a}{\delta + b + d} \qquad (10.17)$$

Table 10.1 illustrates the path that key variables take in the passage to full employment.

Table 10.1 also underlines how the competitive equilibrium of this

Table 10.1   A numerical illustration of the approach to the neoklassikal steady state

K	C	I	Y	ρ	w	π	q
100	30.0	10.4	40.4	408.0	0.093	0.66	4.35
213	63.8	19.3	83.1	99.2	0.275	0.50	1.42
283	84.8	17.4	102.3	50.1	0.397	0.42	0.91
327	98.0	13.0	111.0	32.2	0.473	0.36	0.72
354	106.3	8.9	115.2	23.6	0.521	0.32	0.62
371	111.4	5.9	117.3	19.0	0.551	0.30	0.57
382	114.6	3.8	118.5	16.4	0.569	0.28	0.54
389	116.6	2.4	119.1	14.9	0.581	0.27	0.53
393	117.9	1.5	119.4	14.0	0.588	0.26	0.52
396	118.7	1.0	119.7	13.4	0.592	0.26	0.51

Note: a = 0.3, b + d = 0.375, δ = 0.125, ç = 0.5, Σ = 150, q ≡ wK/Y

neoklassikal model mimics the standard neoclassical model: a falling profile of profit, a rising profile of the wage, a rising capital per head; all flattening out at steady state values.

The question that remains is: will the neoklassikal model mimic the standard neoclassical model under conditions of labour monopoly?

WAGE BILL MAXIMIZING WAGE DETERMINATION: AN UNEMPLOYMENT MODEL

Suppose now that the wage is not set competitively, but to maximize the wage bill in the current period.

Employment is now an endogenous variable, but employment cannot be a matter of the equality of the real wage with a (non-existent) marginal product of labour. Employment is the outcome of two separate considerations. Employment is the sum of 'consumption sector labour':

$$L_{C,t} = bK_t \tag{10.18}$$

plus 'investment sector labour':

$$L_{I,t} = K_{t+1} - [1 - d]K_t \tag{10.19}$$

Consumption sector labour is completely inelastic to the wage rate, at least until the wage is so high that profit on producing consumer goods has shrunk to zero. Investment sector labour, however, is negatively related to the wage rate. The logic is that a higher wage spells a lower profit rate, and so a lower growth rate in consumption, and so a lower growth rate in capital, and so less investment, and so less investment labour. And so less total labour. Algebraically:

$$\frac{a + [1 - b - d]w_{t+1}}{[1 + \delta]w_t} = \frac{1 + \rho_t}{1 + \delta}$$

and invoking in turn:

$$\left[\frac{1 + \rho_t}{1 + \delta}\right]^\varsigma = \frac{C_{t+1}}{C_t}$$

and:

$$\frac{C_{t+1}}{C_t} = \frac{K_{t+1}}{K_t}$$

and:

$$\frac{K_{t+1}}{K_t} = \frac{L_t}{K_t} + 1 - b - d$$

yielding:

$$\frac{L_t}{K_t} = \left[\frac{a + [1 - b - d]w_{t+1}}{w_t[1 + \delta]}\right]^\varsigma - 1 + b + d_t \qquad (10.20)$$

Equation (10.20) is the neoklassikal labour demand function. As we might expect of a labour demand function, total demand for labour is in any given period is negatively related to that period's *w*. This solely reflects the reduction of investment labour as w rises; the demand for consumption labour is perfectly inelastic to w, until w reaches the average product of labour in consumption production, above which the demand for consumption labour shrinks to zero. Figure 10.1 illustrates.

The elasticity of the labour demand implied by (10.20) is:

$$e_t = \frac{\varsigma\left[\dfrac{a + [1 - b - d]w_{t+1}}{[1 + \delta]w_t}\right]^\varsigma}{\left[\dfrac{a + [1 - b - d]w_{t+1}}{[1 + \delta]w_t}\right]^\varsigma - 1 + b + d} \qquad (10.21)[9]$$

Using (10.22), the elasticity may be expressed more compactly as a function of the employment–capital ratio:

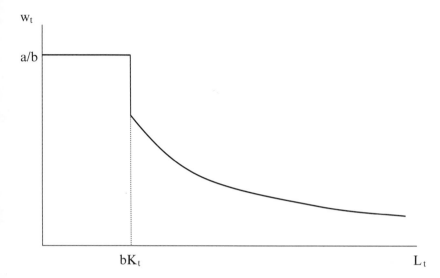

Figure 10.1 The neoklassikal demand for labour schedule

$$e_t = \frac{\varsigma\left[\dfrac{L_t}{K_t} + 1 - b - d\right]}{\dfrac{L_t}{K_t}} \qquad (10.22)$$

The elasticity of labour demand is a negative function of the labour–capital ratio, just as in the standard neoclassical 'twice-differentiable' case. At full employment the elasticity equals:

$$e_t = \varsigma\left[1 + [1 - b - d]\frac{K_t}{\Sigma}\right] \qquad (10.23)^{10}$$

Evidently, the elasticity of labour demand at full employment is a positive function of the ratio of capital to the labour force (see Figure 10.2).

Evidently, there is some critical ratio capital per unit of labour supply $K_{CRITICAL}/\Sigma$ such that the elasticity of demand at full employment equals one:

$$\frac{K_{CRITICAL}}{\Sigma} = \frac{1}{1 - b - d}\frac{1 - \varsigma}{\varsigma} \qquad (10.24)$$

For any quantity of capital greater than $K_{CRITICAL}$, then the elasticity of demand for labour at full employment will exceed one, and a wage bill maximizing labour monopoly would have no incentive to raise the wage

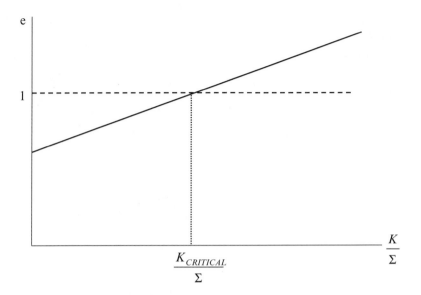

*Figure 10.2   The elasticity of labour demand at full employment rises with
capital intensity*

rate above the full employment rate. So for any quantity of capital greater
than $K_{CRITICAL}$ there is full employment. But for any quantity of capital
less than $K_{CRITICAL}$ the elasticity of demand for labour at full employment
will be less than one. So for any quantity of capital less than the critical
amount a wage bill maximizer would exploit the resulting inelasticity by
contracting employment below full employment until the elasticity of
labour demand equals one.

$$L_t = \frac{\varsigma}{1 - \varsigma}[1 - b - d]K_t \qquad (10.25)$$

Equation (10.25) states the wage bill maximizing level of employment.

Evidently wage bill maximizing employment tracks capital. But K must
grow as C grows, and C will grow according to the relativity of the rate of
profit to the rate of time preference. What will be that relativity? This may
be inferred from the elasticity as it may also be written as:

$$e_t = \frac{\varsigma\left[\dfrac{1 + \rho}{1 + \delta}\right]^\varsigma}{\left[\dfrac{1 + \rho}{1 + \delta}\right]^\varsigma - 1 + b + d} \qquad (10.26)$$

From (10.26) we can infer the 'critical rate of profit' that makes $e = 1$, and which the actual profit equals as long as there is unemployment:

$$\left[\frac{1 + \rho_{CRITICAL}}{1 + \delta}\right]^\varsigma = \frac{1 - b - d}{1 - \varsigma} \qquad (10.27)$$

Therefore recalling

$$\left[\frac{1 + \rho_t}{1 + \delta}\right]^\varsigma = \frac{C_{t+1}}{C_t}$$

we may write:

$$\frac{K_{t+1}}{K_t} = \frac{C_{t+1}}{C_t} = \frac{1 - \beta - d}{1 - \varsigma} \qquad (10.28)$$

K grows until ultimately $K = K_{CRITICAL}$, at which point the elasticity of demand is unit at full employment, and the economy has 'grown out of unemployment', just as the economy did in the Ramsey–Solow model dealt with in Chapter 6.[11]

The fact that $\rho = \rho_{CRITICAL}$ during unemployment allows the determination of the wage rate with the help of (10.15):

$$w_{t+1} = \frac{1 + \rho_{CRITICAL}}{1 - b - d}w_t - a \qquad (10.29)$$

It will be seen that there is no such thing as 'the' wage bill maximizing wage rate. Rather 'the' wage bill maximizing wage rate grows over time according to (10.29), until it equals $w_{CRITICAL}$ in the period that full employment is reached.[12]

RIGIDITY AND VOLATILITY IN WAGE RATES AND EMPLOYMENT

We have seen in the previous section how in the neoklassikal model wage bill maximization may reduce employment, but the wage strategy that secures the wage bill maximizing level of employment has not yet been discussed.

Under the 'twice-differentiable production' wage bill maximization was secured by several distinct strategies, depending on the shock in question. In the face of capital shocks, to illustrate, a strategy of wage rigidity was maximizing. But in the face of technical change a strategy of wage volatility was maximizing.

Some of the wage bill maximization strategies of those of the neo-classical model recur in the neoklassikal model, and some do not.

Wage rigidity is not wage bill maximizing for any shock in the neoklassikal model. In the ordinary neoclassical model wage rate was rigid to shocks in the capital stock, but this is not so here. Employment is unit elastic to the capital stock (as before), but as the wage rate now grows with the capital stock during the phase of unemployment, and we can infer that a higher K entails a higher w.

But wage volatility is wage bill maximizing for some shocks in the neoklassikal model. We can tell this because there are parameters that appear in the demand for labour expression (10.20), but do not appear in the expression for employment (10.25), indicating that these parameters' impacts are entirely neutralized by compensating movements in the wage rate. These are a and δ.

'The Productivity of Capital', a

An increase in the 'productivity of capital' shifts the demand for labour outwards, but in the context of wage bill maximization, this will have no impact on the level of employment (see 10.25). Neither will it have any impact on the growth of the capital stock, either during unemployment or after the achievement of full employment. What it will impact on is on the wage rate. The wage rate takes all the burden of adjustment, when the productivity of capital rises so as to keep employment exactly unaltered, and downwards when the productivity of capital falls, so as to keep employment exactly unaltered. We are evidently in a realm of wage volatility.

The parallel wage volatility of the present neoklassikal model and the wage volatility of Chapter 4's neoclassical model becomes clearer as soon as it is appreciated that to refer to a as the 'productivity of capital' is a misnomer. For an increase in a not only increases product per machine, it also provides an equal proportionate increase in the product per unit of labour in the consumption sector. It is a 'neutral' augmentation of both capital and labour, that we saw in Chapter 4.

The Rate of Time Preference, δ

An increase in the rate of time preference shifts the demand for labour inwards but will have no effect on the level of employment. Neither will it have any impact on the growth of the capital stock, either during unemployment or after the achievement of full employment. What it will impact on is on the wage rate, that takes all the burden of adjustment. So what might be expected to be contractionary in its effect on employment, induces a wage response that neutralizes it. We are still in a realm of wage volatility.[13]

Just as some shocks have their employment impact completely neutralized by the induced wage response, so there are other shocks that have no employment impact in the absence of induced wage response, but creates an employment impact through the wage response it induces. To illustrate, consider now varying the maintained assumption that one unit of labour builds one machine. Suppose that in the current period one unit of investment labour produces Γ units of machine. Evidently:

$$\frac{\Gamma L_t}{K_t} = \left[\frac{a + [1 - b - d]w_{t+1}}{\frac{w_t}{\Gamma}[1 + \delta]} \right]^\varsigma - 1 + b + d_t \qquad (10.30)$$

What is $\partial L/\partial \Gamma$? Evaluated at the wage rate that maximizes the wage bill $\partial L/\partial \Gamma = 0$, that is, holding wage rate at the level that was optimal prior to the shock, a temporary increase in the productivity of labour in producing machines would have no impact on employment. However, the wage rate will not be held at the level that was optimal prior to the shock. Wage bill maximization will induce the wage rate to be increased in response to the shock. And the consequence of that is that employment falls. Formally:

$$e_t = \varsigma\left[1 + [1 - b - d]\frac{K_t}{\Gamma L_t} \right] \qquad (10.31)$$

so to keep e = 1 then an increase in Γ must reduce total employment in proportion. The upshot is that ΓL is completely unaltered. And so total investment is unchanged. Thus K_{t+1} is unchanged. Thus w_{t+1} is unchanged. And inspecting (10.30), we see that if ΓL is unchanged and w_{t+1} is unchanged, then the wage must have risen. The fall in employment is all the work of the reaction of the labour monopolist.

To summarize, in the neoklassikal model wage bill maximization is not simply a matter of wage rigidity. Quite the contrary: for all shocks considered, wage rate will move in response. But, critically, the movement is not to serve the purpose of market equilibration, but to maximize the wage bill. Thus employment does not match the labour supply, but: (1) will move unit elastically to capital; (2) will have a zero elasticity to neutral change; and (3) will move with a negative unit elasticity to augmentations of labour in the investment sector.

THE GOVERNMENT SPENDING MULTIPLIER: THE PEGGED WAGE CASE

The previous sections' 'neoklassikal model' has painted a picture of the impact of wage bill maximization on employment similar to that implied by the neoclassical growth model. But the neoklassikal labour demand function does not merely replicate the neoclassical model. It awards significance to a range of variables in affecting labour demand beyond current technology and capital stock. Recall (10.20):

$$\frac{L_t}{K_t} = \left[\frac{a + [1 - b - d]w_{t+1}}{w_t[1 + \delta]} \right]^{\varsigma} - 1 + b + d$$

There are preference variables present: δ and ς There are variables which are future-orientated: w_{t+1}. There are variables that come down to predictions about future technology: for a is not a current variable but refers to how much a machine is believed to produce in the future. And the b that pre multiplies w_{t+1} also refers to the amount of labour that is believed to be needed to operate a machine in the future. Evidently, for given w_t and w_{t+1}, favourable movements in expectations about a and future b will stimulate investment and so employment.

The responsiveness of neoklassikal labour demand to perceptions of the future makes the neoklassikal model a better vehicle than the neoclassical model for explaining cyclical movements in unemployment that seem to be so much a matter of perceptions. It might also make it a better candidate vehicle for scrutinizing mooted remedies for cyclical unemployment, such as government spending.

This section therefore turns to appraising the government spending multiplier in the context of the neoklassikal model of labour demand. We first examine the implications of the neoklassikal model for the multiplier under the assumption that the wage rate is arbitrarily pegged. In the following section we endogenize the wage rate by invoking labour monopoly.

A Fiscal Framework

A sound analysis of the government spending multiplier calls for some of characterization of the spending. The simplest way to think about G is to suppose that the government purchases G of consumption output, and throws it away. To conceive of G as the government purchasing consumer goods, and throwing them away, may seem an assumption that is 'biased' against the Keynesian doctrine. But the Keynesian doctrine of the government spending multiplier should not be identified with the mere contention that more government spending might be a good thing. Everyone, presumably, will allow that in certain circumstances it might be a good thing for the government to build (say) more bridges. The Keynesian doctrine is much more surprising: it contends that in times of unemployment it will be good thing to spend money 'uselessly'; to pay people to dig holes, and fill them up again.[14] To pay someone to do that is no different from paying someone to make a widget, and then smash it. So we will proceed in this section on the assumption that this is what government 'demand' amounts to, and later analyse the multiplier when G consists of the hiring of persons onto the government payroll and their payment.

A sound analysis of the government spending multiplier also requires a characterization of the financing of G. The simplest way of thinking about that is to suppose a flat tax. But the analysis would be unaltered if we supposed G was financed by a consumption tax at such a rate as to yield revenues of G. And, if householders have foresight of their future tax liabilities, then the analysis would also be unaltered if we supposed that G was financed by government borrowing, as long as the future tax burden is financed by a consumption tax.

A Temporary Shock to G

Suppose now that the government decides to spend G, in real terms, in the current period, but not other periods. Under the fiscal framework assumed in the preceding subsection, the consumption growth rate equation is now altered to:

$$\frac{C_{t+1}}{C_t} = \frac{aK_{t+1}}{aK_t - G} \tag{10.32}$$

Thus the employment equation becomes:

$$\frac{L_t}{K_t} = \left[1 - \frac{G}{aK_t}\right]\left[\frac{a + [1 - b - d]w_{t+1}}{w_t[1 + \delta]}\right]^\varsigma - 1 + b + d \tag{10.33}$$

Evidently, employment for a given wage is reduced by G. Equivalently, the wage rate for a given level of employment is reduced by G. Why? Anyone who pays labour to build a machine is effectively sacrificing current consumption for the sake of future consumption. How much you are willing to pay that labour is dictated by how much you value future consumption, in terms of current consumption. But the value of future consumption, in terms of current consumption, is reduced on account of the reduction in current consumption forced by higher G. Thus the demand price of labour is reduced by higher G. Thus, for a given wage, employment falls.

A Permanent Shock to G

Suppose now that the government decides to spend G, in real terms, in all periods.

The consumption growth rate equation is now altered to:

$$\frac{C_{t+1}}{C_t} = \frac{K_{t+1} - G/a}{K_t - G/a} \tag{10.34}$$

and so:

$$\frac{L_t}{K_t} = \left[1 - \frac{G}{aK_t}\right]\left[\frac{a + [1 - b - d]w_{t+1}}{w_t[1 + \delta]}\right]^s - 1 + b + d + \frac{G}{aK_t} \tag{10.35}$$

Evidently, the net effect of a permanent increase in G on labour demand is negative; employment for a given wage is reduced by G. This is because, in a growing economy, any permanent reduction in C of a given absolute magnitude will increase the ratio of C_1 to C, and so reduce the valuation of future consumption in terms of current consumption. Thus the demand price of labour is reduced by permanently higher G.

THE GOVERNMENT SPENDING MULTIPLIER: THE LABOUR MONOPOLY CASE

The previous section analysed the multiplier on the assumption that the real wage is arbitrarily pegged. The present work is premised on the unsatisfactory character of the assumption, so we now turn to the case where wage rate is not arbitrarily pegged but has a degree of intelligence; we suppose that it is set so as to maximize the wage bill.[15]

A Temporary Shock to G

Under wage bill maximization the critical thing is the elasticity of labour demand. Given:

$$\frac{L_t}{K_t} = \left[1 - \frac{G}{aK}\right]\left[\frac{a + [1 - b - d]w_{t+1}}{w_t[1 + \delta]}\right]^s - 1 + b + d$$

we can infer that the elasticity of demand is exactly the same as before:

$$e_t = \varsigma\left[1 + [1 - b - d]\frac{K_t}{L}\right]$$

Thus employment per unit of capital is entirely unchanged by a temporary shock to government spending:

$$L_t = \frac{\varsigma}{1 - \varsigma}[1 - b - d]K_t$$

This further implies that the economy's capital stock in the next period is unchanged by the G shock. (And so we have the same wage rate in the next period as we would have had.) This implies that the economy's consumption in the next period is unchanged by the G shock. The impact of this temporary shock is temporarily to reduce consumption in this period. That reduces the valuation of next-period consumption, in terms of current consumption. And profits rise. And so the wage falls. We see that the wage rate is depressed by government spending.[16] The contractionary effect of government spending is arrested by a fall in the wage rate sufficient to preserve employment. Labour monopoly here has alleviated in part the negative impact of G.

In summary, under wage bill maximization the G shock does not do anything but waste consumption, and impose the waste entirely upon the wage-earning section of the population.

Permanent G

The wage bill is:

$$w_t\frac{L_t}{K_t} = w_t\left[1 - \frac{G}{aK_t}\right]\left[\frac{a + [1 - b - d]w_{t+1}}{w_t[1 + \delta]}\right]^\varsigma - w_t[1 - b - d] + w_t\frac{G}{aK_t}$$

Thus:

$$\frac{\partial W_t}{\partial w_t} = w_t^{-\varsigma}[1 - \varsigma]\left[1 - \frac{G}{aK_t}\right]\left[\frac{a + [1 - b - d]w_{t+1}}{[1 + \delta]}\right]^\varsigma$$

$$- [1 - b - d] + \frac{G}{aK_t}$$

To evaluate this at the wage bill maximizing rate in the absence of G:

$$w_t = \left[\frac{1 - b - d}{1 - \varsigma}\right]^{-1/\varsigma}\left[\frac{a + [1 - b - d]w_{t+1}}{1 + \delta}\right]$$

Substituting back in implies:

$$\frac{\partial W_t}{\partial w_t} = \frac{G}{K_t a}[b + d] > 0$$

Thus the wage is not kept at its former level when G rises permanently from zero. Rather, G increases the wage rate. This exacerbates the negative impact on employment of G.

In summary, while the wage volatility of labour monopoly operates so as to nullify the negative impact of a temporary increase in G, it also operates to magnify the negative impact of a permanent increase in G.

A SHOCK TO G IN THE FORM OF INCREASED GOVERNMENT INVESTMENT

We now turn to analyse the case where tax revenues are used by the government to hire people. So we move to the situation where the G consists of 'public works' and 'job creation schemes'.

We could suppose that these employees are paid to construct machines. The income stream of these machines, we might suppose, is used to reduce tax liabilities. We can model this as the government giving away the machines.

What will be the impact on total employment of this sort of 'nation-building' initiative? To the extent that this type of G shock increases total employment in t, K_{t+1}/K_t must rise. But, critically, the implication of this new characterization of G has restored the equality of the growth in consumption to the growth in the capital stock, as G does not waste capital's output if consumer goods:

$$\frac{C_{t+1}}{C_t} = \frac{K_{t+1}}{K_t}$$

Thus to the extent that this type of G shock increases total employment in t, it increases C_{t+1}/C_t, and that will reduce the valuation placed on future consumption. And that will reduce the wage. But the wage cannot be reduced.

The conclusion is that employment cannot rise at all. Government investment employment exactly displaces an equal amount of private 'investment employment'. In effect, households – seeing the government tax them (say) $1 million to build machines that they will give back to them – just let the government do their investment for them to the extent of $1 million, and scale back their own investment by $1 million.

CONCLUDING COMMENT

The chapter demonstrates that a twice-differentiable aggregate production function is inessential to the labour monopoly story.

Yet there may be some disappointment in the yield of the neoklassikal model with fixed coefficients. If the neoklassikal version of labour monopoly supplies no less than the neoclassical version, it is not clear that the neoklassikal version adds more. For although the neoklassikal labour demand function promises less 'employment rigidity', labour monopoly does not exploit that promise. We have seen that employment is immunized from the impact of all future-orientated variables by the wage adjustment chosen by the labour monopolist. The neoklassikal labour monopoly is a picture of wage volatility in the face of fluctuating perceptions, rather than wage rigidity.

What neoklassikal labour monopoly does seem to add is the critique of the government spending multiplier. For in the neoklassikal labour monopoly the elasticity of labour demand is affected by government spending, and affected in a way such that a permanently higher G induces the labour monopoly to raise the wage rate, to the detriment of employment. We are left with the conclusion that labour monopoly not only creates unemployment, but also adds to the ineffectiveness of trying to cure it by fiscal policy. But if fiscal policy is useless, what of monetary policy?

NOTES

1. The neologism 'neoklassikal' is modelled on T.W. Hutchison's coinage 'Klassikal economics' to denote the conception of Keynes and his followers of classical economics, as distinguished from classical economics itself. As 'Klassikal economics' both resembles and (at points) diverges from classical economics, so 'neolassikal' indicates an approach that both resembles and, in some aspects, diverges from a the standard neoclassical approach (see Hutchison 1978, 123).
2. Obviously 'neoclassical' models can deal with fixed coefficients. Obviously, Leon Walras and Bohm-Bawerk used fixed coefficients. Nevertheless, 'neoclassical aggregate production function' is synonymous with putty capital and flexible capital–labour ratios.
3. Instead of being the 'rate of evaporation', d could be equivalently interpreted as the amount of labour that needs to be spent to 'repair the machine', without which the machine would be useless. Thus both b and d can be interpreted as operating coefficients. This is why b appears summed with d throughout the model. It also explains why b + d < 1: if b + d > 1, then building a machine is irrational, as the amount of labour that builds a machine exceeds that amount required to operate it. Its construction, therefore, will necessitate the abandonment of other machines in order to free up sufficient labour to operate it.
4. $$aK_{t+1} = a\Sigma + (1 - b - d)aK_t$$

$$C_{t+1} = a\Sigma + (1 - b - d)C_t$$

$$C_t = a\left[K(0) - \frac{\Sigma}{b + d} \right][1 - b - d]^t + \frac{a\Sigma}{b + d}$$

5. More specifically, if the rate of profit exceeds the rate of time preference (that is, consumption is growing), then $\partial\rho/\partial\delta > 1$. Thus the rate of time preference has an immediate and strong impact on the rate of profit, unlike in growth models built on the twice-differentiable production function

6. The declining rate of profit reflects the declining rate of consumption growth, that reflects the declining rate of capital growth. The growth rate of capital (evaluated at constant prices) declines as the steady state is approached:

$$\frac{K_{t+1} - K_t}{K_t} = \frac{[b + d]\left[\dfrac{1}{b + d} - K(0) \right][1 - b - d]^t}{\left[K(0) - \dfrac{1}{b + d} \right]\left[[1 - b - d]^t + \dfrac{1}{b + d} \right]}.$$

7.
$$1 + \rho_{t+k} = \left[\frac{\Sigma}{K_{t+k}} + 1 - b - d \right]^{1/\varsigma}[1 + \delta]$$

8.
$$\frac{K_{t+i}}{\Sigma} = \left[\frac{K(t)}{\Sigma} - \frac{1}{b + d} \right]\left[[1 - b - d]^i + \frac{1}{b + d} \right]$$

9. Notice that (10.21) implies that $e_t > \varsigma$ and $\partial e_t/\partial w_t > 0$, and that as $\rho \to \delta$, $e \to \varsigma/[b + d]$.

10. As K tends to zero the elasticity tends to ς, and as K heads to its steady state value the elasticity tends to $\varsigma / [b + d]$. There is no necessity that $\varsigma/[b + d] > 1$.

11. Can we be sure that capital will grow rather than decline? No. But if the elasticity of labour demand exceeds one at full employment, then the right hand side of (10.28) exceeds one. So as long as wage bill maximization does not make the steady state impossible, then K grows.

12.
$$w_{CRITICAL} = \frac{a}{1 + \rho_{CRITICAL}}\left[1 + \frac{[1 - b - d]}{[1 + \rho_1]} + \frac{[1 - b - d]^2}{[1 + \rho_1][1 + \rho_2]} + \ldots \right],$$

where $\rho, \rho_1, \rho_2 \ldots$ are the sequence of profit rates subsequent to the achievement of full employment. Notice that $w_{CRITICAL}$ must exceed the steady state solution of the wage rate of (10.29),

$$\frac{a}{\dfrac{1 + \rho_{CRITICAL}}{1 - b - d} - 1}.$$

For:

$$w_{CRITICAL} > \frac{a}{1 + \rho_{CRITICAL}}\left[1 + \frac{[1 - b - d]}{[1 + \rho_{CRITICAL}]} + \frac{[1 - b - d]^2}{[1 + \rho_{CRITICAL}]^2} + \ldots \right]$$

$$= \frac{a}{1 + \rho_{CRITICAL} - [1 - b - d]}$$

Thus

$$[1 - b - d]w_{CRITICAL} > \frac{a}{\dfrac{1 + \rho_{CRITICAL}}{1 - b - d} - 1},$$

and so $w_{CRITICAL}$ exceeds the steady state solution (10.29). Since (10.29) is an unstable first-order difference equation we can infer that the wage rate must grow during the period of unemployment.

13. Inspection of (10.20) indicates that labour demand is shifted out by higher elasticity of intertemporal substitution, ς. Further, the elasticity expression $e_t = \varsigma[1 + [1 - b - d]K_t/L_t]$ indicates an increased elasticity at any level of employment, and so increased employment in consequence of ς. Evidently, a higher ς does not induce a neutralizing wage rise.

14. Or, in Keynes's comparison, to pay them to fill holes and dig them out again: 'If the Treasury were to fill old bottles with bank-notes, bury them at suitable depths in disused coal-mines, which are then filled up to the surface with town rubbish, and leave it to private enterprise on well-tried principles of *laissez faire* to dig the notes up again [. . .] there need be no more unemployment and, with the help of the repercussions, the real income of the community [. . .] would probably become a good deal greater than it actually is. It would, indeed, be more sensible to build houses and the like; but if there are political and practical difficulties in the way of this, the above would be better than nothing' (Keynes 1936, 129).

15. To assume an arbitrary peg of the wage is incoherent. For, one way or another, the wage rate after taxes is reduced by increased G. Does it make sense to assume a pegged wage, and then give the government free movement to reduce the wage by means of fiscal policy? If the government has that power, why not just reduce wages as a policy measure?

16.
$$\frac{\Delta w}{w} = -\frac{\Delta G/C}{\varsigma}.$$

11. Labour monopoly as the source of money wage rigidity: a hypothesis

This chapter reinforces Chapter 10 by further exploring the implications of alternative theories of labour demand for labour monopoly and, in doing so, discovering certain Keynesian echoes. But whereas Chapter 10 was, like the entire analysis so far, concerned with real wage rigidity, the present analysis turns to the issue of nominal wage rigidity.

The distinction between real wage rigidity and nominal wage rigidity might be drawn as follows:

- Under real wage rigidity real wages do not respond to the shocks that shape the market-clearing real wage.
- Under nominal wage rigidity nominal wages do not respond to the shocks that shape the market-clearing nominal wage.

Despite the parallelism in definition there is a key incongruence between the two rigidities: for whereas real wage rigidity can easily be rationalized purely in terms of violation of competition, nominal wage rigidity seems to imply a violation of rationality. For if nominal wages are not responding to nominal shocks, then real wages are responding to nominal shocks, at least insofar as money prices are themselves responding in some measure to nominal shocks. Thus nominal wage rigidity seems to amount to a non-neutrality in real wages with respect to money. And non-neutrality is not obviously rationalizable in terms of rational behaviour.

This chapter seeks to offer an explanation of nominal wage rigidity in terms of the rational behaviour of the labour monopolist. It outlines a model in which a 'labour monopolist' will have an incentive to impose rationally a rigidity in the nominal wage.

But the chapter's aspiration is not simply to advance an answer to the 'puzzle' of nominal rigidity. For nominal rigidity is more than just puzzling. It is also of deep import, since most notions of non-neutrality of money with respect to economic activity, and therefore activist monetary policy, turn upon some rigidity in nominal wages. The chapter therefore suggests that the impact of activist monetary policy might be traced to the operation of labour monopoly.

The critical feature in the analysis that creates an incentive for the labour monopolist to choose nominal rigidity is, on the face of it, remote from labour markets. It is the absence of indexed bonds. For unindexed bonds mean that the bond market cannot in a monetary economy perform a critical function: the welfare-efficient sharing between workers and capitalists of the turbulence in national income. And it will be argued that nominal wage rigidity provides a remedy to this inadequacy of nominal, unindexed bonds. One non-neutrality, it seems, deserves another.[1]

The argument begins with the observation that where there are unpredictable shocks to both technology and money, then bonds are inflation-vulnerable as long as they are not inflation-indexed. That has deleterious consequences for the capacity of capital owners to relieve themselves, by means of their purchase of bonds, of the risk arising from their hire of labour. It thereby reduces the demand for labour. In such an economy the labour monopolist, instead of indexing money wages to money prices, might strictly prefer real wages to vary with money prices. By this means is introduced some responsiveness of real wages to economic conditions, which consequently unburdens firms of some of the risk of employing labour, and so increases the demand for labour, to the benefit of the labour interest.

The argument requires a considerable preparatory stage, and that occupies the first sections of this chapter. These sections outline the labour monopoly's optimal wage policy in the case where technological shocks are present, but money shocks are absent. In this situation money wage rigidity is shown to be no better or worse than money wage flexibility; the two strategies over the nominal wage come down to the same thing as far as the labour monopolist is concerned.

The next sections develop the analysis to allow for money shocks, but retain the existence of indexed bonds. In that circumstance a strategy of money wage rigidity is shown to be inferior to money wage flexibility, as far as the labour monopolist is concerned.

It is only in the last sections of the chapter that there appears the key assumption of bonds not being inflation-indexed. It is under that circumstance that money wage rigidity is shown to be potentially superior to money wage flexibility.[2]

IN THE PRESENCE OF TECHNOLOGY SHOCKS BUT THE ABSENCE OF MONEY

We begin at the very beginning, by considering an economy with unpredictable technology but without money. This clears the way for analysing a monetary economy with full indexation of wage and bond contracts, which itself is a preliminary to exploring rigidities in nominal wages.

As we have often done before, we assume a one-period economy. All decision-makers maximize expected utility, which is an identical and homothetic function of consumption:

$$EU = E\frac{C^\alpha}{\alpha} \qquad \alpha < 1 \qquad (11.1)$$

As before, we assume that output is produced by labour and capital by means of a standard production function, but subject to Hicks-neutral shocks:

$$\frac{Y}{K} = \eta q\left(\frac{L}{K}\right) \qquad (11.2)$$

η = random technological shock

We assume that employment is decided by competitive wage-taking capital owners, who own all the capital. We also suppose the owners of capital make employment decisions without knowledge of the realization of η (perhaps on account of some sort of lag between employment and output). Given this, we cannot suppose that capital owners optimize by adjusting employment to equate the marginal product of labour with the real wage. For, since η is not known, the level of employment that equates the marginal product of labour with the real wage is not known.

The upshot is that the capital owners' problem is not a profit-maximizing one, but a utility-maximizing one, in which they simultaneously choose their hire of labour, L, and their purchases of indexed bonds, B (offering a secure real return r) so as to maximize the expected utility of their consumption.

To explicate their expected utility of their consumption, the capital owner consumes the profit on whatever capital remains after the sale of a portion of their endowment to buy bonds, plus the profit on that capital that remains, plus the principal and interest on the bonds they have bought:

$$^jC_C = \left[^j\eta q\left(\frac{L}{K}\right)K - wL + ^j\eta K\right]\frac{[K - B]}{K} + B[1 + r] \qquad (11.3)$$

^jC_C = capital owners consumption in state of the world j

K = capital owners endowment of capital

B = capital owners purchase of bonds

Thus the capital owner's maximization problem is:

$$\max_{L,B} Eu(C_C) = \sum^j pu\left(\left[{}^j\eta q\left(\frac{L}{K}\right)K - wL + {}^j\eta K\right]\frac{[K - B]}{K} + B[1 + r]\right)$$

(11.4)

The worker's problem is analogous, but their only choice variable is how many bonds they sell in order to finance purchases of capital:

$$\max_{B} Eu(C_W) = \sum^j pu\left(wL + \left[{}^j\eta K + {}^j\eta q\left(\frac{L}{K}\right)K - wL\right]\frac{B}{K} - B[1 + r]\right)$$

(11.5)

The implications of these optimization problems can be more easily understood if we suppose that there are just two states: a high-productivity state, ${}^1\eta$, and a low-productivity state, ${}^0\eta$; as under that assumption a diagrammatic analysis becomes fruitful.[3] Figure 11.1 plots the 'profit possibility locus' implied by these two possible states for a given wage: the possible combinations of ${}^1\Pi + {}^1\eta K$ and ${}^0\Pi + {}^0\eta K$.

This plotting of Figure 11.1 begins at the point of zero employment, and consequently zero product, labour cost and profits. As L rises above zero we can assume that the average product of labour exceeds w in both technology states, so profit increases with employment in both states: the plotting heads 'north-east'. But at some point L will become so large that the marginal product of labour will equal the wage in the low state, even though the marginal product of labour will still exceed the wage in the high state. Further additions to employment will reduce profit in the low state, while increasing it in the larger one: so the plotting bends backwards, and heads 'north-west'. At some further point, L is so large that the marginal product of labour will equal the wage even in the high state. Any further increase in L will only reduce profits in both states, and the plotting now heads 'south-west'.

Figure 11.1 can be adapted to represent the general equilibrium, as in Figure 11.2. This is an Edgeworth Box in factor incomes, with the point of origin for wages being the north-east corner. The proportions of the box are as ${}^1\eta$ is to ${}^0\eta$.[4] Consumption outcomes can also be represented in the box, as we suppose that all output is consumed. The indifference curves indicate the combinations of consumption in the two states that yield equal expected utility.

Figure 11.2 represents equilibrium because both workers and capital owners are maximizing utility, given some assumed real wage. To explicate

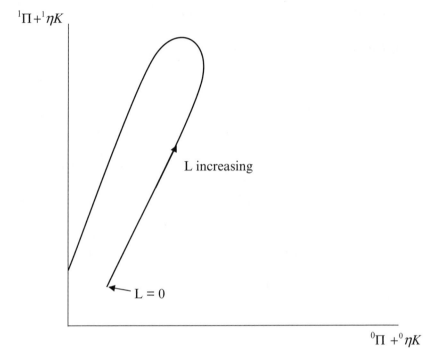

Figure 11.1   The profits possibility locus

how Figure 11.2 represents equilibrium, note that any chosen level of employment must produce a risky profit bill outcome, as the wage bill is given but technology is not. But that chosen employment level also yields a riskless wage bill outcome (trivially, as the real wage is given). This conjunction of a risky income on one side, and a riskless income on the other, will present an opportunity for the 'sale' of risk by capital owners to workers, as capitalists assume the position of hedger, and workers the position of speculator. The hedging capitalist sells capital, and buys bonds; the speculating worker buys capital and sells bonds. To put it another way, the capitalist lends to the worker to finance workers' purchase of part of the capitalists' capital.

This sale of risk means that the income (and so the consumption) of the capital owners no longer corresponds to the profit bill; and the income (and so the consumption) of the labour interest no longer corresponds to the wage bill. Rather, for every capital-financed purchase of bonds, the consumption of the capital-owner declines by $^1\eta + {}^1\rho - [1 + r]$ in state of the world 1, and increases by $1 + r - [{}^0\eta + {}^0\rho]$ in state of the world 0. Thus in terms of

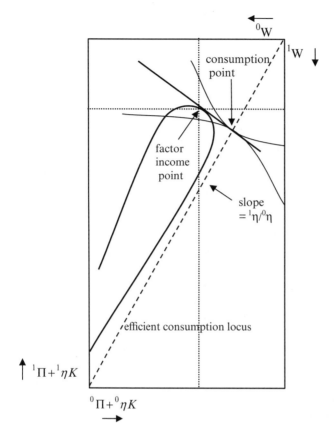

Figure 11.2   The employment decision

Figure 11.1 capitalist consumption heads south-east from the factor income point according to the ratio $[[^1\eta + {}^1\rho] - [1 + r]]/[[1 + r] - [^0\eta + {}^0\rho]]$. The opportunity that capital owners have to do this is represented by the solid straight line in Figure 11.2.

Obviously this line also constitutes a budget line for workers, who are the counter-party to the capitalist in the trade of bonds. It will be seen that in Figure 11.2 both capital owners and workers are maximizing utility subject to their budget constraint, and that the bond market is in equilibrium. Evidently, the slope of the budget line $[[^1\eta + {}^1\rho] - [1 + r]]/[[1 + r] - [^0\eta + {}^0\rho]]$ equals the magnitude of the 'marginal rate of substitution' between consumption in state 1 and consumption in state 0, where consumption in state 1 is $^1\eta/^0\eta$ the size of consumption in state 0:

$$\frac{['\eta + '\rho] - [1 + r]}{[1 + r] - [^0\eta + ^0\rho]} = \frac{^0u'^0p}{^1u'^1p} = \left[\frac{^1C}{^0C}\right]^{1-\alpha}\frac{^0p}{^1p} = \left[\frac{^1\eta}{^0\eta}\right]^{1-\alpha}\frac{^0p}{^1p}. \quad (11.6)$$

^jp = probability of state of the world j

The upshot of this trade in risk is that consumption outcomes are on the diagonal. Thus, in accordance with efficient risk-sharing, the ratio of worker consumption across the two states equals the ratio of capitalist consumption across the two states, which equals the ratio of total consumption across the two states, $^1\eta/^0\eta$. To put the same thought in different words: the trade in risk is such that, in accordance with welfare-efficient risk-sharing under the assumed utility function, workers' consumption is the same fraction of total consumption in both the high and low states; and capitalist consumption is the same fraction of total consumption in both the high and low states.

That Figure 11.2 represents the equilibrium (conditional on some assumed wage) is underlined by considering the disequilibrium depicted in Figure 11.3.

Figure 11.3 represents a situation with a lower level of employment than in Figure 11.2. The sale of risk proceeds on the same terms as before: $[['\eta + '\rho] - [1 + r]]/[[1 + r] - [^0\eta + ^0\rho]]$ equals, and is determined by, the 'marginal rate of substitution' between consumption in state 1 and consumption in state 0, $[^1\eta/^0\eta]^{1-\alpha}\,^0p/^1p$, which has not been altered by the altered level of employment. So the budget line has the same slope as before (dictated by the slope of the indifference curves at the diagonal). Only the position of the budget line has changed; it has shifted inwards, to the obvious detriment of capital owners.

It is easy to see that in Figure 11.3 capital owners can shift out their budget line by increasing employment, and thereby improve their expected utility. They can continue to increase their expected utility by increasing employment until the budget line, with slope $[^1\eta/^0\eta]^{1-\alpha}\,^0p/^1p$, is tangential to the profit possibility locus; this is the tangency solution depicted earlier in Figure 11.2. Since:

$$^1\Pi = {}^1\eta Kq\left(\frac{L}{K}\right) - wL \qquad ^0\Pi = {}^0\eta Kq\left(\frac{L}{K}\right) - wL \quad (11.7)$$

this tangency condition of employment optimization can be stated as:

$$-\frac{\partial^1\Pi}{\partial^0\Pi} = \frac{^1\eta q'\left(\frac{L}{K}\right) - w}{w - {}^0\eta q'\left(\frac{L}{K}\right)} = \left[\frac{^1\eta}{^0\eta}\right]^{1-\alpha}\frac{^0p}{^1p} \quad (11.8)$$

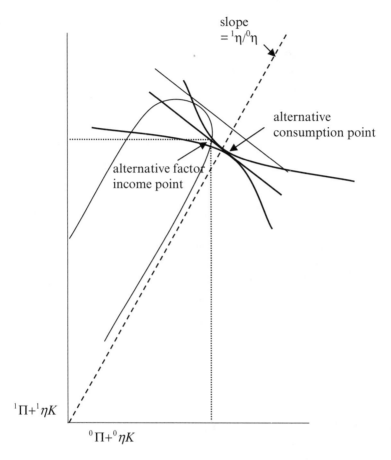

Figure 11.3   A suboptimal employment decision

This condition for employment optimization be rearranged to imply a negative relation between w and L; a demand schedule for labour:

$$
{}^{0}\eta q'\left(\frac{L}{K}\right) = w\left[\frac{1 + \left[\frac{{}^{1}\eta}{{}^{0}\eta}\right]^{1-\alpha}\frac{{}^{0}p}{{}^{1}p}}{\frac{{}^{1}\eta}{{}^{0}\eta} + \left[\frac{{}^{1}\eta}{{}^{0}\eta}\right]^{1-\alpha}\frac{{}^{0}p}{{}^{1}p}}\right] \tag{11.9}
$$

It can be seen from (11.9), and still more easily from (11.8) that:

$$
{}^{1}\eta q'\left(\frac{L}{K}\right) > w > {}^{0}\eta q'\left(\frac{L}{K}\right) \tag{11.10}
$$

Equation (11.10) says that the real wage does not equal the marginal product of labour, but is smaller than the marginal product during the positive shocks, and greater than the marginal product during the negative shock. Nevertheless, (11.9) constitutes a standard, negative and deterministic relation between labour demand and the real wage rate. Thus the competitive equilibrium wage satisfies:

$$^0\eta q'\left(\frac{\Sigma}{K}\right) = w \left[\frac{1 + \left[\frac{^1\eta}{^0\eta}\right]^{1-\alpha}\frac{^0p}{^1p}}{\frac{^1\eta}{^0\eta} + \left[\frac{^1\eta}{^0\eta}\right]^{1-\alpha}\frac{^0p}{^1p}}\right] \qquad (11.11)$$

What of the wage under labour monopoly? All workers share the same wage and utility function, and the labour monopolist chooses the wage to maximize their common expected utility.[5] That comes down to choosing the wage to maximize the wage bill. That amounts to choosing a w so that the L/K implied by (11.7) satisfies:

$$-q''\left(\frac{L}{K}\right)\frac{L}{K} = q'\left(\frac{L}{K}\right).$$

and so maximizes the wages bill. It will be seen that the chosen level of employment is completely invariant to the size of the various shocks, and their probabilities.[6]

RISKLESS MONEY AND RISKLESS BONDS

Having analysed a real economy, we now introduce money. We suppose money to be the medium of transaction and the unit of account, and that labour, bonds and goods now have money prices. The money wage is V. The money interest rate is i, but is assumed for now to be indexed to the rate of inflation. Money prices, P, are explained by a simple quantity theory relation:

$$P = \frac{M}{Y} \qquad (11.12)$$

P = price level

M = money supply

Importantly, we will suppose in this section that the money supply is perfectly known, and so price level unpredictability is solely due to technological shocks increasing Y. So for each technology shock there is a single corresponding price level:

$$^jP = \frac{M}{^j\eta q\left(\frac{L}{K}\right)}$$ (11.13)

What, then, is the optimal strategy for the nominal wage? If the labour monopolist indexes the nominal wage rate to the price level, then the labour monopolist is simply choosing a real wage, as it did in the moneyless economy, and so can replicate all the results of the moneyless economy. The only difference is that, in accordance with indexation, V falls with P in the face of a positive technology shock, and rises with P in the case of a positive technology shock; this is nominal wage flexibility.

But suppose now, instead, that the labour monopolist sets the money wage unconditional on movements in prices; that is, it makes the nominal wage rigid. Under this schema the maximization problem of capitalists is:

$$\max_{L,B} \sum{}^j pu\left(\left[^j\eta q\left(\frac{L}{K}\right)K - \frac{V}{^jP}L + {}^j\eta K\right]\frac{[K - B]}{K} + B[1 + r]\right)$$ (11.14)

Optimization over L implies:

$$\sum{}^j p^j u'\left[^j\eta q'\left(\frac{L}{K}\right) - \frac{V}{^jP}\right] = 0$$ (11.15)

Equation (11.15) is satisfied by:

$$^j\eta q'\left(\frac{L}{K}\right) = \frac{V}{^jP} \quad \text{all } j$$ (11.16)

That is, the marginal product of labour equals the real wage. This equality was impossible to satisfy when the money wage was flexible, and indexed to P; because the flexibility meant that the real wage was pegged at some magnitude, and so could not possibly equal the several magnitudes that the marginal product of labour will assume according to the size of the technological shock. But now the real wage is not pegged at some magnitude; it varies on account of the impact of technology shocks on P in the face of a predetermined money wage. With money wages rigid, but real wages variable, it seems at least possible for the real wage to equal the marginal product of labour in each contingency.

But how to make that possibility an actuality? How to ensure that the various real wages (arising from technology shocks confronting a predetermined money wage) do equal the corresponding marginal products (resulting from a predetermined L in the face of technology shocks)? There is, in truth, a unique level of employment that will ensure that the real wage equals the marginal product in all contingencies. The equalities of (11.16) will be secured if employment is positively related to M, and negatively related to V, in the following particular manner:

$$\frac{q\left(\dfrac{L}{K}\right)}{q'\left(\dfrac{L}{K}\right)} = \frac{M}{V} \tag{11.17}$$

Equation (11.17) secures (11.16) because, given the quantity of money relationship (11.13), if (11.17) then (11.16). So (11.17) ensures that the real wage in any state j equals the marginal product of labour in that state j. Thus in making the money wage rigid the labour monopoly has made the real wage 'flexible', and conditional on technology, in such a way that the that marginal product of labour equals the real wage.

Further, by appropriate choice of V the labour monopoly can, through (11.17), choose that unique level of employment that satisfies $-q''(l)l = 'q(l)$ that will be wage bill maximizing for all shocks.[7] And, since the wage rate equals the marginal product of labour under all shocks, the wage bill comes to the same share of total consumable resources under all shocks: the factor income point lies on the diagonal of the Edgeworth Box (factor shares are invariant to Hicks-neutral shocks). Thus nominal wage rigidity secures the welfare-efficient sharing of consumption risk, without recourse to bonds. Nominal wage rigidity has made the bond market redundant.

The beginning of this section showed that complete nominal wage flexibility, in replicating the moneyless economy, also secured welfare-efficient sharing of consumption risk, but by means of bond markets. Complete nominal wage flexibility, in replicating the moneyless economy, also secures that level of employment that satisfies $-q''(l)l = 'q(l)$. It seems that the outcome the labour monopoly achieves by a strategy of nominal wage rigidity bears a strong similarity to the outcome the labour monopoly achieves by a strategy of nominal wage flexibility. In fact, the two outcomes are identical.[8] Thus in a monetary economy where there is no unpredictability in the money supply or the real return on bonds, labour monopoly is indifferent between complete nominal wage flexibility and complete nominal wage rigidity.

UNPREDICTABLE MONEY, RISKLESS REAL INTEREST RATE

The preceding analysis of the monetary economy facing technological shocks appears to have arrived at a conclusion of some significance: that money wage rigidity would serve the labour monopoly no worse than money wage flexibility. However the section drew conclusions about 'nominal wage rigidity' in only a weak sense of that term. For in the preceding section there were no money shocks. Obviously 'nominal wage rigidity' in any substantial sense is all about not responding to money shocks. But in the preceding there were no money shocks to 'not respond' to.

This section therefore turns to addressing what the model has to say about 'nominal wage rigidity' in a stronger sense by exploring the situation where there is unpredictability in the money supply, while still supposing that bonds are inflation-indexed.

Let M have ι possible, and unpredictable, states. The price level is therefore now a function of both technology shocks and money shocks:

$$^{j}P^{i} = \frac{M^{\iota}}{^{j}\eta q\left(\dfrac{L}{K}\right)} \tag{11.18}$$

In this environment of an unpredictable money supply, will nominal wage flexibility and real wage rigidity remain equally rewarding to the labour monopolist?

Clearly, if the labour monopolist chooses nominal wage flexibility (and indexation of V to P) it can peg the real wage as it pleases, and so secure all the results that hold under the moneyless economy. Which is to say: it can secure all the results that nominal wage flexibility delivered under a predictable money supply. Thus the pay-off to a strategy of money wage flexibility is unaffected by unpredictability in the money supply.

But what of the pay-off to a rigid money wage in the face of an unpredictable money supply? A rigid nominal wage can still secure the relevant first-order optimization condition for capitalists. For given:

$$\sum {}^{j}p{}^{j}u'\left[{}^{j}\eta q'\left(\frac{L}{K}\right) - \frac{V}{^{j}P^{i}}\right] = 0 \tag{11.19}$$

the function:

$$\frac{q\left(\dfrac{L}{K}\right)}{q'\left(\dfrac{L}{K}\right)} = \frac{M^i}{V} \qquad (11.20)$$

can secure (11.19) given (11.18). But (11.20) does not now achieve replication of the results of wage rigidity under predictable money. For given the shocks in M, any choice in V does not now imply a unique outcome in l. For any choice of V, the l that satisfies $-q''(l)l = q'(l)$ would be obtained only by luck. Thus, luck aside, the wage bill is not now maximized under wage rigidity.[9] The pay-off to a strategy of money wage rigidity is reduced by unpredictability in the money supply.

So unpredictable money shocks treat unequally two strategies that were equally ranked by the labour monopolist in the absence of money shocks. The pay-off to money wage flexibility is unaltered, but the pay-off to money wage rigidity is reduced.

Thus we conclude that in the context of unpredictable money shocks, but riskless real interest rates, a nominal wage flexibility strategy dominates a nominal wage rigidity strategy. In this environment, evidently, there is no incentive for the labour monopoly to make the money wage rigid.

But if, for some reason, bonds are nominal, and the real interest rate is consequently risky, an incentive to make nominal wages rigid may appear.

UNPREDICTABLE MONEY, RISKY REAL INTEREST RATE

We now turn to the case that is the point of the chapter; the case where money wage rigidity may dominate money wage flexibility. This is the case where bonds are not indexed to P, and the real interest rate is consequently inflation vulnerable.

We compare in turn the labour monopoly's two strategies for the nominal wage.

Money Wage Flexibility

If the money wage is indexed to the price level, then the real wage is being decided unconditional on the technology shock, just as before, and employment is decided unconditional on the technology shock, just as before. But now the real return on bonds has become unpredictable, as the contracted return on bonds is (by assumption) nominal but money shocks are imparting some unpredictability to P.[10] This means that the purchase of bonds by capital owners, from the proceeds of the sale of their capital, will no longer necessarily contract the variance of capital owners' consumption opportunities, as the purchase of bonds now involves making the purchase subject to inflation risk. The upshot is that the unpredictable real return on bonds impairs the sale of risk, since the attempt to spread 'factor income risk' efficiently now means incurring 'bond income risk'. To illustrate the consequences, imagine that inflation is so extremely unpredictable, and that the consequent bond income risk is so severe, that capital owners decide it is best simply living with factor income risk, and choosing employment to maximize expected utility in the absence of any resort to bond markets.

Figure 11.4 shows that such a 'living with factor income risk' strategy reduces employment.

Without needing to assume that the bond market is completely abandoned, we may surmise that unpredictable inflation will disrupt bond markets with consequences that are harmful to both workers and capital owners. The disruption of bond markets reduces employment for a given real wage. The disruption of bond markets means that workers must take on more risk to obtain a given expected return, and capitalists necessarily reduce their risk by less for any given reduction in expected return. Thus unpredictable inflation appears harmful to labour on several counts.

Money Wage Rigidity

A rigidity in nominal wages holds out the promise of correcting some of the discouragement of employment arising from the inflation vulnerability of non-indexed bonds. For, as we have seen from (11.16) to (11.18), the attainment of the capital owners' employment optimization condition in the context of nominal wage rigidity amounts to a 'flexibility' of real wages in the face of shocks. By reducing the riskiness of employing labour, that flexibility encourages the employment of labour, relative to the situation where the real wage is given, and capital owners cannot lay off the risk of labour hire through bond purchases.

On the other hand, we have also seen that the attainment of the capital owners' employment optimization condition spells a variability in employment in the face of shocks, which produces a variability in the wage bill. It was this last consideration that made nominal wage rigidity inferior to nominal wage flexibility in the context of indexed bonds.

We contend that in the full light of these contrasting considerations, the labour monopolist might find it in their interest to make the money wage rigid.

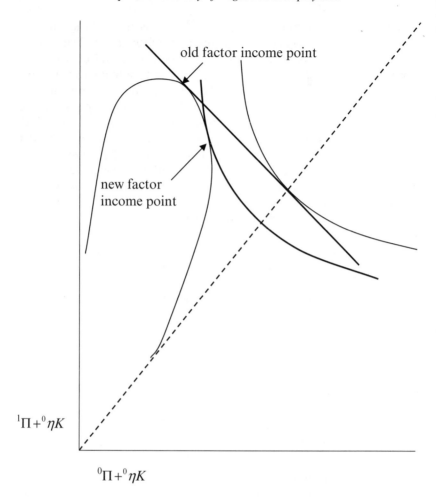

Figure 11.4   The impact on employment of an absence of a bond market

The key part of the argument is the contention that the riskiness produced by money and technology shocks can be efficiently shared out by
bond markets even if bonds are nominal. To argue this contention, we
restrict ourselves to just two possible technology states, $^1\eta$ and $^0\eta$, and just
two money supply states: a low-money-supply state, M^-, and high-money-
supply state, M^+. We begin by supposing that the money shock and the
technology shock are independent events, statistically. These two money
shocks imply two possible employment levels (from 11.18), and so four
possible outputs (see Table 11.1).

What consumption efficiency requires is that the capitalist share of total

Table 11.1   Output (per unit of capital)

	M^-	M^+
$^1\eta$	$^1\eta q(\dfrac{L^-}{K})$	$^1\eta q(\dfrac{L^+}{K})$
$^0\eta$	$^0\eta q(\dfrac{L^-}{K})$	$^0\eta q(\dfrac{L^+}{K})$

consumption is the same in all four states. We begin by asking: is the capitalist share of total income the same in all four states? If this is the case, then consumption efficiency is obtained by simply by consuming factor income, and bond markets are redundant.

There are two conflicting considerations. First, because the real wage now equals the marginal product of labour, we may conclude that the profit share is invariant to the Hicks-neutral technology shock. Thus consumption is efficiently shared, at least with respect to technology shocks. And this is on account of rigid money wages; for (recall) the profit share was not invariant when the real wage was rigid, as profits absorbed all the technology shock. It is the rigidity in nominal wages, with the consequent 'flexibility' in real wages, that makes for the invariance of the profit share with respect to technology shocks.

However, it may appear that money wage rigidity has 'solved' risk-sharing with respect to technology shocks only at the cost of creating a risk-sharing problem with respect to money shocks. For given the rigid money wage, the profit share will vary with the state of the money supply; the share being higher under M^+ than under M^- on account of higher employment (given that the elasticity of technical substitution is less than unity).

In summary, the capitalist share of total consumable resources is not the same in all four states, and so consumption efficiency cannot be obtained by each factor simply consuming their factor income. Factor markets cannot be relied upon, without the aid of bond markets, to allocate consumption in a way that shares out risk in a welfare-efficient manner (that is, the share going to profits being the same in all states). Rather, profit incomes rise disproportionately with income under a money shock, and there is a benefit in transferring risk from profits to wages.

Figure 11.5 underlines the 'problem' the money shock creates for efficient risk-sharing, and the imperative to shift risk from profits to wages if efficient risk-sharing is to be secured. Figure 11.5 does this by presenting incomes in the two money states (M^- and M^+), and conditioned on some common realization of η.

This box is different from earlier boxes, as it represents the impact of M

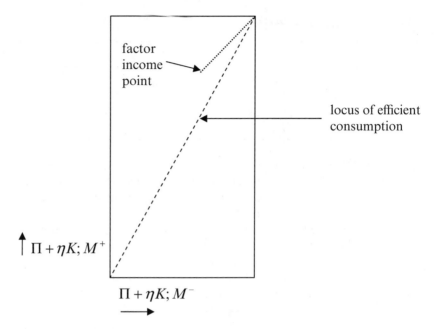

Figure 11.5   A box for different money states

volatility not η volatility; and so the slope of the diagonal of this box is not $^1\eta/^0\eta$, but depends upon M^+/M^- and the elasticity of Y to M.[11] But the important point for the present discussion is that the factor income point is off the locus of efficient consumption.

The question arises: as factor markets cannot by themselves secure efficient consumption (that is, equal capitalist share of consumption in all states), can nominal bond markets secure efficient consumption? Is there a nominal rate of interest and a nominal quantity of bonds that would produce an equal capitalist share of consumption in all states? And if there was, would this nominal rate of interest and nominal quantity of bonds actually be a market equilibrium?

As factor shares are invariant to technological shocks under nominal wage rigidity, we concentrate on the money shock. We begin with the observation that the sale of capitalists' capital for bonds would help equalize consumption shares across M shocks only insofar as the profit rate exceeds the real interest rate in the high-money state, and the real interest rate exceeded the profit rate in the low-money state. And this is true: the real interest rate tends to be lower in the high M state, and profit is certainly higher in the high-money state.

The prospect that bond markets can efficiently allocate risk in the face of an M shock raises a further hope: if buying bonds can secure equal shares in consumption, across the two M states, for a given realization of η, can then that same action also secure equal shares in consumption, across the two M states, in the other realization of η? Since a Hicks shock, a change in η, simply expands profits and wages in proportion to total consumption, this seems at least possible.

The idea of the possibility can be represented with the help of Figure 11.6, that consists of two boxes. In both boxes the horizontal axis measure outcomes under the low realization of M, M⁻, and the vertical axis measure outcomes under the high realization of M, M⁺. But the smaller box pertains to the smaller realization of η, and the larger pertaining to a larger realization of η.

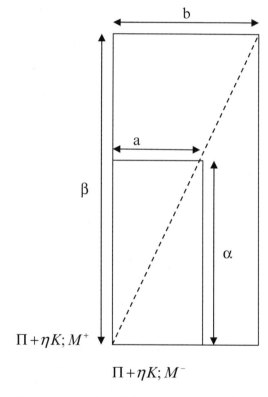

Figure 11.6   The two categories of shocks represented by two boxes

In this box $^1\eta/^0\eta$ = b/a= β/α. Wages in each technology realization are read off from the north-east corner of the respective boxes.

Figure 11.7 adds the two factor income points, one for each box.

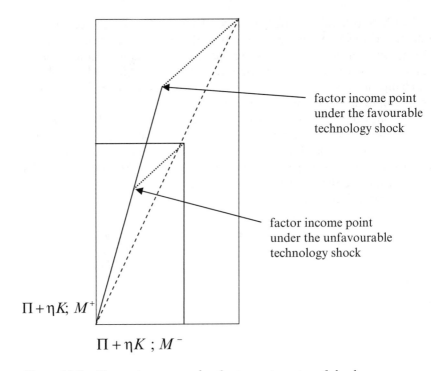

$\Pi + \eta K; \; M^+$

factor income point
under the favourable
technology shock

factor income point
under the unfavourable
technology shock

$\Pi + \eta K \; ; \; M^-$

Figure 11.7   Factor incomes under the two categories of shocks

Figure 11.8 conveys how bond markets might efficiently spread consumption.

Figure 11.8 suggests bond markets can efficiently spread consumption, and an algebraic analysis corroborates the suggestion (see the Appendix). As the efficient marginal rate of substitution between money states is the same regardless of the technology state, we want the trade-off between consumption in the money states that is offered by bond–capital trades, to be the same regardless of the technology state, and some algebra shows that it is (see the Appendix).

But what about the scale of the bond–capital swaps? Successful risk-sharing requires a certain volume of bond–capital swaps. And it would seem that in the high η state a greater real quantity is required, while in the low η state, a smaller real quantity is required. To explicate: we see by inspection of Figure 11.8 that there is some vertical displacement in capitalist consumption $\Delta^0 C_C$ when $\eta = {}^0\eta$, and some vertical displacement in capitalist consumption $\Delta^1 C_C$, when $\eta = {}^1\eta$, which is necessary to shift the endowment to the diagonal of Figure 11.8. We can tell that the ratio of the displacements must conform to:

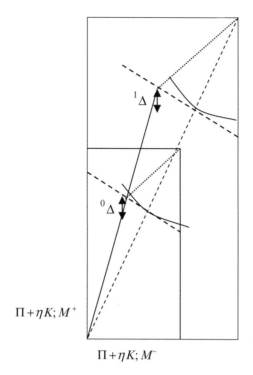

$\Pi + \eta K; M^+$

$\Pi + \eta K; M^-$

Figure 11.8   Efficient consumption?

$$\frac{\Delta^0 C}{\Delta^1 C} = \frac{{}^0\eta}{{}^1\eta} \qquad (11.21)$$

But is this the case? Yes. Budget constraint arithmetic implies:

$$\Delta^0 C_C = \Delta K \left[{}^0\eta + {}^0\rho^+ - \frac{1 + i}{{}^0 P^+} \right] \qquad (11.22)$$

and:

$$\Delta^1 C_C = \Delta K \left[{}^1\eta + {}^1\rho^+ - \frac{1 + i}{{}^1 P^+} \right] \qquad (11.23)$$

which imply (11.21) (see Appendix).

This concludes the argument that consumption is efficiently shared by rigid money wages when bonds are not indexed.

To locate the point of this section: whereas under flexible (indexed) money wages the difference in real interest rates between money states created a pointless turbulence in consumption of capital owners and labour in the face of money shocks, under rigid nominal wage rates the resultant responsiveness of total output to the money shock gives the difference in real interest rates between money shocks a function: it allows worker debtors to be the beneficiaries of the high M state (and so get a larger of consumption that their factor incomes alone would warrant in the high M state); and capitalist creditors to be the beneficiaries of the low M state (and so get a higher share of consumption than their factor incomes alone would warrant in the low M state). In this way money bonds efficiently share consumption in the context of rigid money wages.

Thus a schema of nominal wage rigidity secures a range of consumption opportunities which will be efficiently distributed across the different economic interests in the presence of nominal bond markets.

But what is the significance of this conclusion? The conclusion does not by itself imply that nominal wage rigidity dominates nominal wage flexibility as far as the labour monopolist is concerned. For while the now functional bond markets allow workers and capitalists to deal with turbulence in national income in a welfare-efficient manner, it remains the case that money supply shocks will create a turbulence in national income which would not have occurred under money wage indexation. And this is costly not only in expected utility, but also because the variations in L caused by variations in M (a given V) cause L to miss the wage bill maximizing employment level. For the wage bill maximizing level of employment is invariant to the money supply, and the realization of η. So the elasticity of L to M that rigid V implies means that the wage bill maximizing level of employment is being missed: either too high, or too low.

The critical question is: while the absence of indexed bonds reduces the pay-off to a money wage flexibility strategy (on account of the incapacity to trade the risk created by technology shocks, and the consequent discouragement to employment) does it reduce the pay-off so much that it is now inferior to the money wage rigidity strategy, which it previously dominated in the presence of indexed bonds?

There appears to be one circumstance in which the answer is 'yes'. There appears to be one circumstance in which the benefits of efficient risk-sharing secured by rigid money wages outweighs any suboptimality in the wage bill caused by money wage rigidity. This is where the money shock is 'small'. For small variations in M, the deviation from the maximum wages bill on account of nominal rigidity is 'second-order'. But there is no presumption that loss to the labour monopoly arising from the disruption of bond markets by small variations in M are merely 'second-order'.[12] We conclude that for sufficiently small shocks to M, a labour monopolist will prefer rigid nominal wages.

THE SCOPE AND IMPLICATIONS OF THE MONEY WAGE RIGIDITY

The preceding section has told a story where, under certain circumstances, a labour monopolist will rationally prefer money wage rigidity over real wage rigidity. More precisely, it has told a story where the labour monopolist will wish the money wage to be rigid in the face of a *shock* to the money supply. The thesis, in other words, is that money wage is rigid with respect to any unexpected element in the change in the money supply. By contrast, the money wage the labour monopolist selects will be flexible with respect to its expectations of the money supply. More formally, the model says that a change in the mean realization of M (that is, a change in the rational expectation of M) would yield a matching change in the V chosen by the labour monopolist.[13]

The rigidity of the preferred money wage in the face of surprise changes in the money supply, but its flexibility in the face of anticipated changes, clearly has implications for the non-neutrality of money implied by the model. As a shock change in the money supply leaves the money wage unchanged, a shock change spells a positive elasticity of employment and output to such shock changes, and an elasticity of money prices to money shocks of less than one.[14] In other words, a labour monopolist creates a non-neutrality in money with respect to money surprises. But as a fully anticipated change in the money supply will change the labour monopolist's chosen money wage in proportion, the elasticity of employment and output to such a change is zero. Thus while there are Keynesian echoes in the implications of the model, it would appear that a much louder echo is that of the New Classical models of the 1970s.

Yet the model also exhibits an important deviation from New Classical models, and one in the direction of the Keynesian outlook: the model has no implication of full employment, on average, or ever. For the labour monopolist selects a V, so as to maximize the wage bill, not to secure full employment. That selection may spell unemployment. And not just unemployment associated with a negative money surprise, but unemployment regardless of whether the money surprise is positive, negative or zero.[15]

NOTES

1. See Coleman (2007, 138–57) for another illustration of the potential for two non-neutralities usefully to correct each other.
2. The reasoning and ideas of this chapter call to mind Baily (1974), and to a lesser degree Azariadis (1975).
3. The equimarginal conditions of capital owners and workers are:

$$\sum {}^j p^j u'\left(\left[{}^j\eta K + {}^j\eta q\left(\frac{L}{K}\right)K - wL\right]\frac{[K - B]}{K} + B[1 + r]\right)\left[{}^j\eta + {}^j\eta q'\left(\frac{L}{K}\right) - w\right] = 0$$

$$\sum {}^j p^j u'\left(\left[{}^j\eta K + {}^j\eta q\left(\frac{L}{K}\right)K - wL\right]\frac{[K - B]}{K} + B[1 + r]\right)$$

$$\left[{}^j\eta + {}^j\eta q\left(\frac{L}{K}\right) - w\frac{L}{K} - [1 + r]\right] = 0$$

$$\sum {}^j p^j u'\left(wL + \left[{}^j\eta K + {}^j\eta q\left(\frac{L}{K}\right)K - wL\right]\frac{B}{K} - B[1 + r]\right)$$

$$\left[{}^j\eta + {}^j\eta q\left(\frac{L}{K}\right) - w\frac{L}{K} - [1 + r]\right] = 0$$

These evidently constitute three equations in three unknowns: L, r and B.

4. The ratio of total C in one state relative to the other is $[{}^1\eta q K + {}^1\eta K]/[{}^0\eta q K + {}^1\eta K] = {}^1\eta/{}^0\eta$.

5. Any heterogeneity in income outcomes of workers will prove problematic for the labour monopolist's maximand; for if some workers are employed, and some are unemployed, whose welfare does the labour monoplist care about? We assume away heterogeneity in income outcomes of workers by supposing that any excess supply of labour is shared out equally amongst all workers by work rationing; or complete unemployment insurance; or work being randomly allocated across workers in tiny packets so often during the period that the 'law of large numbers' ensures that each worker receives the mean wage income. The upshot is that labour monopoly is interested in the wage bill W; that is, mean wages.

6. As in preceding chapters we assume the labour monopolist knows the functional form of q, and therefore the functional form of $e = e(l)$. But it does not know aggregate K, or the K of any firm. And it does not know the realization of η. We could imagine the labour monopoly setting a 'schedule' of wage rates conditional upon the realization of η, even without it knowing the realization of η, and inviting capital owners to pay a wage according to the realization of η. But this would be to invite the labour monopoly's deception by capital owners.

7. Given that now ${}^j w = {}^j\eta q(L/K)$, the magnitude of L that maximizes the wage bill, ${}^j\eta q(L/K)L$, is the same for all realizations of η. This simply reproduces the conclusion of Chapter 4 that, assuming the wage equals the marginal product, Hicks-neutral technical shocks have no impact on the wage bill maximizing level of employment.

8. Let (11.8) be written

$$ {}^0\eta q'(l)l = wl\left[\frac{1 + \Xi}{\frac{{}^1\eta}{{}^0\eta} + \Xi}\right]. \text{ Then } \frac{{}^1\eta q'(l)l + {}^0\eta q'(l)l\Xi}{1 + \Xi} = wl, $$

and so

$$ {}^1\eta q'(l)l - \frac{[{}^1\eta - {}^0\eta]q'(l)l\Xi}{1 + \Xi} = wl. $$

But the left hand side of this expression equals the magnitude of the wage bill which is secured in both states with a sufficient 'sale' of wages in state 1 for wages in state 0, at the going value of state 1 consumption in terms of state 0 consumption. (Proof: the sale that secures an equal wages bill satisfies

$$ {}^1\eta q'(l)l - sale = {}^0\eta q'(l)l + \frac{sale}{\Xi}. $$

Thus $sale = [^1\eta - {}^0\eta]\dfrac{q'(l)l}{1 + \Xi}$, thus the resulting equal wages bill is

$$^1\eta q'(l)l - \frac{[^1\eta - {}^0\eta]q'(l)l\Xi}{1 + \Xi}.)$$

But the right hand side is simply the wage bill under money wage flexibility. Thus the wage bill under money wage rigidity is equivalent to the wage bill under money wage flexibility.

9. And the wage bill is now more variable than under wage rigidity and predictable money; whereas previously there were j wage bill outcomes, there are now jı.

10. Technology shocks also impart some unpredictability to P. But the unpredictability that technology shocks thereby impart to real interest rates is not significant. For if there was no variance in the money supply, the real interest rate would still be perfectly predictable, conditional on the state of technology.

11. The slope of the diagonal equals

$$\frac{M^+}{M^-}\left[1 + \frac{\partial Y}{\partial L}\frac{L}{Y}\frac{\partial L}{\partial M}\frac{M}{L}\right],$$

where the elasticity of L to M is implied by

$$\frac{q\left(\dfrac{L}{K}\right)}{q'\left(\dfrac{L}{K}\right)} = \frac{M}{V}.$$

12. To analogize, consider the marginal cost to a monopolist's profits of a tax, evaluated at the zero tax rate. If $P + T = 1 - aQ$ then $\Pi = Q - aQ^2 - TQ$, and

$$\frac{\partial \Pi}{\partial T} = \frac{T-1}{2a}. \text{ At } T = 0 \ \frac{\partial \Pi}{\partial T} = \frac{-1}{2a} \neq 0.$$

13. More correctly, the solutions values of P and V for the system (11.16) to (11.18) are unit elastic to any equiproportionate increase in the realization of M for each state ı.

14. $\dfrac{q(l)}{q'(l)} = \dfrac{M}{V}$ implies $\dfrac{\partial M}{\partial Ml} = \dfrac{1}{\dfrac{lq'}{q} - \dfrac{q''l}{q'}} = \dfrac{1}{1 - \pi + \dfrac{1}{e}}.$

$$\frac{\partial qM}{\partial Mq} = \frac{l\partial q}{q\partial l}\frac{M\partial l}{l\partial M} = \frac{1 - \pi}{1 - \pi + \dfrac{1}{e}}.$$

As $\dfrac{\partial PM}{\partial MP} + \dfrac{\partial qM}{\partial Mq} = 1, \dfrac{\partial PM}{\partial MP} = \dfrac{\dfrac{1}{e}}{1 - \pi + \dfrac{1}{e}}.$

15. If the elasticity of the demand for labour is greater than one at full employment, what incentive would labour monopoly have to create unemployment? In that situation the

labour monopoly may always secure full employment by indexing the nominal wage to P; and choosing a full-employment real wage. In the context of nominal bonds, the consequent variability in V has the costs listed before; damaged risk-sharing. But that cost might be worth the benefit of the enlarged wage bill. The upshot is that just as capital richness may induce a labour monopoly to choose real wage flexibility (as a consequence of the impact on the elasticity of labour demand at full employment), so it may also induce a labour monopoly to choose an associated nominal wage flexibility.

APPENDIX: THE TRADE-OFF IN CONSUMPTION ACROSS STATES

As units are chosen so that at the beginning of the period the price level is unit, the trade-off between consumption in a low M state and consumption in the high M state is:

$$\frac{{}^{0}\eta + {}^{0}\rho^{+} - \dfrac{1 + i}{{}^{0}P^{+}}}{-[{}^{0}\eta + {}^{0}\rho^{-}] + \dfrac{1 + i}{{}^{0}P^{-}}} \qquad \text{for } \eta = {}^{0}\eta$$

and:

$$\frac{{}^{1}\eta + {}^{1}\rho^{+} - \dfrac{1 + i}{{}^{1}P^{+}}}{-[{}^{1}\eta + {}^{1}\rho^{-}] + \dfrac{1 + i}{{}^{1}P^{-}}} \qquad \text{for } \eta = {}^{1}\eta$$

respectively.

But as:

$$
{}^{0}\eta + {}^{0}\rho^{+} - \frac{1 + i}{{}^{0}P^{+}} = {}^{1}\eta\frac{{}^{0}\eta}{{}^{1}\eta} + \frac{{}^{0}\eta}{{}^{1}\eta}{}^{1}\rho^{+} - \frac{1 + i}{{}^{1}P^{+}}\frac{{}^{0}\eta}{{}^{1}\eta}
$$

$$
= \frac{{}^{0}\eta}{{}^{1}\eta}\left[{}^{1}\eta + {}^{1}\rho^{+} - \frac{1 + i}{{}^{1}P^{+}}\right]
$$

we can say:

$$
\frac{{}^{0}\eta + {}^{0}\rho^{+} - \dfrac{1 + i}{{}^{0}P^{+}}}{{}^{1}\eta + {}^{1}\rho^{+} - \dfrac{1 + i}{{}^{1}P^{+}}} = \frac{{}^{0}\eta}{{}^{1}\eta}
$$

and by a parallel logic we may also conclude:

$$
\frac{{}^{0}\eta + {}^{0}\rho^{-} - \dfrac{1 + i}{{}^{0}P^{-}}}{{}^{1}\eta + {}^{1}\rho^{-} - \dfrac{1 + i}{{}^{1}P^{-}}} = \frac{{}^{0}\eta}{{}^{1}\eta}
$$

Thus:

$$\frac{{}^0\eta + {}^0\rho^+ - \dfrac{1+i}{{}^0P^+}}{-[{}^0\eta + {}^0\rho^-] + \dfrac{1+i}{{}^0P^-}} = \frac{{}^1\eta + {}^1\rho^+ - \dfrac{1+i}{{}^1P^+}}{-[{}^1\eta + {}^1\rho^-] + \dfrac{1+i}{{}^1P^-}}$$

and the trade-off between consumption in the money states, offered by bond markets, is the same regardless of the technology state.

12. A concluding comment

These pages began with the assertion that the abiding problem of macro-economics was to explain why there is unemployment.

But it may be thought, to judge from the central tendency of macro-economic theorizing of the past several decades, that the key task of macroeconomics has been to explain how there is *not* unemployment; to explain how, against near universal belief, there are no periods of a general excess supply of labour; there are no circumstances that spell 'too many applicants for available jobs'; and that any belief to the contrary is the fruit of an illusion, delusion or simplicity of mind. For since about 1970 sophisticated thinking about macroeconomics has been dominated by various rationalizations of labour market behaviour that, as if from first principles, shun the possibility that there could be 'too many applicants for available jobs'.

The impetus behind these theories, and the credence that adheres to them, has not arisen from any success of theirs in empirical contests with the alternatives; there has been no such success. Rather, the underlying current that impels them is a discomfort with Keynesian and Classical theories on account of their apparent violation of the tenets of rational behaviour.

This book has a different response to the shortcomings of Keynesian and Classical doctrines, and adopts a different end. The goal of this work is to advance and develop a rational explanation of the presence of a socially wasteful excess supply of labour. To that end it airs and sustains the doctrine that unemployment is rooted in the rewards to wage earners from acting collectively to restrict competition amongst themselves. It aims to clarify and articulate the circumstances under which wage earners benefit from restricting competition, thereby gaining a higher price for their labour than the market-clearing price, but at the cost to the quantity of labour sold.

To that end it has worked to establish credible underpinnings of such a 'labour monopoly' approach, and also to suggest a fertility in that approach's implications.

The analysis concludes that labour monopoly does not rely on unions to be the instrument of restricting competition; it does not require the bulk of the workforce to be subject to any restrictions on competition; it does not require that wage earners irrationally neglect the consequences for their future opportunities to accumulate wealth; it does not require the workforce to lack any capital of its own to defend; it does not suppose that the business interest lacks any influence over wage outcomes; it does not even assume the usual neoclassical substitutability of capital for labour.

It does show that labour monopoly theory predicts rigidity in the real wage rate in several common and important circumstances, while predicting volatility in others. It demonstrates how the theory can yield a unified explanation of public sector and private sector employment; and an integrated theory of the unemployment rate and unemployment benefits, and social security contributions. It argues that labour monopoly theory can supply a rationalization of money wage rigidity and therefore monetary policy; and it also provides a critique of the Keynesian government spending multiplier.

The links of labour monopoly approach to monetary and fiscal policy underline one additional merit of the whole approach: it makes it possible for economic theory to enter into the debate over economic policy in the wake of the Global Financial Crisis. In refusing an 'excess supply of labour' conception of unemployment economics has written itself out of that policy debate. For it is not credible to assert that, say, one-tenth of the workforce being unemployed involves no social waste; it is not credible to object to government spending or monetary easing as a remedy for unemployment on the grounds that there is no unemployment. Whatever particular merits these denials of excess supply of labour might possess, the denial will certainly go unheeded, and attention instead be awarded to whatever section of economic opinion has the readiest politic nostrum for unemployment. And here we arrive at the leading irony of the rejection of any concept of unemployment as an excess supply of labour: it has not delivered an unanswerable blow to Keynesian economics but instead has left macroeconomic policy a preserve of Keynesian economics; the baldest, glibbest, most *simpliste* form of Keynesian economics at that.

But apart from an attendant and circumstantial utility which the labour monopoly approach may have in the policy battles of the Global Financial Crisis, does it actually bear significant insight? A full assessment of this question will require a more extensive development of the approach than it has received so far, and certainly more than is found in these pages. For this work is no more than a little book of models; a series of studies in quick strokes, to fix ideas, make points and raise possibilities. Their conclusions are necessarily based on assumptions that are bare and stark, and call for elaboration.

But the function of any empirical ultimate assessment of labour monopoly theorizing should not be misconceived. That assessment will not be to select the right theory, or the best model. The true task of empiricism in economics is to humble all theory, and mute all pat self-assurance of their devotees; to leave all doctrines in a rough equality of mediocrity, each, in spite of their difficulties, offering some insight; and each doing so despite of mutual inconsistency on account of the inconsistency in human experience. For that experience displays a degree of heterogeneity across space and time; a heterogeneity that is easy to recognize, even if not easy for economists to acknowledge and make peace with, on account of its coexistence with those pervasive (if amorphous) unities that are the stuff of economics. The previous pages are advanced in an attempt to do justice to one aspect of that taxing variety.

References

Ashenfelter, O. (1994), 'H. Gregg Lewis Memorial', *Journal of Labor Economics*, **212**(1), 138.

Aspromourgos, T. (1997), 'Keynes on wage flexibility and the Australian wages system', *Australian Economic Papers*, **36**(68), 114–26.

Azariadis, Costas (1975), 'Implicit contracts and underemployment equilibria', *Journal of Political Economy*, **83**(6), 1183–202.

Baily, Martin Neil (1974), 'Wages and employment under uncertain demand', *Review of Economic Studies*, **41**(1), 37–50.

Bewley, Truman F. (1999), *Why Wages Don't Fall During a Recession*, Cambridge, MA: Harvard University Press.

Biddle, Jeff E. (1996), 'H. Gregg Lewis', in Warren J. Samuels (ed.), *American Economists of the Late Twentieth Century*, Cheltenham, UK and Brookfield, VT, USA: Edward Elgar.

Blais, Andres, J.-M. Cousineau and K. McRoberts (1989), 'The determinants of minimum wage rates', *Public Choice*, **62**(1), 15–24.

Booth, Alison L. (1985), 'The free rider and a social custom model of trade union membership', *Quarterly Journal of Economics*, **100**(1), 253–61.

Booth, Alison L. (1995), *The Economics of the Trade Union*, Cambridge: Cambridge University Press.

Brakman, Steven and Ben J. Heijdra (2004), *The Monopolistic Competition Revolution in Retrospect*, New York: Cambridge University Press.

Brecher, R.A. (1974), 'Minimum wage rates and the pure theory of international trade', *Quarterly Journal of Economics*, **88**(1), 98–116.

Brems, Hans (1976) 'From the years of high theory: Frederik Zeuthen (1888–1959)', *History of Political Economy*, **8**(3), 400–411.

Bronfenbrenner, Martin (1939), 'The Cobb–Douglas function and trade union policy' *American Economic Review*, **29**(4), 793–6.

Brown, Vivienne (1991), 'On Keynes's inverse relations between real wages and employment: a debate over excess capacity', *Review of Political Economy*, **3**(4), 439–65.

Browning, Edgar K. (1978), 'More on the appeal of minimum wage laws', *Public Choice*, **36**(2), 91–3.

Carlin, Wendy and David Soskice (2006), *Macroeconomics: Imperfections, Institutions and Policies*, Oxford: Oxford University Press.

Carruth, Alan A. and Andrew J. Oswald (1987), 'On union preferences and labour market models: insiders and outsiders', *Economic Journal*, **97**(386), 431–45.

Chamberlin, Edward H. (1951), 'The monopoly power of labor', in David McCord Wright (ed.), *The Impact of the Union: Eight Economic Theorists Evaluate the Labor Union Movement*, New York: Kelley and Millman.

Citrine, Walter (1964), *Autobiography*, London: Hutchinson.

Clay, Henry (1929a), 'The public regulation of wages in Great Britain', *Economic Journal*, **39**(155), 323–43.

Clay, Henry, Sir (1929b), *The Post-War Unemployment Problem*, London: Macmillan.

Coleman, William (1985), 'Wicksell on technological change and real wages', *History of Political Economy*, **17**(3), 355–66.

Coleman, William (1998), 'Should we wait to "grow out of" unemployment? The implications of a neoclassical calibration analysis', *Economic Record*, **74**(225), 162–70.

Coleman, William (2007), *The Causes, Consequences and Compensations of Inflation: An Investigation of Three Problems in Monetary Theory*, Cheltenham, UK and Northampton, MA, USA: Edward Elgar.

Coleman, William, Selwyn Cornish and Alf Hagger (2006), *Giblin's Platoon: The Trials and Triumph of the Economist in Australian Public Life*, Canberra: ANU E Press.

Creedy, John (1986), *Edgeworth and the Development of Neoclassical Economics*, Oxford and New York: Blackwell.

Creedy, John and Ian M. McDonald (1991), 'Models of trade union behaviour: a synthesis', *Economic Record*, **67**(199), 346–59.

Danziger, Leif (2009), 'The elasticity of labor demand and the minimum wage', *Journal of Population Economics*, **22**(3), 757–72.

de Menil, George (1971), *Bargaining: Monopoly Power versus Union Power*, Cambridge, MA: MIT Press.

De Vroey, Michel (2004), *Involuntary Unemployment: The Elusive Quest for a Theory*, London and New York: Routledge.

Dimand, Robert W. and Mary Ann Dimand (1996), *A History of Game Theory*, London and New York: Routledge.

Dixit, A.K. (1968), 'Optimal development in a labour-surplus economy', *Review of Economic Studies*, **35**(1), 23–34.

Dixit, A.K. (1973), 'Models of dual economies', in J.A. Mirrlees and N.H. Stern (eds), *Models of Economic Growth*, New York: John Wiley & Sons.

Dow, Louis A. and Lewis M. Abernathy (1963), 'The Chicago School on economic methodology and monopolistic competition', *American Journal of Economics and Sociology*, **22**(2), 235–49.

Dunlop, John (1938), 'The movement of real and money wage rates', *Economic Journal*, **48**(191), 413–34.

Dunlop, John (1942), 'Wages policies in trade unions', *American Economic Review*, **32**(1), 290–301.

Dunlop, John (1944), *Wage Determination under Trade Unions*, New York: Macmillan.

Dunlop, John and Benjamin Higgins (1942), '"Bargaining power" and market structures', *Journal of Political Economy*, **50**(1), 1–26.

Friedman, Milton (1951), 'Some comments on the significance of labor unions for economic policy', in D. McCord Wright (ed.), *The Impact of the Union: Eight Economic Theorists Evaluate the Labor Union Movement*, New York: Harcourt, Brace.

Galbraith, J.K. (1936), 'Monopoly power and price rigidities', *Quarterly Journal of Economics*, **50**(3), 456–75.

Grossman, Gene M. and Elhanan Helpman (2001), *Special Interest Politics*, Cambridge, MA and London: MIT Press.

Hamermesh, Daniel S. (1993), *Labour Demand*, Princeton, NJ: Princeton University Press.

Hansen, Alvin (1940), 'Price flexibility and full employment of resources', *The Structure of the American Economy*, Washington, DC: US Government Printing Office.

Harsanyi, John C. (1956), 'Approaches to the bargaining problem before and after the theory of games: a critical discussion of Zeuthen's, Hicks', and Nash's theories', *Econometrica*, **24**(2), 144–57.

Hayek, F.A. (1980), *1980s Unemployment and the Unions: Essays on the Impotent Price Structure of Britain and Monopoly in the Labour Market*, Hobart Paper 87, London: Institute of Economic Affairs.

Heijdra, Ben J. and Frederick van der Ploeg (2002), *The Foundations of Modern Macroeconomics*, Oxford: Oxford University Press.

Hicks, J.R. (1963 [1932]), *The Theory of Wages*, London: Macmillan.

Horvat, Branko (1986), 'The theory of the worker-managed firm revisited', *Journal of Comparative Economics*, **10**(1), 9–25.

Hutchison, T.W. (1978), *On Revolutions and Progress in Economic Knowledge*, Cambridge: Cambridge University Press.

Hutt, W.H. (1930), *The Theory of Collective Bargaining: A Critique of the Argument that Trade Unions Neutralise Labour's 'Disadvantage' in Bargaining and Enhance Wage-rates by the Use, or Threat, of Strikes*, London: King.

Kaufmann, Bruce E. (2002), 'Models of union wage determination: what have we learned since Dunlop and Ross?', *Industrial Relations*, **41**(1), 110–58.

Kaufmann, Bruce E. and John Dunlop (2002), 'Reflections on six decades in industrial relations: an interview with John Dunlop', *Industrial and Labor Relations Review*, **55**(2), 324–48.

Keech, William R. (1977), 'More on the vote winning and vote losing qualities of minimum wage laws', *Public Choice*, **29**, 133–7.

Keynes, John Maynard (1936), *General Theory of Employment Interest and Money*, London: Macmillan.

Layard, David and Stephen Nickell (1990), 'Is unemployment lower if unions bargain over employment?', *Quarterly Journal of Economics*, **105**(3), 773–87.

Layard, Richard, Stephen Nickell and Richard Jackman (1991), *Unemployment: Macroeconomic Performance and the Labour Market*, Oxford: Oxford University Press.

Leontief, W. (1946), 'The pure theory of the guaranteed annual wage contract', *Journal of Political Economy*, **54**(1), 76–9.

Lewis, Gregg H. (1946), 'Henry Calvert Simons', *American Economic Review*, **36**(4), 668–9.

Lewis, Gregg H. (1951), 'The labor-monopoly problem: a positive program', *Journal of Political Economy*, **59**(4), 277–87.

Lewis, Gregg H. (1965), 'Competitive and monopoly unionism', in Philip D. Bradley (ed.), *The Public Stake in Union Power*, Charlottesville, VA: University Press of Virginia.

Manning, Alan (2003), *Monopsony in Motion: Imperfect Competition in Labor Markets*, New Haven, CT: Princeton University Press.

Marshall, Alfred (1892), *Elements of Economics of Industry: Being the First Volume of Elements of Economics*, London: Macmillan.

Marshall, Alfred (1919), *Industry and Trade*, London: Macmillan.

Means, Gardiner (1935a), 'Price inflexibility and the requirements of stabilizing monetary policy', *American Statistical Journal*, **30**(190), 401–13.

Means, Gardiner (1935b [1992]), 'The major causes of the depression', in Frederic S. Lee and Warren J. Samuels (eds), *The Heterodox Economics of Gardiner C. Means: A Collection*, Armonk, NY: M.E. Sharpe.

McDonald, I.M. and Robert Solow (1981), 'Wage bargaining and employment', *American Economic Review*, **71**(5), 896–908.

McDonald, I.M. and Robert Solow (1984), 'Union wage policies: reply', *American Economic Review*, **74**(4), 759–61.

Mill, John Stuart (1848 [1878]), *Principles of Political Economy with Some of Their Applications to Social Philosophy*, 8th edn, London: Longmans, Green, Reader & Dyer.

Mill, John Stuart (1869) 'Thornton on labour and its claims', *Fortnightly Review*, (May), 505–18; 'Part II', (June), 680–700.

Naylor, Robin (1992), 'Review of *Macroeconomics and the Wage Bargain* by Wendy Carlin and David Soskice', *Economic Journal*, **412**(102), 642–4.

Oswald, Andrew J. (1982), 'Trade unions, wages and unemployment: what can simple models tell us?', *Oxford Economic Papers*, **34**(3), 526–45.

Oswald, Andrew J. (1993), 'Efficient contracts are on the labour demand curve: theory and facts', *Labour Economics*, **1**(1), 85–113.

Petridis, R. (1990), 'The trade unions in the *Principles*: the ethical versus the practical in Marshall's economics', Working paper, Murdoch University, Economics Programme, no. 36.

Pigou, A.C. (1905), *Principles and Methods of Industrial Peace*, London: Macmillan.

Pigou, A.C. (1933), *The Theory of Unemployment*, London: Cass.

Pissarides, Christopher A. (2002), *Equilibrium Unemployment Theory*, Cambridge, MA and London: MIT Press.

Reynolds, Morgan (1981), 'Whatever happened to the monopoly theory of labor unions?', *Journal of Labor Research*, **2**(1), 163–74.

Robertson, Peter E. (1999), 'Economic growth and the return to capital in developing economies', *Oxford Economic Papers*, **51**(4), 577–94.

Robinson, Joan (1947 [1937]), *Essays in the Theory of Employment*, Oxford: Blackwell.

Rothschild, Kurt W. (1994), 'The theory of wages revisited', in Harald Hagemann and O.F. Hamouda (eds), *The Legacy of John Hicks: His Contributions to Economic Analysis*, London: Routledge.

Samuels, Warren J. and Steven G. Medema (1990), *Gardiner C. Means. Institutionalist and Post Keynesian*, Armonk, NY: M.E. Sharpe.

Sgro, P.M. and A. Takayama (1981), 'On the long-run growth effects of a minimum wage for a two-sector economy', *Economic Record*, **57**(157), 180–85.

Shackle, G. (1957), 'The nature of the bargaining process', in J.T. Dunlop (ed.), *The Theory of Wage Determination*, London: Macmillan.

Simons, Henry C. (1936), *A Positive Program for Laissez Faire: Some Proposals for a Liberal Economic Policy*, Chicago, IL: The University of Chicago Press.

Simons, Henry C. (1942), 'Hansen on fiscal policy', *Journal of Political Economy*, **50**(2), 161–96.

Simons, Henry C. (1944) 'Some reflections on syndicalism', *Journal of Political Economy*, **52**(1), 1–25.

Sobel, Russel (1999), 'Evidence on the political economy of the minimum wage', *Journal of Political Economy*, **107**(4), 761–85.

Solow, Robert (1985), 'Insiders and outsiders in wage determination', *Scandinavian Journal of Economics*, **87**(2), 411–28.

Steindl, Frank G. (1973), 'The appeal of minimum wage laws and the invisible hand in government', *Public Choice*, **14**, 133–6.

Stigler, G. (1985), *Memoirs of an Unregulated Economist*, New York: Basic Books.

Swanson, James and Kim Andrews (2007), 'Testing the monopoly union model: a stochastic frontier approach', *Industrial Relations*, **46**(4), 781–98.

Sweezy, Paul M. (1939), 'Demand under conditions of oligopoly', *Journal of Political Economy*, **47**(4), 568–73.

Upmann, Thorstten and Anke Gerber (2003), 'The Kalai–Smorodinsky solution in labor-market negotiations', CESifo Working Paper Series No. 941.

West, E.G. (1977) 'Shifting public choice on minimum wages', *Public Choice*, **29**(1), 143–7.

Wicksell, Knut (1934), *Lectures on Political Economy, Public Choice*, London: G. Routledge & Sons.

Wright, D. McCord (ed.) (1951), *The Impact of the Union: Eight Economic Theorists Evaluate the Labor Union Movement*, New York: Harcourt, Brace.

Zeuthen, F. (1930), *Problems of Monopoly and Economic Warfare*, London: G. Routledge & Sons.

Index